Here's a list of the keystrokes you can use to quickly choose the most popu... a mouse and like to use it, almost everything here also can be accomplishe... various toolbars.

Common Windows Tasks

If you want to...	Press...
Show the next workbook that's open in Excel	Ctrl+F6
Close a workbook that's on your screen	Ctrl+F4
Leave Excel for the moment, and go to another Windows program that's running on your computer	Alt+Tab
Quit Excel	Alt+F4

Common Workbook Tasks

If you want to...	Press...
Insert a new, blank workbook	Ctrl+N
Insert a new, blank sheet into a workbook	Shift+F11
Open a saved workbook	Ctrl+O
Save a workbook	Ctrl+S
Change the name of a saved workbook	F12
Print a workbook	Ctrl+P

Common Movement Tasks

If you want to...	Press...
Move down to the next row	↓
Move up to the preceding row	↑
Move to the beginning of a row	Ctrl+Home
Move to cell A1 from anywhere in the active sheet	Home
Move down one screen	PgDn
Move up one screen	PgUp
Move to the end of a cell range that contains data	End+Arrow key
Move to the last cell in the active sheet that contains data or formatting	End+Home

Common Entering & Editing Tasks

If you want to...	Press...
Edit the contents of a cell	F2
Clear the contents of a cell	Del
Copy a cell	Ctrl+C or Ctrl+Insert
Cut a cell	Ctrl+X or Shift+Delete
Paste the cell you just cut or copied	Ctrl+V or Shift+Insert
Undo an operation	Ctrl+Z
Sum a range of cells	Alt+=, then Enter, when the first blank cell below the range you want to sum is the active cell
Check the spelling of text in a workbook	F7

Common Formatting Tasks

If you want to...	Do this...
Display the Format Cells tabbed dialog box	Ctrl+1
Make cells bold	Select the target cells and press Ctrl+B
Make cells italic	Select the target cells and press Ctrl+I
Make cells underline	Select the target cells and press Ctrl+U
Choose a different font	Select the target cells, press Ctrl+Shift+F, press the down-arrow key, select the name of the font from the drop-down list, and press Enter
Choose a different font size	Select the target cells, press Ctrl+Shift+P, press the down-arrow key, select the size from the drop-down list, and press Enter
Select a built-in style from the Style dialog box	Alt+' (apostrophe)

Common Function Keys: The Best of the Rest

If you want to...	Press...
Display a help window	F1
Activate the menu bar so that you can open a menu	Alt or F10
Show the shortcut menu for a cell	Shift+F10
Recalculate all workbook formulas	F9
Go to any cell in the workbook	F5
Move to the next pane of a split window	F6
Display Function Wizard so you can paste a function in the formula bar	Shift+F3

I HATE

EXCEL 5

Patrick J. Burns

I Hate Excel 5

Copyright © 1993 by Que® Corporation

Library of Congress Catalog No.: 93-86864

ISBN: 1-56529-532-3

96   95   94   6   5   4   3   2

Interpretation of the printing code: the rightmost double-digit number is the year of the book's printing; the rightmost single- digit number, the number of the book's printing. For example, a printing code of 93-1 shows that the first printing of the book occurred in 1993.

Screen reproductions in this book were created by using Collage Compute from Inner Media, Inc., Hollis, NH.

I Hate Excel 5 is based on Microsoft Excel Version 5.0.

Publisher: David P. Ewing

Director of Publishing: Mike Miller

Managing Editor: Corinne Walls

Marketing Manager: Ray Robinson

Dedication

Three people in my life, each a stranger to the other, have been kind enough to share their wit and wisdom. Jack Burns, who convinced me to plant my feet firmly in the ground before allowing my mind to drift off to the stars. Kenny Baca, who taught me to stop and smell the roses before I bundled them up and shipped them out. Patty Vergara, the first person I ever met who hated computers more than I did. My eternal soul mate. One day I'd like to get you all together in one place and say, "Now look what you've gone and done!"

I HATE EXCEL FOR WINDOWS!

Credits

Publishing Manager
Don Roche, Jr.

Acquisitions Editor
Nancy Stevenson

Product Director
Robin Drake
Joyce J. Nielsen

Production Editor
Thomas F. Hayes

Technical Editor
N. Christine Pichereau

Book Designer
Amy Peppler-Adams

Cover Designer
Tim Amrhein

Novice Reviewer
Sandy Covington

Production Team
Jeff Baker
Angela Bannan
Danielle Bird
Paula Carroll
Charlotte Clapp
Karen Dodson
Brook Farling
Michelle Greenwalt
Carla Hall
Joy Dean Lee
Elizabeth Lewis
Nanci Sears Perry
Amy L. Steed
Tina Trettin
Donna Winter
Michelle Worthington
Lillian Yates

Indexer
Johnna VanHoose

Editorial Assistant
Jill Stanley

Composed in *Goudy* and *MCPdigital* by Que Corporation.

About the Author

Patrick J. Burns is a well-entrenched author, a self-professed spreadsheet guru, and a really happy guy. A founder and principal of Burns & Associates, a professional consulting firm, Patrick has authored lots of 400-pound computer books. It's the experience he's garnered from his other professions—wrapping fruit, cutting grass at a golf course, and selling flowers—that has allowed him to become so conversant in matters of silicon chips and plastic mice. He welcomes all comments and criticisms about the book. Send them in care of Waterside Productions, 2191 San Elijo Avenue, Cardiff-by-the-Sea, California 92007.

When Patrick gets bored with writing, he hops on a plane and darts off to exotic locations around the world. Always one to adapt to local culture, he's played cards with banditos in a Mexican jail, trekked the Himalayas on camel, and explored a sunken Greek freighter 110 feet below the ocean surface off the coast of Barbados. One time he ended up in a gigantic black stew pot deep in the jungle of a South Pacific island. Patrick loves to play beach volleyball, hates snails and gigantic black stew pots, is 6'1" tall, has brown hair and eyes, sometimes dreams in French, and adores his blond-haired and blue-eyed, 5'9" fiancée, Cathy.

Acknowledgments

Where do I begin? It's like being shipwrecked on a deserted island with 30 strangers who suddenly become your closest friends. Half the time is spent imagining so-and-so smothered in a creamy béarnaise sauce, while the rest is spent exchanging ideas, solving problems, or just talking dirty. Then suddenly you're rescued, and it's time to bid everyone farewell.

At Que: Many thanks to Shelley O'Hara, my alter ego on this book. My sincere wishes for continued success after you leave the pod. Thanks to Don Roche and Nancy Stevenson for excellent coaching. And thanks to Robin Drake and Joyce Nielsen, for your friendly voices, easy-to-answer questions, and your careful attention to detail.

At home: Thanks, Cathy, for being such a good sport throughout this shipwreck. You listened to me, read for me, advised me, coaxed me, consoled me, cajoled me, and celebrated with me without complaining (too much) or quitting (ever). You deserve 100 medals!

At Waterside: Thanks, Bill and Matt, for the vote of confidence on this one. Carol, thanks for managing the money. Lavander, Margo, and Justine, thanks for understanding when I get your voices mixed up on the phone.

Trademark Acknowledgments

All terms mentioned in this book that are known to be trademarks or service marks have been appropriately capitalized. Que cannot attest to the accuracy of this information. Use of a term in this book should not be regarded as afffecting the validity of any trademark or service mark.

Microsoft Excel and Microsoft Windows are registered trademarks of Microsoft Corporation.

Contents at a Glance

Introduction		**1**
I	**All You Really Need To Know**	**5**
II	**Making It Look Good**	**79**
III	**Formulas for Success**	**195**
IV	**Graphs and Data Lists**	**239**
V	**That's the Way I Like It**	**281**
VI	**Quick & Dirty Dozens**	**317**
	Index	**357**

Table of Contents

Introduction   **1**

Icons 2

I All You Really Need To Know   **5**

1 Getting Started   **7**

The Secret of a Spreadsheet 8
Giving Excel the Green Light 9
    I See C:\> or Some Variation 10
    I See Windows 10
Looking Under the Hood 12
Checking Out the Dashboard 15
Moving Around 16
How To Enter Information 18
What You Can Enter 19
    Putting It into Words 19
    I've Got Your Number 20
Keeping Track of Dates Every Time 21
    Formulas (Numbers that Think) 23

2 Making Changes   **25**

No, No, No...It's All Wrong! 26
    Fixing While You Work 26
    Fixing after the Fact 27
Deleting Entries 28
Undoing Changes 28
Selecting a Range 31
Getting Help 32

3 Saving and Exiting   35

Save It or Lose It 36
Saving Your Workbooks 37
   Saving the Second Time, Third Time, and So On 40
   Changing a Workbook's Name
     (Excel's witness-protection program) 41
Closing Workbooks and Exiting Excel 42

4 Opening, Closing, and Deleting Workbooks   45

Opening an Existing Workbook 46
Closing a Workbook 50
Getting a Fresh New Workbook 50
Getting Rid of a Workbook 51

5 Formatting Your Workbook   55

Changing Type Styles 56
   To Boldly Go Where No Type Has Gone Before 57
   Italic (Text on the slant) 58
   Sizing Up Your Type 59
Displaying Numbers That Make Sense 61
Goldilocks and the Three Alignment Tools 65
Widening Columns 66
   AutoFit Selection (One size fits all) 67
   Dragging the Column 68

6 Printing Basics   71

Checking Out Your Printer 72
Using Print Preview 73
Printing the Whole Thing 76
Printing Only Part of a Workbook 77
Shooting Trouble 78

II Making It Look Good 79

7 Formulas and Functions 81

What's a Formula Look Like? 82
Creating Smarter Formulas 84
  Showing Up at the Right Address 84
  It's Okay To Point 86
Home, Home on the Range 89
Changing Your Address 90
A Formula's Pecking Order 92
Formulas That Go Bump in the Night 93
Error Message Blues 94
What's a Function, and What Does It Look Like? 96
  The Arguments for Using Functions 96
  Entering a Function 97
  Warp Speed Addition with the AutoSum Button 99

8 Editing 101

Repeating History 102
Inserting More Space in a Workbook 103
  Inserting Rows, Columns, and Sheets (Move over) 104
  What Happens to Your Formulas? 107
Deleting Space from a Workbook 108
  Clearing Cells (To make room for new prisoners) 109
  Deleting Rows, Columns, and Sheets (Out of my way!) . . 110
  What Happens to Formulas? 113
Other Exciting Editing Techniques 114
  Moving Somewhere Fast 114
  Selecting Specific Types of Cells (picky, picky) 115
  Finding Information 116
  Replacing Information (Tit for tat) 118

9 Moving and Copying Data 121

Moving Cell Data 122
   Dragging and Dropping (with your mouse) 122
   Cutting and Pasting (with your keyboard) 124
Copying and Pasting Cell Data 127
   Dragging and Dropping (à la mouse) 127
   Copying and Pasting (à la keyboard) 129
Copying Formulas 131
Filling Cells with Data 133
Cool Pasting Techniques 135
Switching Rows and Columns 137

10 More Workbook Formatting 139

What the Heck Is WYSIWYG, Anyway? 140
Selecting the Makeover Candidate 141
Parallel Parking and Other Popular Alignments 142
   Centering Titles 143
   It's a Wrap! 145
   Stacked and Sideways Text 146
Fonts Are Our Friends 146
   Fonts Have Feelings, Too 147
   Stylizing a Font 149
   Special Font FX (spesh-el fänt effects) 150
   Color Me Blue (Or yellow, or red, or...) 151
Headin' for the Borders 151
Restin' under a Shady Cell 154
Auto-Formatting Tables of Data 156

11 Beyond Basic Printing 159

Basic Printing Revisited 160
Printing More Than One Copy 161
Controlling What Excel Prints 162
   Printing a Range of Pages 163
   Printing a Particular Area of a Sheet 163

Bestowing Titles upon Your Sheet 164
Adding Page Breaks 168
Tinkering with Printing Special Effects 168
Changing the Headers and Footers 172
Help! I Can't Seem To Manage Printing in Excel 174
    Turning On the Print Manager 174
    Choosing a Printer 175

12 Excel Does Windows   **177**

Controlling Your Workbook Window 178
Looking at the Same Workbook Twice 181
    Opening a Second Window 182
    Arranging the Windows 183
    Hiding and Unhiding Windows (Peekaboo with panes) . . 185
Working on Two Files at Once 186
Splitting a Window in Two 187
Freezing Windows 189
Who's Zooming Who? 192

III Formulas for Success   **195**

13 Those Fab Functions   **197**

Why Functions? 198
SUM Day It'll All Add Up 201
Just Your AVERAGE Run-of-the-Mill Function 202
You Can COUNT on It 204
How 'bout a DATE? 206
The Date and Time Is NOW 208
Collect $200 Only IF You Pass Go 209
Sorry, I'm NA Quite Ready 212
Let's Just ROUND It Off a Bit 212
UPPER-Case Appeal 214
I'm How Many DAYS Late on That Payment? 215

I HATE EXCEL FOR WINDOWS!

14 Functions You'll Profit From 219

Why Financial Functions Are Special 220
Financial Arguments 221
How Much Is That Loan Payment? 223
How Much Money Can I Borrow? 225
How Many Payments Do I Have To Make? 227
What's the Interest Rate I Need? 228
Here's What I'm Really Interested In 229
Here's the Principal Thing I'm Interested In 231
What'll It Be Worth Tomorrow? 234
Will I Really Make Any Money? 236

IV Graphs and Data Lists 239

15 You Say Chart, I Say Graph 241

All You Really Need to Know about Charts 242
Chart Magic with the ChartWizard 243
Creating Chart Sheets 251
Tinkering with the Chart 252
Changing the Chart 253
Saving Your Chart 255
Formatting a Chart 255
   Changing the Chart Type 256
   Bestowing Titles (And other meaningful text) 257
   A Legend in Its Own Mind 258
   Objects of Desire (Making chart objects pretty) 260
Printing a Chart 261

16 Dynamic Data Lists 263

A Few Terms To Gnaw On 264
Making Out a List 266
   Typing into a List 267
   Putting on the List Hat 268
Changing Your List 269

The A to Z's of Arranging Records 270
   The Key to the Sort 271
   Sorting 272
   Undoing a Sort Operation 275
Cruising Your List with Data Form 276
Finding Records 279
   Match-Maker, Match-Maker, Make Me a Match 279
   Close Enough 280

V That's the Way I Like It   281

17 The Miracle of Macros   283

Demystifying Macros 284
   What's So Special about a Macro? 285
   Where Do Macros Live? 286
   What Can My Macros Do? 287
Your First Recording Session 288
   Starting the Recorder (Lights, Camera...) 288
   Recording Your Actions (...Action!) 291
Playing Back the Macro 292
Changing Instructions in a Macro 293
Creating Additional Macros 294
Saving the Personal Macro Workbook 295
Some Macro Recording Ideas 296

18 Excel, Made To Order   297

Changing Appearances 298
   Déjà View All Over Again 299
   Organizing Your Workspace 304
Hanging Out in Your Favorite Toolbar 307
   The Toolbar Family 307
   Organizing Your Toolbars 310
   Making Additions to the Toolbar Family 312

I HATE EXCEL FOR WINDOWS!

VI Quick & Dirty Dozens   317

Quick & Dirty Dozens   319

12 Cool Things Nobody Knows You Can Do with Excel ... 320
12 Things You Should Never Do in Excel 329
12 Heart-Stopping Messages and What To Do
  about Them 335
12 Most Common Mistakes 341
12 Best Excel Shortcuts 345
12 Features You Can Monkey with If You Have
  Time To Kill 349

Index   357

Introduction

"Hey, what happened to my mouse pointer?"

"My data disappeared!!"

"I hate Excel!"

"#$?/%@!"

Famous first and last words. They roll off every computer user's tongue at one time or another. Hey, computers are tricky. Excel can be tricky. But, it really isn't too difficult to outsmart both of them. All you need is this book. This is a book about Excel for people who hate the thought of learning Excel. Of learning anything. This is a book for people who just want to get things done.

I HATE EXCEL FOR WINDOWS!

Throughout this book, I do my best to talk *to* you—not *at* you. If ever you feel that I've let you down in this regard, tear out the offending pages and mail them back to me. I'll promptly rewrite them and send them back. You see, when confronted with six different ways of doing the same thing in Excel, I choose to ignore at least five of them. You'll learn only the stuff that gets you immediate results, like a great-looking budget report, a well-organized printout, and a hefty raise. Well, I can't promise that last one.

Icons

(What those little pictures really mean)

I promised you that I'd only discuss the things that are relevant to the basics of using Excel. By and large, this goal has been accomplished. But every so often, it gets tough to complete a thought without mentioning some technical buzzword, esoteric computer function, or obscure mathematical concept. That's why you'll see a bunch of little picture icons.

The pictures that appear in the margins of this book are dedicated to completing thoughts, filling in blanks, stopping you from self-destructing, and ushering you into nerddom. Actually, feel free to skip over all the stuff flagged with icons, because it won't impair your ability to successfully work in Excel. But, if you're feeling a little bit adventurous some morning, take a look at the information in those parts.

Here are the pictures and what they mean:

TIP

This icon alerts you to shortcuts, tricks, and time-savers.

BUZZWORDS

BUZZWORD

This icon warns you that you're about to learn an impressive technicobabble word.

"I HATE THIS!"

This icon points out all the frustrating, annoying problems you might encounter.

CAUTION

This icon says: Hey! Watch Out! Stop! Falling Rocks Ahead!

EXPERTS ONLY

This icon flags the really technical stuff. If you are curious, read this information. And remember, curiosity killed the cat, but satisfaction brought him back.

PART I

All You Really Need To Know

Includes:

1: Getting Started

2: Making Changes

3: Saving and Exiting

4: Opening, Closing, and Deleting Workbooks

5: Formatting Your Workbook

6: Printing Basics

CHAPTER 1

Getting Started
(The Secrets of a Spreadsheet, Uncovered)

IN A NUTSHELL

▼ What's a spreadsheet?
▼ Starting Excel
▼ Checking out the territory
▼ Moving around in a workbook
▼ Typing stuff (or stuffing type) into a workbook

The original inspiration for a spreadsheet arose from a pretty basic need: the need to count things. It didn't matter what you were counting—beans, sheep, rocks, money—you just needed a way to know how many beans, or whatever, you had. The counting started on fingers, moved to those bead things called abacuses, and then took a leap onto paper.

The original spreadsheets were big pieces of ruled paper you could spread out on a table top. You would scribble numbers on each sheet, being very careful to stay between the lines, and then total them with a calculator. Then along came computers, and spreadsheets became high-tech and electronic.

Today's spreadsheets can do lots more than count stones and rice grains. This chapter introduces you to the modern-day spreadsheet.

BUZZWORDS

SPREADSHEET

A spreadsheet is a program designed to let you tinker around with numbers. It's the high-tech equivalent of a ledger sheet and calculator.

The Secret of a Spreadsheet

(One secret you should never keep to yourself)

The best way to get a feel for a spreadsheet program like Excel is to start with something familiar, like a personal budget. The following budget shows a short list of expenses that should look familiar to you. The number at the bottom of these expenses is their total.

A typical personal budget

The Monthly Bills Budget
for June, 1994

	Budgeted	Actual	Over/ Under (−)
Mortgage payment	$1,250.25	$1,250.25	$0.00
Vacation fund	100.00	100.00	0.00
College fund	200.00	0.00	−200.00
Fun stuff	200.00	600.00	400.00
Food	225.00	294.21	9.21
Car payment	225.57	225.57	0.00
Gas & electric	37.00	62.87	25.87
Cable	40.00	41.54	1.54
Telephone	68.00	59.66	−8.34
Car gas & upkeep	75.00	89.99	14.99
Totals:	$2,420.82	$2,664.09	$243.21

You can easily total the numbers in this budget with a calculator, but what if something changes? What if you want to add something? What if you are a multimillionaire and your budget includes lots of categories such as furs, diamonds, Jaguars, and so on? For any of these scenarios, you'd have to peck, peck, peck through the numbers all over again on the calculator.

With Excel, you just change, add, or delete a number, and the totals are recalculated automatically. That, my friends, is the beauty of a spreadsheet program!

Giving Excel the Green Light

(Pushing the pedal to the metal)

To put that magic to work, you first must start Excel. That involves figuring out where you are starting from. If you turn on the computer and Excel is already started, you are lucky! Skip this entire section. If you see

something like C:\>, you have to start Windows first. Read the next two sections. If you see Windows, go directly to the section called "I See Windows." Do not pass Go.

I See C:\> or Some Variation

If you see pretty much a blank screen with C:\> or something like that, you are at the DOS prompt. You first have to start Windows. Type **win** and press Enter. You should see a bunch of little pictures on-screen. That's the Program Manager, alias Windows. (If you want to learn all the ins and outs of Windows, get a copy of *I Hate Windows*. I've got enough to worry about teaching you Excel.)

I See Windows

OK. Somehow or other, you see Windows. Either you started it yourself or you turned on your computer and it magically appeared (someone—the person who sold you the computer, your sister-in-law the computer whiz, or your son—has set up the computer so this happens automatically). Now you are ready to start Excel.

Look around on your screen for an icon (a little picture) that says *Microsoft Excel 5.0* or something like that.

Now grab hold of your mouse and slide it on your desk or mouse pad until the arrow on your screen is positioned directly on the icon. Press the left mouse button twice, really quickly. This is called *double-clicking*. A window will open and inside you should see an icon called *Microsoft Excel*. Double-click on this icon and Excel starts!

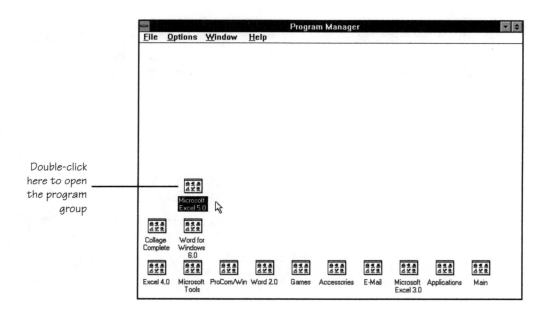

Double-click here to open the program group

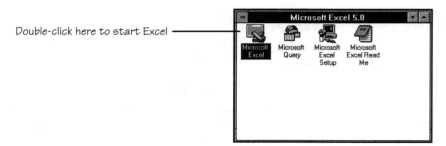

Double-click here to start Excel

TIP

In Excel, you can use a mouse to do things like move around on-screen, click icons to start activities, and scroll the workbook on your screen. All this—and more—is possible when you acquaint yourself with the three dance steps necessary to tango with your mouse:

Click	Press and release the mouse button in one continuous motion.
Double-click	Press and release the mouse button, then do it again, really quickly.
Drag	Press and hold down the mouse button and drag the mouse pointer around on your screen; when you're finished dragging, release the button.

Looking Under the Hood

(What makes this thing go?)

The Excel workbook is really nothing more than a collection of individual pages, affectionately called sheets. Each sheet is made up of a grid of columns and rows. It's the electronic version of an accountant's ledger sheet, with the columns and rows identified.

HUH?

BUZZWORDS

SHEET

A sheet is the grid of columns and rows. It's where you type your numbers. The tab sticking out from the bottom of a sheet shows a sheet's name, like Sheet1 or Sheet2.

A column in a sheet is identified by a letter. The first column is column A, the second is column B, and so on. Each row is identified by a number: 1, 2, 3, 4, and so on. Take a look at this sheet:

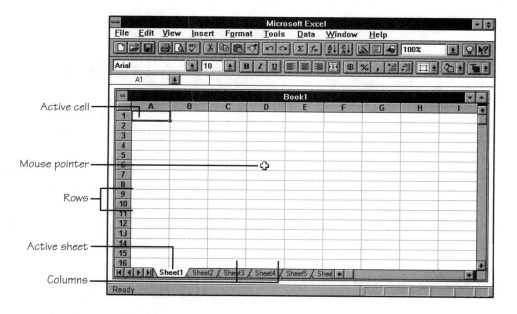

"I HATE THIS!"

Your screen might look different

The configuration of toolbars and screen regions shown in this figure is the typical setup for the toolbar. Your screen may be customized to look different.

Now take a look at where column A meets row 1 in the sheet. This is called a *cell*. The "address" of the cell is formed by snapping together the column letter and row number, such as A1. Notice that cell A1 has a dark rectangle around it. The cell with the dark rectangle is called the *active cell*.

BUZZWORDS

CELL ADDRESS

A cell address is the name of the cell and is formed by combining the column letter and row number.

BUZZWORDS

ACTIVE CELL

The active cell is where Excel will store words and numbers when you type them from your keyboard.

You probably see only nine or so columns and 18 or so rows, but this is really only the top left corner of a much larger beast. Each sheet in an Excel workbook has 256 columns and 16,384 rows! You will only see a few rows and columns on-screen at any one time because your screen isn't large enough to show everything.

TIP

If you bump the keyboard and the active cell suddenly changes location and you can no longer see your original sheet area, press the Home key. Pressing Home yanks the active cell back to A1. Sort of like bungee jumping in and out of the Grand Canyon.

BUZZWORDS

WORKBOOK

A workbook is a collection of 16 sheets, suitably named Sheet1 through Sheet16. In Excel, a workbook sits in its own window.

Checking Out the Dashboard

(What's all this stuff on my screen?)

The area just above the workbook on your screen is Excel's equivalent of an automobile dashboard. The gadgets you see are the controls you use to "drive" Excel.

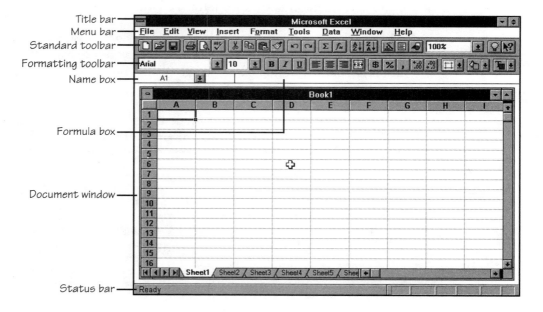

Excel's dashboard

✔ The top title bar displays the name of the program, Microsoft Excel.

✔ The menu bar lists the menus: **File**, **Edit**, **Help**, and so on.

✔ The toolbars contain lots of little icons you can use to do stuff quickly in Excel. More about that later.

continues

✔ The name box displays the address of the active cell.

✔ The formula bar is one of two places where Excel displays what you type, before you stick it in the active cell.

✔ The Irish Bar (not shown here) is on Carmel Mountain Road in San Diego, California. Ask for John. Tell him Ted sent you.

✔ The document window contains the workbook and its sheets—the grids of rows and columns. This window also has a title bar, which displays a default workbook name like Book1, Book2, Book3, and so on.

✔ The status bar displays plain-English descriptions of many activities that take place while you're driving around in Excel.

TIP

When you can't figure out what's happening in Excel, check the status bar first. The message you see there might call attention to a problem or condition that isn't readily evident to the untrained eye.

Moving Around

(Finger-twisting fun)

Before you can begin typing away, you first have to pick the active cell—the cell where you want to put something. There are a bunch of different ways to move the active cell around the sheet that happens to be showing on your screen.

To move the active cell with your mouse, move the mouse pointer (the four-pointed cross that looks like a plus symbol) around the sheet on your screen until it rests on the cell you want to make active. Then click the left mouse button.

To move the active cell with your keyboard, just press one of the four keys marked with an arrow. The active cell moves in the direction of the arrow, one cell at a time.

Other keys you can use to cruise

✔ To make cell A1 the active cell, press the Home key.

✔ To quickly move more than one cell in any direction, tab the End key, and then press the arrow key that points in the direction you're heading. If you get numbers instead of moving, your Num Lock key is on. Press the Num Lock key again to turn it off, and press Esc to get rid of the numbers.

✔ Press the PgUp and PgDn keys to scroll up and down inside the current sheet, one screen at a time.

✔ To go to a specific cell, press the F5 function key, type the cell's address, and press Enter.

✔ To go to the next sheet in the workbook, press Ctrl+PgDn.

✔ To go to the previous sheet in the workbook, press Ctrl+PgUp.

How To Enter Information

(Sticking stuff in the cells)

Entering information into a new workbook is as easy as selecting the lucky cell, doing a little typing, and then pressing Enter.

Golden rules for entering stuff into cells

✔ Whenever you begin typing anything on your keyboard, the characters will appear in the formula bar, as well as in the active cell. You can watch as you type. If you make a mistake, press Backspace to delete the error, and then retype the information.

✔ To store stuff in the active cell after you finish typing it, just press Enter.

✔ If you change your mind before pressing Enter, press Esc. Nothing is entered in the cell. If you've already pressed Enter, read Chapter 2, "Making Changes," to find out how to correct your mistake.

✔ To store stuff in the active cell and then advance to a cell in a particular direction, just press the up-, down-, left-, or right-arrow key instead of pressing Enter. If the active cell is at the edge of a sheet when you press an arrow key, Excel may beep at you. No big deal, just press an arrow key that moves you in a different direction

✔ As you type, you will see four boxes to the left of the text: one contains an X and the other shows a check mark. (Ignore the other two for now.) You can click on the check mark, rather than pressing Enter, to enter the information into the cell. Click on the X box to cancel the entry.

What You Can Enter

(The stuff that Excel lets you stick)

You know how to enter stuff; now you need to figure out what to enter. Basically, you can enter words, numbers, dates, or formulas.

"I HATE THIS!"

> ### Is it a number? Is it text?
> Excel handles different types of information differently. For instance, Excel can subtract two dates or two numbers, but it can't subtract text. It's important that you and Excel "agree" on the type of information you are entering. If you think you are entering a number, Excel better think it's a number, too. If you think you have entered a date, Excel better think it's a date, too. Most of the time, you don't have to worry about this, because Excel and you will be in agreement.

Putting It into Words

To type text into a cell, select the cell and type the text you want. For instance, click on cell B1, type **My Finances**, and press Enter. Excel enters the text into the selected cell.

Tongue twisters and verbal barbs

✔ As long as the entry contains at least one letter, or a character such as * ! & # or ?, Excel will treat your entry as text. (That is, unless Excel thinks it's a negative number, scientific notation, date, time, or formula. Read the rest of the chapter for the gory details on this.)

continues

✔ You can type other characters (ones that aren't letters of the alphabet) as part of the entry. This includes things like numbers and punctuation characters.

✔ Excel automatically aligns text to the left edge of the cell.

✔ When the entry is so long that it won't fit into the width of the current cell, Excel allows the extra characters to spill over into the cell immediately to the right, as long as that cell is empty. (The extra characters aren't actually *in* the adjacent cell; they're just displayed there.) If that cell does contain information, you won't see your entire cell entry, because part of it won't be displayed. But all of the text is still in the current cell.

✔ When Excel cuts off an entry at the right edge of a cell, you can widen that column to view that text. But that's a topic best left to Chapter 5, "Formatting Your Workbook."

I've Got Your Number

To type a number, select the cell you want and type a number. For instance, to enter 455 into cell C2, click on cell C2, type **455**, and press Enter.

It's all in the numbers

✔ You might think that 89PT100 is a number, but Excel thinks it's text. That isn't a problem unless you want to use the number in a calculation. If you want to use an entry in calculations, it can include only numbers. (How would you add 25 and 37oboe9, anyway?)

✔ Excel aligns numbers to the right edge of the cell. And nothing fancy is displayed initially—no commas, no currency signs, nothing. Don't worry, you learn how to add this kind of stuff in Chapter 5, "Formatting Your Workbook."

✔ To type a negative number, type a minus sign, and then the number.

✔ When the entry is so long that it won't fit into the width of the current cell, Excel displays something like

　　1.2E+10

This is *scientific notation*. You must be working on the national debt, because you have some pretty big numbers. You can widen the column, a trick you learn in Chapter 5, "Formatting Your Workbook."

BUZZWORDS

SCIENTIFIC NOTATION

Scientific notation is a shorthand method of displaying a big number. For example, 1.2E+10 is 1.2 times 10^9 (1 with 9 zeros behind it).

Keeping Track of Dates Every Time

(After all, if you snooze you lose)

To include dates and times in your workbooks, you just need to type them in a form that Excel recognizes. Excel recognizes several different date and time formats.

Excel's Date and Time Formats

Type the date like this	Shorthand	Explanation
4-Apr	d-mmm	day, month
9/23/62	m/d/yy	month, day, and year
23-Sep-62	d-mmm-yy	day, month, and year
Sep-62	mmm-yy	month and year
12:01 AM	h:mm AM/PM	hour, minute, and AM or PM
12:01:00 AM	h:mm:ss AM/PM	hour, minute, second, and AM or PM
12:01	h:mm	hour and minute
12:01:00	h:mm:ss	hour, minute, and second
9/23/62 12:00	m/d/yy h:mm	month, day, year; then hour and minute

Other things to ponder when entering dates and times

✔ You can include the slash (/) or hyphen (-) character as part of an entry, as in 1/23/93 or 23-Jan-93.

✔ Excel always displays the date in the style you type, but "thinks of" the date in the format m/d/yy.

✔ Excel converts your entry into a *serial number*. This number represents the number of days from the beginning of the century until the date you type. Doing so enables you to do calculations on dates and to ask that all-important question: "How many days until the next payday?"

✔ Excel converts times to a fraction of a 24-hour day so that you can do calculations on times and answer that daily question: "How many minutes until lunch?"

✔ You can enter dates and times into the same cell, as in the entry 1/23/94 1:35 AM. Be sure to separate the date portion from the time portion with a space.

✔ Excel ignores capitalization when you are entering dates and times; therefore, the date 23-JAN-94 is the same as 23-jan-94.

✔ You can enter military times. For example, the entry for eleven o'clock at night is 23:00.

✔ When you include AM or PM as part of a time entry, Excel assumes that you want to use the 12-hour (not the military) clock. Likewise, without an AM or PM as part of a time entry, Excel assumes military time.

Formulas (Numbers that Think)

Let's face it. Nobody likes talking about formulas. They remind us too much of seventh-grade math, when we had that first "eyes glazing over numbers" experience. But Excel formulas have nothing to do with nor look anything like the formulas from our algebra/trigonometry/calculus/ theoretical particle physics/teenage days. Formulas provide the magic in a spreadsheet program!

To enter a formula, click the cell where you want the result to appear. Then type an equal sign (=). The equal sign tells Excel that what comes next is a formula. Then type the equation you want and press Enter.

The key to formulas is using cell references. Suppose that cell B1 contains 5 and cell B2 contains 10. You could create a formula like

=5+10

but this isn't any better than a calculator!

Instead, you can tell Excel to use the cell's value, like this:

=B1+B2

Excel will total the numbers in each cell. If you change a number in either cell, the formula automatically updates the answer.

If nothing else, remember this

✔ Excel displays the correct answer (not the formula you typed) in the cell.

✔ When the cell with the formula is active, you see the formula in the formula bar.

✔ This is just the bare bones of formulas. You will put formulas through their paces in Chapters 7, 13, and 14.

CHAPTER 2

Making Changes
(Quick-Change Artist)

IN A NUTSHELL

▼ Correcting mistakes
▼ Deleting entries
▼ Undoing changes
▼ Selecting a range
▼ Getting help

The thrill of using a spreadsheet program is the ease with which you can change things. For instance, maybe you thought you were going to sell 200,000 of those "pet sticks," but ended up selling only two. The business calculations you set up in your workbook probably need some major adjustments. Or maybe you need to correct a mistake—a typo, a wrong number, or a glaring error. Or maybe you want to make changes because you simply changed your mind.

This chapter covers the most common editing changes you can make in a workbook. And because you're a preferred customer, I've included a section on how to use Excel's on-line help feature—absolutely free!

No, No, No...It's All Wrong!

There are two ways to correct mistakes in Excel. You can correct them as you make them, or you can correct them after you make them. (Microsoft currently is working on a new Excel feature that enables you to correct them before you make them.)

Actually, you might not be fixing mistakes. Maybe you're just "making changes." Yeah, that's right, they're not mistakes; they're just changes you need to make.

Fixing While You Work

Whenever you're typing on your keyboard, the stuff you're typing appears in the cell as well as in the formula bar. If you notice a typing mistake and haven't pressed Enter yet, you can make a change before you put the entry into the cell. Just press Backspace to delete up to the point where you want to make the change. Then type something new and improved.

Fixing after the Fact

If you press Enter, the entry is already made, and you will have to use a different procedure to change it.

If you want to replace an entry with something entirely new—like changing that budget entry from *Ferrari* to *Volkswagen*—make that cell the active one, retype the information, and press Enter.

If you want to slightly change the entry—like changing that budget entry from *Trip to Spain* to *Trip to Scranton*—you can edit the cell by using a different method.

First, point your mouse at the cell you want to change, and then double-click the mouse button or press F2. The insertion point appears in the cell, where you can make changes. You are now in Edit mode (the status bar reminds you of this by displaying Edit).

To accept the new, edited version of the cell, press Enter. To go back to the original entry, don't press Enter. Press Esc instead.

BUZZWORDS

INSERTION POINT

The insertion point is the vertical line that moves while you're typing in the cell. It indicates where the text that you type will appear.

Cruisin' around the cell

✔ Press the left- or right-arrow key to move the insertion point left or right, respectively, one character at a time.

✔ Press Home to quickly move the insertion point to the front of the entry.

continues

✔ Press End to quickly move the insertion point to the end of the entry.

✔ Press Backspace to delete the character to the left of the insertion point.

✔ Press Del to delete the character to the right of the insertion point.

When you're finished making changes, press the Enter key or click the check mark button ☑ at the left end of the formula bar.

To cancel the whole exercise so that nothing gets entered into the active cell, press the Esc key or use the mouse to click the X button at the ☒ left end of the formula bar.

Deleting Entries

Sometimes you just want to get rid of the entry entirely. To completely erase the contents of a cell, make that cell the active one, and then press the Del key. Now wasn't that easy?

Undoing Changes

(Going back in time)

In Excel, you can undo things that you have just done in a workbook! You can go back in time as if it never happened. Typed over an important formula? You can undo it. Deleted a really important number?

You can undo it. Lost a fortune in the stock market crash of '87? Well, Excel's Undo feature is great, but not that great.

To undo something, open the **E**dit menu and choose the **U**ndo command. Excel undoes the last thing you did, presenting you with the workbook as it looked before your boo-boo. For example, if you made something bold by mistake, click the wounded cell once to select it and choose the **U**ndo command to undo it.

TIP

Read this if you don't know how to choose a menu command:

Excel displays nine menu names in its menu bar. Each menu offers a unique grouping of commands. To open a menu, place your mouse pointer on its name in the menu bar and click the mouse button once. If you're a keyboard fanatic, hold down the Alt key and press the underlined letter in the menu name. For example, press Alt and E to open the **E**dit menu.

Excel "pulls down" the menu, revealing an assortment of commands. To choose a command, point and click the command name with your mouse. Or, from the keyboard, press the underlined letter in the command name. If you decide not to choose a command after all, press Esc twice.

The can's and why not's? of undoing mistakes

✔ To be able to have a shot at successfully undoing something, you must use the **U**ndo command immediately after you screw up, and absolutely before you do a single other thing. You can only undo the last thing you did.

✔ Although Excel can undo most things in a workbook, there are a few things that it simply never will be able to handle, such as

continues

recovering a workbook you accidentally deleted or making a workbook look like it did five days ago at precisely 4:32 in the afternoon.

✔ The description for the Undo command in the Edit menu constantly changes to reflect the action you just took in the workbook. After you type an entry into a cell, for example, the Edit menu entry says **Undo Entry**, but after you use the Del key to erase an entry from a cell, the Edit menu says **Undo Clear**.

✔ Excel doesn't warn you when you have taken an action that can't be undone. The only way you will know is when you open the Edit menu and see the **Can't Undo** message, which means that you're out of luck.

✔ You can quickly undo something by pressing Ctrl+Z, the shortcut key for the Undo command.

 ✔ You also can quickly undo something by clicking the Undo button on the Standard toolbar. (It's the one that looks like an arrow that's looped back and pointing to the left.)

✔ The most destructive thing you can do in Excel that simply cannot be undone with Undo is deleting a file with the File Find File command. (More on this one in Chapter 4, "Opening, Closing, and Deleting Workbooks.")

✔ Every blue moon or so, you'll do something in the workbook that requires more memory than the Undo feature can handle. Before Excel actually completes this "something," it will display an alert box warning you that Excel will be unable to undo the event should you choose to proceed. Click **No** if you want to cancel the activity. If you want to continue the operation, knowing full well that you won't be able to undo it if you need to, click **Yes**.

Selecting a Range

(Target practice)

When you edit a workbook, it's much faster to select all the stuff you want to work with, and then execute a command. If you want to delete several cells, for instance, don't select and delete and select and delete and so on, deleting each cell individually. Instead, select all the cells and delete them all at once.

BUZZWORDS

RANGE ADDRESS

A selection of cells is called a *range* and is identified by a *range address*. The *range address* is the top left cell in the range, a colon, and the bottom right cell in the range. The range A1:B2, for example, includes these cells: A1, A2, B1, and B2.

Cell range gymnastics

✔ To select a range with the mouse, click the cell at one corner of the range and drag to the opposite corner.

✔ To select a range with the keyboard, hold down the Shift key and use the arrow keys to highlight the range.

✔ To select an entire row, click the row number.

✔ To select an entire column, click the column letter.

✔ To select the entire sheet, click the blank rectangle at the top of the row numbers and to the left of the column letters.

continues

Cell range gymnastics (continued)

✔ To select cells that aren't next to each other, click the first cell, and then point to the next cell you want to select. Hold down the Ctrl key and click the mouse button. Continue Ctrl-clicking until you select all the cells you want.

Once you have selected a range, you can do lots of things to all the cells in that range: format them, change their alignment, copy or move them, delete them, and so on. The command you choose is applied to each cell in the range. To deselect a range, click anywhere outside of it.

Getting Help

(It's only an F1-call away)

As you work in Excel, you might reach a situation where you just don't know what to do. Excel can talk you through many problem situations, swiftly and painlessly.

Whenever you need help with anything in Excel, press the F1 key. Excel displays a general help contents window that lists information about everything from *Using Microsoft Excel* to *Programming with Visual Basic* (whatever that means).

To choose a topic, look for the green and/or underlined word that corresponds to that topic, and then click it with your mouse. A second list of topics appears. Click the subtopic you want; a more detailed help window appears with an explanation of the selected topic.

A general help contents window in Excel

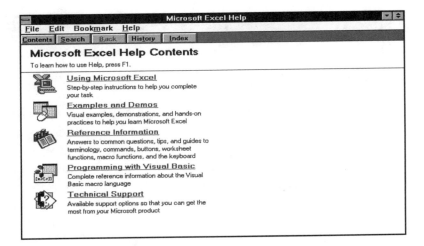

Help topics for the hapless

✔ You can scroll line-by-line through any help window with your mouse or keyboard. With a mouse, click the up or down scroll arrows at the right edge of the help window; with your keyboard, press the Tab key. Use the PgUp or PgDn keys to scroll through the help window one window at a time.

✔ To redisplay the main help window from any other help window, click the Contents button.

✔ When the help you need can be phrased in the form of a how-can-I question, like "How can I move around a workbook?," start by selecting the help topic called *Using Microsoft Excel,* and then choose the *Essential Skills* topic from the next window.

✔ To move back to the previous help window, click the Back button.

✔ To exit help and return to your workbook, open the **F**ile menu from the help window and choose the E**x**it command. Keyboard maniacs can press Alt+F4.

BUZZWORDS

CONTEXT-SENSITIVE HELP

Excel also offers context-sensitive help. This type of help displays a help window that relates exactly to what you were doing the moment you pressed F1.

Best of all, you don't have to go traipsing through lots of topic windows just to get a simple answer to a simple question. (Remember asking mom how to spell a word, and being told to look it up in the dictionary?) Suppose, for example, that you open a menu and aren't sure what a command does. Use the arrow keys to highlight the command. Then press F1. Excel displays a help window that relates to that exact command. To get context-sensitive help about stuff that you can't highlight from the keyboard, click the Help button at the far-right end of the Standard toolbar. Then click the area of the screen you want to know more about.

TIP

Most Excel dialog boxes also contain a **Help** button. Click the Help button to get the same context-sensitive help window.

CHAPTER 3
Saving and Exiting
(File Shenanigans)

IN A NUTSHELL

▼ Saving a workbook
▼ Saving new stuff in an old workbook
▼ Changing the name of a workbook
▼ Turning off the Excel program

A ll the effort you put into a workbook goes for nothing if you don't save the workbook. Saving the workbook ensures that your hard work is tucked away where you can work on it again. This chapter covers the all-important task of saving. After you save, you're free to go—yes, exit Excel and turn off the computer.

Save It or Lose It

(Tough love with your workbooks)

Whenever you stick a file folder into your briefcase, you do so with the expectation that the next time you open the briefcase, the folder will still be there. But imagine opening the file folder expecting to see that beautiful report with the cool color graphs you made, only to find the file folder completely empty.

The one thing you're sure to hate about Excel (and any software program for that matter) is that it's not smart enough to know when it should make a permanent copy of your hard work. An Excel workbook won't become permanent until you tell Excel to make it permanent. The workbooks you create on-screen are temporary and can easily be lost if there's a sudden power failure, if you turn off your computer, or if you exit the program.

To make a permanent record of a workbook, you must "save" the workbook. To save the workbook means to take the workbook and store it on your computer's hard disk. (It isn't called a hard disk because it's hard to find, but because it's inside a hard metal box that sits inside your computer.) Your computer's hard disk is your "electronic briefcase." As soon as you save your workbook, you will be able to retrieve it from your electronic briefcase as often as you like.

Saving Your Workbooks

(From certain doom)

Get into the habit of saving your workbooks at regular intervals during your workday. If you save regularly, you'll never have to experience the pain of re-creating a workbook that's accidentally been lost. For really important work, saving every few minutes or so isn't out of the question. Here's how to save a workbook:

1. Open the **F**ile menu and choose the **S**ave command.

The first time you save a workbook, Excel will display the Save As dialog box.

Type a file
name here

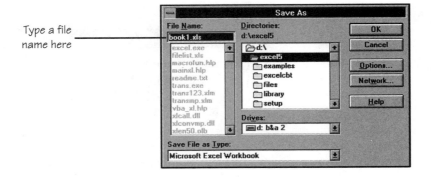

Book1 is a temporary name that Excel gives the workbook. Excel fully expects you to come up with a better one. The name you choose should be more distinctive so that you will be able to tell your workbooks apart.

2. Type a name, like BUDGET94.XLS.

   This name has two parts to it: BUDGET94 is the first name and XLS is the last name (called the *extension*). A period separates the two. You can use up to 8 characters for the first name and 3 characters for the last. Also, don't use any blank spaces, and avoid using punctuation in your workbook names.

3. Click OK. Excel displays the Summary Info dialog box. Then type the information about your workbook into the text boxes.

4. Click OK.

As soon as you click OK, Excel names your workbook and saves it on your hard disk. The new name now appears in the workbooks title bar.

Important stuff about saving workbooks

✔ Every workbook must have a first name (of up to eight characters), but you don't have to type the last name. When you leave off the last name, Excel adds the last name XLS. The file name MONEY, for example, becomes MONEY.XLS. (The letters *XLS* stand for *ex-el-spreadsheet*.)

✔ Excel does not accept more letters than are allowed in a file name. Try using the name EGGSBENEDICT and an alert box appears. Click OK and supply a shorter name.

✔ Choose first names that describe the workbook's information.

✔ When typing a name, you can use either uppercase or lowercase characters. It makes no difference.

✔ Whenever the name you type for a new workbook already belongs to another workbook, Excel displays the message: `Replace existing NODOUGH.XLS?` (in this example, you're trying to create a second workbook named NODOUGH.XLS). Click the Cancel button to stop. Excel returns you to the Save As dialog box. Now type a unique name.

✔ The quickest way to save a workbook is to click the Save button in the Standard toolbar. It's the third icon from the left and looks like a floppy disk. Keyboard enthusiasts can press Shift+F12 to do the same thing.

✔ Excel keeps your workbooks in specific locations on your hard disk. Unless you tell Excel otherwise, it saves the file to the current directory, which is listed at the top of the Save As dialog box. To put the file in a different directory, you must change to that directory. If you aren't sure how to change directories, you need to get your hands on the companion book *I Hate Windows*.

BUZZWORDS

FILE

A file is a collection of data you want to record permanently on your computer's hard disk. In the case of Excel, the data collection happens to be in a workbook. In word processing programs they're in documents, and in database programs they're in, well, databases.

BUZZWORDS

> **DIRECTORY**
>
> A directory is a section of your hard disk set up to store certain types of files. Similar to a folder, a directory keeps all files in an easy-to-find spot. A directory also can contain other directories. Sometimes the term "subdirectory" is used to refer to directories within directories, but basically directory and subdirectory mean the same thing. Only one directory can be current at a time.

Saving the Second Time, Third Time, and So On

The Save As dialog box appears on-screen only the first time you save a workbook. This box appears so that you can name the workbook. Every other time you save the same workbook by using the **F**ile menu's **S**ave command, Excel assumes that you want to keep using the same name, so it doesn't bother with the dialog box. When you want to change the name of a workbook, you must use the **F**ile Save **A**s command.

TIP

> The other quickest way to save a workbook the second, third, and so on time, is to press Ctrl+S—that's the shortcut key for the **F**ile **S**ave command.

CAUTION

> As you work in Excel, keep in mind that the changes you make in your workbook aren't recorded (saved) until you save the workbook on disk again. At any given point in time, the disk version includes only the changes you made up to the last time you saved.

Every time you save a workbook after you've saved it the first time, Excel does very little to show that the workbook's actually being saved. Scary, huh? Here are a couple of road signs you can keep an eye out for when saving your workbooks:

✔ Try watching your computer (not the screen, but the box itself) as you save a workbook. Most computers show a red, blinking light when they're saving to the hard disk.

✔ Try listening to your computer as you save a workbook. Most computers make a chirping, whirring sound when they're saving to the hard disk. Sounds sort of like a squirrel that's had ten cups of coffee.

✔ Look at the very left end of the status bar. Excel displays a progress message here while it saves your workbooks. The problem is that today's computers are pretty darn fast, so this message may appear and disappear in the blink of an eye.

Changing a Workbook's Name (Excel's witness-protection program)

Do you hate the name you just gave to your workbook? You can save it with a new name.

TIP

Saving a file with a new name is also handy when you want to have two similar versions of a workbook. Save the workbook with a new name to create a copy of that workbook. You can make any changes you want to the copy; the original is still intact in its original form.

41

Open the **F**ile menu and choose the Save **A**s command. Keyboard junkies can press F12 instead. As soon as you choose this command, Excel displays the Save As dialog box. (Yes, it's the same dialog box you get when you use the **S**ave command on a workbook for the first time.) Notice that the current workbook name is highlighted below File Name in the dialog box.

Type a new name and click OK. As soon as you click OK, Excel saves a copy of your workbook, using the name you typed. For now, you have two versions of the same workbook, each with a different name, on your hard drive.

Closing Workbooks and Exiting Excel

(Until another day)

If you're like me, you look forward to turning off your computer at the end of the day. It's the office worker's equivalent of the factory whistle. Unfortunately, computers make few noticeable sounds when you turn them off. In fact, things get even more quiet—that is, unless a colleague down the hall accidentally turns off his or her computer before saving stuff and exiting Excel. Then you'll hear that factory whistle blow, or something that sounds pretty much like it.

Before you exit Excel or turn off your computer, save your workbook. Before you turn off the computer, exit both Excel and Windows.

To exit Excel, open the **F**ile menu and choose the E**x**it command. Excel disappears from your screen. You return to Program Manager (Windows).

If you forget to save your workbook, Excel reminds you with an alert box. Click **Yes** to save the workbook and then exit. Click **No** to discard (throw away, ignore, toss out, forget for eternity) all the changes you've made and exit. Click Cancel to return to the workbook to do whatever.

To exit Windows, open the **File** menu and choose the Exit Windows command. When you see an alert box that asks whether you are sure you want to exit, click OK. You are returned to a blank screen with something like `C:\>` at the top. Now you can turn off your computer.

CHAPTER 4

Opening, Closing, and Deleting Workbooks

(File Shenanigans II)

IN A NUTSHELL

▼ Opening a workbook
▼ Closing a workbook
▼ Getting a new, blank workbook
▼ Deleting a workbook

This chapter covers even more useful stuff you can do to your workbooks. Things like opening the workbook you were using the last time you ran Excel and getting a fresh, blank workbook so that you can create something new and exciting. And for the adventurous, you will see how to dispose of those old, worn-out workbooks you no longer need.

Opening an Existing Workbook

(Picking up where you left off)

Naming workbooks and saving them on your hard drive is the equivalent of labeling file folders and stuffing them into your briefcase. This section explains how to reach back into your "electronic briefcase" and pull out your file folders.

When you save a workbook, you store the information in a file, and you store the file on your computer's hard drive. When you want to continue working with that same workbook at a later date—perhaps to type in a few more numbers or change a title—you must reopen it in Excel.

Here's how to open a workbook:

1. Open the File menu and choose the Open command. Excel displays the Open dialog box.

   Notice the highlighted text underneath File Name in this dialog box. The mysterious *.xl* is a coded message that tells Excel what types of files to display below. Decoded, *.xl* means "all Excel files."

Type the name of the file you want here

Or click it in this file list

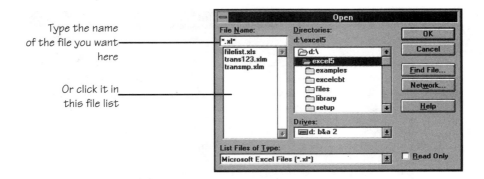

2. Find your workbook name in the files list and click it once.

Its name pops into the File Name box. If you would prefer to type the name instead, go ahead.

3. Click OK. Excel opens the workbook and displays it on-screen.

You can combine steps 2 and 3 by double-clicking the workbook name in the files list.

TIP

If the workbook you want to open is one of the last four that you opened, try the following shortcut. Click the File menu. At the bottom of the menu, you will see a list of the last four workbooks that were opened. Click the one you want.

✔ You can have more than one workbook open at once. If you have a workbook open that doesn't fill up the whole screen and then open another, they both appear on-screen. The one you opened most recently is on top and is the *active* workbook. (You can tell an active workbook by its title bar—it appears in a different color.) See Chapter 12, "Excel Does Windows," for the gymnastics of working with more than one workbook at a time.

✔ Keyboard devotees can press Ctrl+F12 to quickly display the Open dialog box.

✔ When the workbook name you type in the File **N**ame box doesn't exist, Excel displays a message saying so. Click OK to continue. Try again, but this time pick from the file list.

✔ When typing the name of the workbook you want to open, you can use either uppercase or lowercase characters. It makes no difference to Excel.

✔ To open a file that's stored in a different directory, you must change to that directory. If you aren't sure how to change directories, you need to get your hands on the companion book *I Hate Windows*.

✔ When you try to open a workbook that's already open on-screen, Excel displays a message such as `BRUNCH.XLS is already open. Reopening will cause your changes to be discarded. Do you want to reopen?` (This message appears if you're trying to open a workbook named BRUNCH.XLS that's already open.) Click the No button to stop.

EXPERTS ONLY

What's wild about wild cards?

In DOS espionage circles, the secret code *.XL* contains "wild cards." Just as a wild card in poker can match any card, a wild card in Excel can match any character or characters. When you see *, it means "insert whatever you want here." So the code *.XL* means "look for all files with any first name, but whose last name uses X and L for the first two characters and anything for the third character." This code would locate the files BRUNCH.XLS, LUNCH.XLM, and SUPPER.XLC if they existed.

Wild cards are really useful for narrowing the number of files displayed in the Open dialog box.

To use a wild card, open the File menu and choose the Open command. Type the wild card into the File Name box and click OK. Excel immediately displays a list of the matching files. The following table displays some examples of how you can use wild cards in your day-to-day Excel work.

.	Displays all file names in the current directory
*.XLS	Displays Excel workbook names only
DINNER.*	Displays all files whose first name is DINNER, as in DINNER.XLS, DINNER.DOC, and DINNER.YUM
LUNCH*.XLS	Displays all workbooks whose first name begins with the word LUNCH, as in LUNCH91.XLS, LUNCH92.XLS, and LUNCH93.XLS

TIP

To quickly open a workbook, click the Open button in the Standard toolbar. It's the icon second from the left that looks like an open folder. When the Open dialog box appears, double-click the workbook name in the file list.

Closing a Workbook

(I'm done for now)

It's a good idea to close workbooks you aren't working on. Open workbooks take up memory and crowd your electronic desktop (your screen). If you are working on a workbook and want to close it (put it away), save the workbook first. Then open the **F**ile menu and choose the **C**lose command. Keyboarders can press Ctrl+F4 to do the same thing.

Getting a Fresh New Workbook

(Starting from scratch)

You have created a workbook and saved it. Now you're ready to start creating another one. But where does Excel keep all its spare workbooks? To display a new, blank workbook on-screen, open the **F**ile menu and choose the **N**ew command. Excel displays the New dialog box. The word *Workbook* is highlighted.

Click OK. Excel opens a blank workbook on-screen. The name of this workbook says Book1 or Book2 or something similar to that. Excel uses the same dummy naming scheme for each new workbook you open into

the program. The next time you start Excel on your computer, though, the first workbook you'll see will be named Book1. If you want to change this dummy name to something more descriptive, take a look at the section "Changing a Workbook's Name" in Chapter 3, "Saving and Exiting."

TIP

The quickest way to get a new workbook is to click the New Workbook button in the Standard toolbar. It's the icon at the very left end of the toolbar and resembles a sheet of paper with a dog-eared corner. As soon as you click this button, a new workbook appears on-screen.

Getting Rid of a Workbook

(Without doing hard time)

Most workbooks eventually outlive their usefulness. Either you no longer need the data, or the workbook itself is obsolete. Every so often you should draw up a list of workbooks that fit into this category and delete them. If you're sharing your computer with someone else, be sure to check with that person before you delete anything.

When you delete a workbook, you are actually erasing the information from your hard drive. This procedure is like pulling a file folder from your briefcase and tossing it into the trash. Not only does deleting old workbooks make it easier to manage the ones that remain behind, but it also frees up room on your hard drive for saving new information.

To delete a workbook, open the File menu and choose the Find File command. As soon as you choose this command, Excel displays the Find File dialog box.

"I HATE THIS!"

What's this Search dialog box all about?

The first time that anyone uses the Find File command in your copy of Excel, the Search dialog box appears instead of the Find File dialog. To kick-start Excel in its search for files, type the name of the file to search for in the File **N**ame box. Next, type the letter of the hard drive you wish to search, then type the colon character in the Location box. (For instance, type C: to search your "C" drive.) Now click OK. Every time afterwards, when you choose Find File, you get the Find File dialog box.

Click the name of the workbook you want to delete here

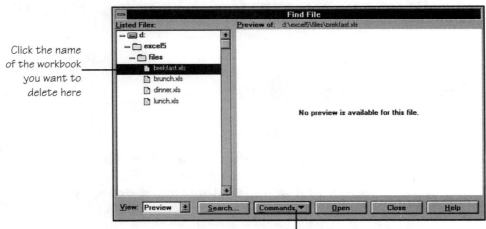

Then click this button to display the **D**elete command

Excel shows you a complete list of all the files in the current directory in the Listed Files box. When you see the name of the workbook you want to delete in the list, click the name. Click the **C**ommands button at the bottom of the dialog box and a pop-up menu appears. Locate the **D**elete command on this menu, and then click it once.

As soon as you click **Delete**, Excel displays a question box asking whether you're sure that you want to delete the file. This is your last chance to change your mind, so think really hard before continuing.

Click the **Yes** button to delete the file from your hard drive. After you delete a workbook, you cannot open it up in Excel ever again, at least not without some special program and the help of a data recovery whiz.

Click the **No** button to stop the delete operation dead in its tracks. Excel returns you to the Find File dialog box. Choose a different file to delete (the one you meant to pick in the first place), and then start the button-clicking process all over again. Or click Close to stop this deleting stuff altogether. Excel returns you to your workbook.

CAUTION

Deleting a workbook is the final commitment. Once a workbook is gone, it's gone for good. Before you actually consummate the deal, double-check that the file name displayed in the question box is, in fact, the name of the workbook you want to delete. Also, never delete a file whose name you do not recognize. The unrecognizable file could be one of the many different files that Excel needs to operate correctly, and you don't want to accidentally delete one of them!

I HATE EXCEL FOR WINDOWS!

"I HATE THIS!"

I accidentally killed my workbook!

It's happened to everyone at least once. You accidentally delete a workbook that you really needed after all. If you're lucky, you are friends with an expert who can raise deleted files from the dead. Call and ask for help. The chances for this voodoo succeeding are excellent as long as you do one thing:

THE MINUTE YOU DELETE THE FILE, STEP AWAY FROM YOUR COMPUTER AND GO CALL YOUR FRIEND!

Do not allow anyone near your computer until the cavalry gets there. Tape a piece of paper to the front of your computer, warning everyone to stay away or else.

CHAPTER 5

Formatting Your Workbook
(From Ugly Duckling to Swan)

IN A NUTSHELL

- ▼ Adding bold and italic style
- ▼ Making text bigger and smaller
- ▼ Aligning text and numbers
- ▼ Using different number styles
- ▼ Aligning and widening columns

All Excel workbooks start out as ugly ducklings. All those words and numbers by themselves do little to inspire the people who read your reports. The best workbooks are accurate and pleasing to the eyes.

Formatting is the key to making a workbook attractive. You start with a plain workbook and spiff it up a bit so that your boss, a colleague, or a client says stuff like, "Wow, it's so clear to me now!" and "What a work of art!"

Excel offers you lots of formatting tools—tools that allow you to widen columns, line up text, and make words bold. This chapter looks at the most popular of these tools.

TIP

Keep in mind that you can open the **E**dit menu and choose the **U**ndo command, press Ctrl+Z, or click the Undo button on the Standard toolbar to reverse any of the formatting commands you'll test drive in this chapter.

Changing Type Styles

(Overhauling your Excel wardrobe)

If you make important words and numbers stand out, you can direct a reader's attention to the important stuff first. There are three good ways to make text stand out: make the type bold, make the type italic, or resize the type.

To Boldly Go Where No Type Has Gone Before

You've just finished creating the year-end sales workbook. The totals are absolutely outstanding. But the numbers just aren't bold enough.

BEFORE: Just a boring old workbook

	Microsoft Excel - EOYSALES.XLS

File   Edit   View   Insert   Format   Tools   Data   Window   Help

MS Sans Serif   10   **B** *I* U

A1

	A	B	C	D	E	F	G	H	I
1									
2									
3		Brash 'n Bold Swimwear							
4		Annual Sales Report							
5									
6				1st Quarte	2nd Quarte	3rd Quarte	4th Quarte	End-Of-Year	
7		One Piece		12407	8581	6199	11805	38992	
8		Bikini		7301	11465	10078	5623	34467	
9		Thong		11470	12349	8481	8530	40830	
10		Dental Floss		11722	11621	6422	11191	40956	
11		Fiber Optic Cable		6816	6726	9502	7930	30974	
12		Totals:		49716	50742	40682	45079	186219	
13									
14									
15									
16									
17									
18									

EOYSALES

Ready

Adding bold to a workbook is easy. Select the cell that contains the type you want to make bold. Click the Bold button in the Formatting toolbar. It's the button with the picture of the bold **B** on it. Excel instantly makes the contents of the cell bold. To remove the bold style from your type, just click the Bold button again.

TIP

Keyboarders can quickly add bold style to the contents of the active cell by pressing Ctrl+B.

Italic (Text on the slant)

Adding italic style is a subtle way of helping the reader figure out what's what in the workbook. You might, for example, want to make your column headings italic.

To use italic style, select the cell that contains the type you want to make italic. Click the Italic button in the Formatting toolbar. It's the button with the picture of the *I* leaning to one side. Excel instantly makes the contents of the cell italic. Do the same for any other cells you want to enhance. To remove the italic style from a cell, just click the Italic button again.

TIP

Keyboarders can quickly add italic style to the contents of the active cell by pressing Ctrl+I.

Font fashion do's and don'ts

✔ There are no laws saying that some type should always be bold and other type should always be italic. It's completely up to you to decide what looks right.

✔ Avoid using bold or italic for all the type in a workbook—that will defeat the purpose of using these "discriminating" tools in the first place.

✔ You also can make text both bold and italic. Click both the Bold and Italic buttons in the Formatting toolbar (one after another, of course).

✔ If you change the type to bold and italic, but see ######## in the cell as a result, you need to widen the column. You'll learn about that in the "Widening Columns," section, later in this chapter.

✔ The Bold and Italic buttons appear "pushed in" after you click them the first time. When you remove the style from a cell, the buttons return to their original "pushed out" appearance. Because of this appearance change, you can easily tell when a particular style has been added to (or successfully removed from) the active cell.

✔ To make a bunch of cells bold or italic at once, select the range of cells before you click the Bold or Italic button. Chapter 2, "Making Changes," explains how to select a range of cells.

Sizing Up Your Type

Changing the size of type in your workbook is useful for emphasizing and de-emphasizing text. Newspapers, magazines, and books, for example, all use bigger type for titles and headlines, and smaller type for main body text and footnotes. You can do the same thing in your workbooks.

Enlarging and shrinking the size of type in a workbook cell is simple. First select the cell whose type size you want to change. You now can proceed in one of two directions to change the type size. First, click in-side the Font Size box on the Formatting toolbar and type the point size value you wish to use (whole numbers only, please), and then press Enter. Or second, click the scroll arrow next to the Font Size box to drop down a list of available sizes, and then click the size you wish to use. You can continue using either of these techniques to achieve even greater increases or decreases in size.

I HATE EXCEL FOR WINDOWS!

AFTER: A new-
and-improved
workbook, with
bold totals, italic
column headings,
and bigger titles

Microsoft Excel - EOYSALES.XLS

| File | Edit | View | Insert | Format | Tools | Data | Window | Help |

100%

MS Sans Serif 10

A1

Brash 'n Bold Swimwear
Annual Sales Report

			1st Quarter	2nd Quarter	3rd Quarter	4th Quarter	End-Of-Year
One Piece			12407	8581	6199	11805	**38992**
Bikini			7301	11465	10078	5623	**34467**
Thong			11470	12349	8481	8530	**40830**
Dental Floss			11722	11621	6422	11191	**40956**
Fiber Optic Cable			6816	6726	9502	7930	**30974**
Totals:			**49716**	**50742**	**40682**	**45079**	**186219**

EOYSALES

Ready

HUH?

BUZZWORDS

FONT

Computer programs use the word "font" to describe unique families of type and all their possible sizes. Courier, for example, is one font family and Arial is another. Windows comes with several built-in fonts, which are available to you in Excel. What I have referred to as "type size" is more accurately described as a font's "point size." The word "point" refers to an age-old measurement system that examines the height of a single character in terms of points. One point is equal to 1/72 inch. Get the point?

To return the contents of a cell to its original size, activate the Font Size box, type the number of the original size, and press Enter.

TIP

The quickest way to remove all special styles you have added to the contents of a cell—including bold style, italic style, and point-size changes—is to make that cell active and click each toolbar button that originally created the formats. To restore the original font name and size, though, you'll have to choose the original name and size from the Font and Font Size list boxes.

Displaying Numbers That Make Sense

(Number makeovers of the rich and famous)

When you enter numbers into cells, you can see that Excel displays the numbers pretty much the way you type them. The number 45.5 appears as 45.5 and the number 2903 appears as 2903. But not all numbers are created equal. If you don't think so, consider accepting payment for a debt owed to you in gallons instead of dollars. This example shows why it's critical that your workbook numbers make sense.

One way to show what a number means is to type a text description, such as "pounds" or "days," near the number in the workbook. A more useful technique is to apply one of Excel's built-in *number formats* to improve the numbers appearance.

Here's how to turn plain-looking numbers into sexy figures:

1. Select the cell or range of cells you want to format. Selecting a range is covered in Chapter 2, "Making Changes."

2. Open the Format menu and choose the Cells command. Excel displays the Format Cells dialog box.

3. Click the Number tab to display the number format options.

4. Click the **C**ategory list choice that best describes the number you're formatting. To format a number to display it as dollars, for example, click Currency.

   As soon as you click an item in the **C**ategory list, Excel displays the formats available for that category in the **F**ormat Codes list.

5. Click a code style in the **F**ormat Codes list box.

First choose a category from this list

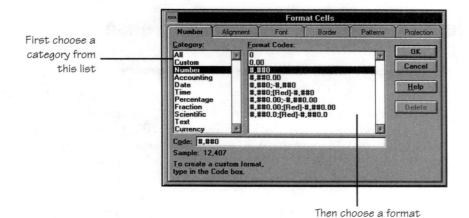

Then choose a format from this list

"I HATE THIS!"

What the heck is #,###0.00?

Excel uses a cryptic numbering scheme to explain the numeric formats. The easiest way to figure out a particular numeric format is to click it and then check the sample in the lower left corner of the dialog box. If the number looks the way you want it, you have the format you want.

6. Click OK. Excel applies the number format to the number in the active cell.

TIP

You can either enter numbers the way you want them formatted or use shortcut keys. If you want the number 1200 shown as currency with two decimal places, for example, either type **$1200** and press Enter, or type **1200**, press Enter, and then press Ctrl+Shift+$. For percentages, you can type something like **10%**, or you can type **.1**, press Enter, and then press Ctrl+Shift+%.

The Number Format categories explained

✔ The All category displays a comprehensive list of the format codes for all of the following categories.

✔ The Number category displays positive and negative numbers, with and without commas and decimal places. Some examples of this category are 2546 and 2,546 and 2,546.00. Excel can display negative numbers like (2,546) in red on-screen.

✔ The Accounting category displays numbers as only professional bean counters can: With commas, dollar signs, decimal points, and cents neatly lined-up according to FASB Rule 355, subsection 27, paragraph 2, rule 3. Some examples of this category are –$246.45 and $2,546.45.

✔ The Date category displays date numbers in one of five date formats. The most popular formats are 6/15/94 and 15-Jun-94.

continues

The Number Format categories explained (continued)

✔ The Time category displays time numbers in one of the five time formats. The most popular formats are 12:03 and 12:03:12 AM.

✔ The Percentage category displays numbers as percents, with or without decimal places. Examples of this format include 5.24% and 5%.

✔ The Fraction category displays numbers as fractions, like 1/4, or mixed numbers, like 2 11/25.

✔ The Scientific category displays numbers in scientific notation. For example, the number 50,000 displays as 5.00E+04.

✔ The Currency category displays positive and negative dollar values. Excel can display negative numbers in red on-screen.

TIP

You also can apply three popular number formats by clicking the Currency Style button 🖫, Percent Style button 🖫, or Comma Style button 🖫 on the Formatting toolbar.

Then, to increase or decrease the number of decimal places showing in your number, you can click the Increase Decimal button 🖫 or Decrease Decimal button 🖫, also located on the Formatting toolbar. If you want the number .1255 shown as a percent with two decimal places, for example, select the cell, click the Percent Style button to display the number as **13%**, then click the Increase Decimal button twice to display the number as **12.55%**.

Goldilocks and the Three Alignment Tools

(Someone's been shifting my data)

Excel automatically aligns text at the left edge of a cell and aligns numbers at the right. But these alignments may not work for your workbook. You might want to use a different alignment. Aligning makes things neat and orderly so that you (and everyone else) can easily read and understand what's in a workbook.

You can change alignment styles by selecting the cell you want to change and then clicking one of the alignment buttons on the Formatting toolbar:

Button	Name	Purpose
	Align Left button	Shifts data to the left edge of the active cell
	Center button	Shifts data to the center of the active cell
	Align Right button	Shifts data to the right edge of the active cell

Left-aligned titles

Centered column headings

Right-aligned text

| | | Microsoft Excel - EOYSALES.XLS | | | | | |

File   Edit   View   Insert   Format   Tools   Data   Window   Help

MS Sans Serif   10   B I U $ % ,   100%

A1

	A	B	C	D	E	F	G	H	I
1									
2									
3		**Brash 'n Bold Swimwear**							
4		Annual Sales Report							
5									
6				1st Quarter	2nd Quarter	3rd Quarter	4th Quarter	End-Of-Year	
7		One Piece		12,407	8,581	6,199	11,805	$38,992	
8		Bikini		7,301	11,465	10,078	5,623	$34,467	
9		Thong		11,470	12,349	8,481	8,530	$40,830	
10		Dental Floss		11,722	11,621	6,422	11,191	$40,956	
11		Fiber Optic Cable		6,816	6,726	9,502	7,930	$30,974	
12		Totals:		$49,716	$50,742	$40,682	$45,079	$186,219	
13									
14									
15									
16									
17									

EOYSALES

Ready

Widening Columns

(And other workbook-altering tricks)

There are two occasions when you'll get the urge to widen a workbook
column. The first is when you've entered text into a cell whose neighbor
to the right also contains some stuff. As you'll recall from Chapter 2,
"Making Changes," Excel lops off the tail end of the first entry in such
circumstances so that you can't see it anymore. The second is when
you've entered a really long number into a cell and all that shows is a
whole slew of number signs (########).

Two examples of when you'd want to widen a column

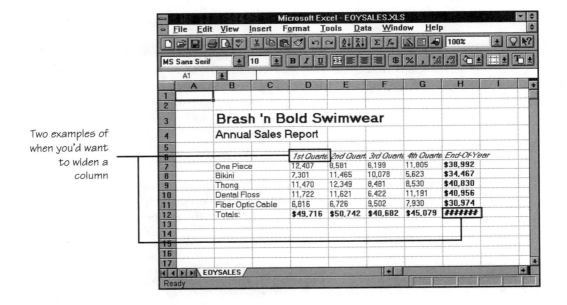

Excel gives you plenty of alternatives when it comes to changing the width of a column. The two most popular of these are using what Excel calls the AutoFit Selection option and dragging the column.

AutoFit Selection (One size fits all)

If you want Excel to figure out how big to make the column (big enough to fit the widest entry, plus a little breathing room), use the AutoFit Selection option:

1. Select any cell in the column you want to widen.

2. Open the Format menu and choose the **C**olumn command.

Excel displays the **C**olumn cascading menu. You'll see the AutoFit Selection option near the top of this menu. (You could choose the **W**idth option, and then type a width into the **C**olumn Width text box, but if you're not quite used to eyeballing column widths yet, let Excel size the column for you.)

3. Choose the AutoFit Selection option.

Excel automatically sizes the column so that it's slightly wider than the contents of the active cell. You can see everything that's in the cell, but the column is not so wide that there are miles of blank workbook until the next column.

TIP

There's even a quicker way to use the AutoFit Selection option. When you know the column you would like to use the AutoFit Selection option on, point your mouse pointer at the vertical bar on the right side of the column heading and double-click there. That's it!

Dragging the Column

The other way to widen a column is to drag the column by using your mouse:

1. Point your mouse at the vertical bar next to the column letter for the column whose width you want to change.

If you intend to widen column B, for example, you would move the mouse pointer to the vertical bar between B and C in the column heading. Your mouse pointer changes into a vertical bar that has two opposing arrows: one pointing left and one pointing right.

2. Drag the vertical bar to the right to increase the column width or to the left to decrease the column width.

To drag the bar, click and hold the left mouse button while your pointer is on the vertical bar, and then move the mouse to the left or right.

3. When the column width is where you'd like it, release the mouse button.

CHAPTER 6
Printing Basics
(Staying between the Lines)

IN A NUTSHELL

- ▼ Preparing to print
- ▼ Previewing a workbook
- ▼ Printing a whole workbook
- ▼ Printing different parts of a workbook
- ▼ Stopping a runaway printer

I HATE EXCEL FOR WINDOWS!

When you create a workbook that looks good enough to eat, it's time to think about printing it onto paper. Printing a workbook creates a permanent work record you can file away, give to a colleague, or turn into an origami masterpiece.

For many, the thought of printing conjures up images of ancient Aztec rituals: pouring out libations of toner and sacrificing paper in the hopes that something (anything!) actually pops out of the printer.

Printing in Excel, fortunately, doesn't require an advanced degree in mysticism. You only need to learn how to use one or two commands to be able to successfully print your workbooks and graphs. This chapter shows you how.

Checking Out Your Printer

(Is it alive?)

Before tackling any printing exercise, check out your printer to see whether it's in good working order. The following items might seem obvious to you, at least until you spend the better part of an afternoon trying to print when the power cord is unplugged.

Important things to look out for before you print

✔ Look behind the printer to see whether the power cord is plugged into the back of the printer and into the wall. If it isn't, plug it in. And make sure that the power cord between the back of the printer and the back of the computer is plugged in at both ends. You might have to wiggle these power cords a little to make sure that there's a good connection. (Cats and small children have a funny way of getting back there and undoing power cords.)

✔ Check out the front of your printer. See whether the printer is turned on and ready for printing. A printer makes a whirring, grinding noise when you first turn it on. Then a series of lights on the front or top of the printer will come on, indicating that your printer is ready to go.

✔ Make sure that the printer has an ample supply of paper. Some printers use paper trays, like copy machines; others use tractor-feed paper, the stuff with hole-punched, tear-away sides. Feed in the paper carefully. For laser printer paper, fan the stack before you cram it into the paper tray. For dot matrix printers, make sure the paper's not cockeyed when you place it onto the tractor-feed pins. If you don't know how to do any of this, ask someone who does.

✔ Most printers have an On-Line or Selected button located near the front or top of the unit. When this button is illuminated, your printer is on-line, which means that it's ready to print. When the On-Line or Selected button is not illuminated, the printer is off-line. Printers can't print when they're off-line, so press the button once to put it back on-line before you try to print.

Using Print Preview

(Sneak a peek)

You're ready to print. All the right lights are lit, the cords are plugged in, and you've fed in enough paper to print 500 copies of your workbook. Even though you're ready to start printing, you're a little bit hesitant. You remember your last printing experience. You printed, and nothing happened. You printed again, but half of your information didn't show up. So you tried a third time, but the printing started halfway down the first page. (Where's that sledgehammer?)

The easiest way to guard against PTPD (post-traumatic printing disorder) is to cure all the annoying problems ahead of time. Start by previewing the workbook.

With your workbook active in Excel, and the particular sheet you want to print displaying in the workbook, open the **F**ile menu. Then choose the Print Preview command. Excel displays the active sheet from your workbook on-screen. (This action may take from two to five seconds, depending on the speed of your computer.) The next thing you will see on-screen is a simulation of your printed workbook.

Previewing a workbook before printing it

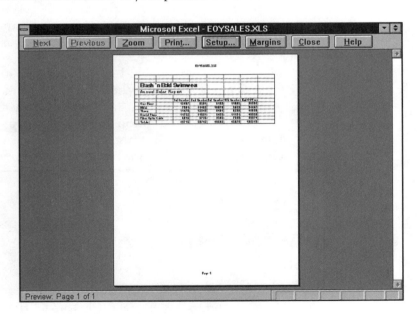

Click the **C**lose button to quit previewing. Excel returns you to the workbook.

TIP

Here's a quicker way to preview a workbook: With the workbook open in Excel, and the sheet you wish to preview showing in the workbook, click the Print Preview button in the Standard toolbar. (It's the fifth button from the left and shows a magnifying glass atop a sheet of paper.) Poof! You're off to the Print Preview environment.

Things you can do while previewing

✔ Press PgUp or PgDn to scroll up or down the active sheet in the workbook to reveal any information (or pages) not showing on-screen.

✔ If you want to magnify an area of the active sheet, click the Zoom button. You can accomplish the same thing by moving the mouse pointer into the sheet area—where the mouse pointer becomes a magnifying glass—and clicking once on the part of the sheet you want to zoom in on. Click once more on the sheet to zoom out.

✔ To change the margins, click the Margins button. Excel displays column markers and a grid over the sheet. This grid reveals the top, bottom, left, and right margin settings that Excel will use when printing the workbook. To change a margin, click the margin line you want to change, and drag it to a new location.

✔ When you're ready to print the workbook, click the Print button.

Printing the Whole Thing

(And nothing but the whole thing)

To print a workbook in its entirety, open the workbook. Then open the File menu. Choose the **P**rint command. When the Print dialog box appears, click the Entire Workbook button in the Print What block, then click OK. Each sheet in your workbook that contains text or numbers will begin printing within a few seconds.

Notice that Excel provides some other information on the printout. The name of the sheet appears at the top. The page number appears at the bottom. You can change these settings, but they are handy. Particularly when you've just dropped a stack of sheets on the floor and they're no longer in order.

TIP

Here's a quicker way to print a workbook: With the workbook open in Excel, click the Print button in the Standard toolbar. (It's the fourth button from the left and looks just like a little printer.)

Excel handles everything else for you, from deciding where the margins should be to where to start printing a second page for larger workbooks. Sure, Excel allows you to control all of that stuff if you really want to, but for now, who wants to?

Printing Only Part of a Workbook

(And other tree conservation tricks)

You can control how much stuff gets printed from your workbook by making the appropriate selection inside the Print What block of Excel's Print dialog box.

To print only a single sheet in a workbook, open the workbook and click the tab of the sheet you want to print. Then open the **File** menu and choose the **Print** command. When the Print dialog box appears, click OK. Excel prints only the current sheet because Selected Sheet(s) is the default option in the Print dialog box.

To print only some cells, select the cells in your workbook. Then open the **File** menu and choose the **Print** command. When the Print dialog box appears, click the Selection button, and then click OK. Excel prints only the selected cells.

Here's even another variation on printing part of a workbook. Suppose you decide that you need to reprint a couple of pages somewhere in the middle of a long printout, say pages 7 and 8 of a 15-page printout.

To print only a few pages of the same long sheet, open the **File** menu and choose the **Print** command. When the Print dialog box appears, click the Page(s) button inside the Page Range block. The cursor moves into the box labeled **From**. Type the starting page number, press the Tab key to move the cursor to the **To** box, and then type the ending page number. Click OK to begin printing the selected pages.

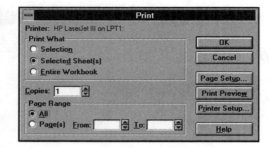

Choose your printer selections in the Print dialog box

Shooting Trouble

(Right between the eyes)

Ninety-nine percent of the things that can go wrong with printing takes place at the printer, nowhere near your fingers, your computer keyboard, or the sledgehammer you occasionally raise above your head. So when something does go wrong, don't start banging on the keyboard or hitting buttons on the computer. Remain calm and relaxed, and try a few of the following quick fixes.

How to stop a print operation gone haywire

✔ To cancel a printout before you click OK in the Print dialog box, just click the Cancel button.

✔ To cancel a printout after you click OK but before your printer starts printing, click the Cancel button in the Printing dialog box. This dialog box always appears for a moment or two immediately after you click OK to start printing.

✔ To cancel a printout after your printer starts printing, turn off the printer, wait 5 to 10 seconds, and then turn the printer back on. Your printer should spit out one final page and then stop.

PART II

Making It Look Good

Includes:

7: Formulas and Functions

8: Editing

9: Moving and Copying Data

10: More Workbook Formatting

11: Beyond Basic Printing

12: Excel Does Windows

CHAPTER 7

Formulas and Functions

(Doing Work That Adds Up to Something)

IN A NUTSHELL

- ▼ Creating formulas
- ▼ Using cell addresses in formulas
- ▼ Dealing with formula entry problems
- ▼ Using functions, Excel's built-in formulas
- ▼ Using the AutoSum button

Formulas are the backbone of your workbooks. But as workbook features go, the formula is the most misunderstood and maligned of them all. Mention this word to computer novices and watch their faces go blank and their eyes roll back into their heads.

In techie terms, a formula is something that uses math symbols to describe a relationship between numbers. A formula can be something as simple as this:

$$10 + 5 = 15$$

or something as bizarre as this:

$$\delta\theta = \frac{1}{2}\,(\delta x + \delta y) + \frac{1}{2}\,(\delta x - \delta y)\cos 2\theta + \tau xy \sin 2\theta$$

In *your* terms, formulas are equations that answer questions like "What's 10 plus 5?" or "What's the average of these 12 sales totals?" or "Just how much money does Uncle Sam take from me?"

What's a Formula Look Like?

(Give me some useful examples, please)

The most basic kind of Excel formula looks a lot like the calculations you would scribble on a piece of paper when figuring out your paycheck. Notice the following classic example:

$$750-200 = 550$$

This formula says that your total pay minus the government's cut equals the cash you can stick in your pocket. To enter that information into an Excel workbook, pick any cell in a worksheet, and then type the formula

$$=750-200$$

and press Enter. As soon as you press Enter, Excel displays the value 550 in the cell. Now look up in the formula bar. Your formula is still there. Excel stores formulas in cells exactly as you type them, but shows the answer in your worksheet.

The facts and figures of formulas

✔ Excel formulas always start with the equal sign. The equal sign tells Excel to show you the answer.

✔ Occasionally you will slip and type a formula in a form that resembles the handwritten, cocktail-napkin variety, such as 750–200=. When you type a formula this way, Excel won't show you an answer. As far as Excel is concerned, the entry 750–200 = is text, because you didn't start by typing an equal sign.

✔ Avoid typing blank spaces in formulas. Even though you can use blank spaces in many kinds of formulas (just like the ones you write out on paper), leaving the spaces out of the formulas you type into cells makes things look cleaner.

✔ There are six math symbols you can use to tell Excel which math operation to perform. The plus (+) symbol means add; the minus (–) symbol means subtract; the asterisk (*) symbol means multiply; the slash (/) symbol means divide; the caret (^) symbol means raise to the power of; and the percent symbol (%) means divide by 100.

✔ Formulas can do more than one math operation at a time. Just string together the numbers you want to calculate. The formula =5+32*120–345/12 performs four different math operations. Can you spot them all?

BUZZWORDS

Creating Smarter Formulas

(Cell addresses and pointing techniques)

Of course, there's more to creating formulas than typing an equal sign and a few numbers. You will eventually want to create formulas that calculate with lots of numbers all over your workbooks. The smartest Excel formulas use the addresses of cells that contain values, rather than the values themselves. And you can create formulas in ways that are more efficient than typing formulas into the formula bar.

Showing Up at the Right Address

Suppose that you've entered our sample paycheck formula into a worksheet. Your supervisor comes by and tells you that starting next week, your payroll taxes will increase by $23.52 per week. Now you have to edit the formula so that it looks like this:

=750–223.52

This change is easy enough to make when you are dealing with a couple of short formulas. But what happens when you have to change 50 formulas every other day during your work week? Ouch! To make these changes easier, create a formula that references values you have typed into your worksheet. Imagine, for example, that you have typed your total pay number into cell A5 and your total taxes number into cell A6. You could now type the formula

=A5–A6

into cell A7. Again, Excel displays the answer to the formula in the cell where you typed it, cell A7 in this case. If your payroll taxes go up, just type the new amount into cell A6. The boss gave you a weekly raise of $200? Enter that new value into cell A5. Each time you change one of the values that's referenced in the formula, Excel calculates a new answer in cell A7. That's the thrill of an electronic worksheet.

	A	B
5	750.00	750.00
6	200.00	200.00
7	=750–200.00	=B5–B6
formula result displayed in cell	500.00	500.00

	A	B
5	750.00	750.00
6	223.52	223.52
7	=750–223.52	=B5–B6
formula result displayed in cell	526.48	526.48

```
─────────────────────────────────────────────────────────────
                       Microsoft Excel                    ▼ ▲
File  Edit  View  Insert  Format  Tools  Data  Window  Help
─────────────────────────────────────────────────────────────
[icons toolbar]                                    100%   ▼ ♀ ▶?
─────────────────────────────────────────────────────────────
MS Sans Serif   ▼  10  ▼  B I U ▤ ≡ ≡ ≡ $ % , ⁺⁰⁸ ⁰⁸⁺ ...
─────────────────────────────────────────────────────────────
      C11       ▼
─────────────────────────────────────────────────────────────
□                    RECORD.XLS                          ▼ ▲
     A      B        C      D      E      F      G      H    I
 1
 2          The Media Revolution
 3          Monthly Sales Report
 4
 5                   Jan    Feb    Mar    Apr    May    Jun
 6
 7          Record  3,268  3,200  2,538  4,246  9,425  2,939
 8          CD      6,180  7,864  8,791  8,762  12,314 6,336
 9          Cassette 2,050   587  1,413  1,262  4,080  1,426
10          Video   2,351  2,784  4,914  6,203  4,614  4,392
11            Total:
12
13
14
15
 ◄ ◄ ► ►► RECORD
─────────────────────────────────────────────────────────────
Ready
─────────────────────────────────────────────────────────────
```

The formulas will go in row 11, starting in cell C11

It's Okay To Point

Okay. You've figured out that it makes much more sense to use cell addresses in your formulas. The next trick is to point to the cell rather than type the address. Suppose, for example, that you want to total up each month's sales dollars in the following worksheet.

Here's how to add the January sales values in cells C7, C8, C9, and C10:

1. Click cell C11 to make it the active cell. This is where you want to put the formula for January's total sales.

2. Type the equal symbol (=) to start the formula.

3. Click the mouse pointer inside cell C7, the first cell address you want to put in the formula. Excel displays Point at the left end of the Status bar whenever you're pointing this way.

A rotating outline appears around the cell you clicked. Excel then copies the address for cell C7 into the formula bar next to the equal sign. You have just pointed out the first cell address!

TIP

> Keyboard lovers can press the arrow keys to select the cells they want.

4. Type the plus (+) symbol so that Excel knows to add numbers.

The rotating outline disappears from cell C7. The original cell, C11, again becomes the active one.

5. Click the mouse pointer inside cell C8, the next cell address you want in your formula.

The rotating outline appears again, this time around cell C8. Excel copies the address for cell C8 into the formula bar next to the plus sign. You've just pointed out the second cell address!

6. Type a plus, click the mouse pointer in cell C9, type another plus, and click in cell C10. The cell addresses for C9 and C10 are now included in the formula bar.

7. Press Enter.

Excel enters the formula into cell C11 and displays the answer: 13,849. You can use this same technique to create formulas for the other blank cells in this worksheet, cells D11 through H11.

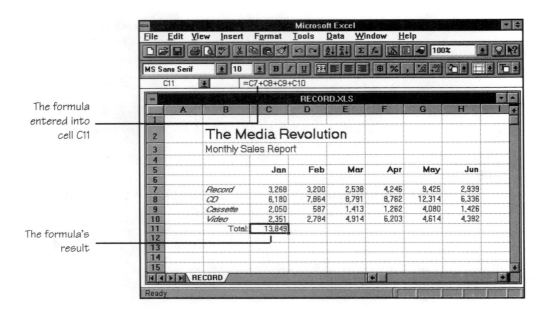

The formula entered into cell C11

The formula's result

TIP

For a fast method of entering the same formula into other cells, copy it. See Chapter 9, "Moving and Copying Data," for information on how to do this.

HUH?

BUZZWORDS

MARQUEE

The proper terminology for that rotating outline is "marquee," just like the flashing neon marquees you see around movie theater signs.

Home, Home on the Range

(Where the cells and their addresses play)

In some formulas, you want to work on a *range* (a selected group of cells). Chapter 2, "Making Changes," covers ranges in more detail, but here are some key range facts:

These are the key range facts

✔ The most common way to select a range is to click and hold down the mouse button on the first cell you want to include (the top left cell of the range). Then drag the mouse to the last cell you want to include (the range's bottom right cell). Release the mouse button. Go back and read Chapter 2, "Making Changes," if you want to know other methods of selecting a range.

✔ Ranges are useful when you want to sum a group of cells.

✔ Ranges, like cells, are designated with a shorthand address. The first cell address describes the cell in the top left corner of the group, and the second cell address describes the cell in the bottom right corner of the group. For example, B2:C4 is a range that includes the cells B2, B3, B4, C2, C3, and C4.

BUZZWORDS

CELL RANGE

"Cell range" is one of the top 10 Excel catch phrases you should never forget. In workbook hackers lingo, a cell range is a shorthand way to describe a group of cells. A range can be one cell, a column of cells, a row of cells, or any other block of cells.

		RECORD.XLS						
	A	B	C	D	E	F	G	H	I
1								
2		The Media Revolution						
3		Monthly Sales Report						
4								
5			Jan	Feb	Mar	Apr	May	Jun
6								
7		Record	3,268	3,200	2,538	4,246	9,425	2,939
8		CD	6,180	7,864	8,791	8,762	12,314	6,336
9		Cassette	2,050	587	1,413	1,262	4,080	1,426
10		Video	2,351	2,784	4,914	6,203	4,614	4,392
11		Total:	13,849					
12								
13								
14								
15								

Formula bar: C11 =C7+C8+C9+C10

A selected range —

Changing Your Address

(Editing cell addresses in formulas)

Not surprisingly, editing a formula is just like editing anything else in the formula bar, and you use all the same keys and techniques. In addition, when you're editing a formula in the formula bar, you can continue pointing out new cell addresses to add to the formula.

Suppose that you've added another category to the sample record store worksheet. The new information appears on row 6, just above the Record category. Typing in the new numbers is a start, but for your formula answers to be on the mark, you will have to edit them to include this new row of information.

Make cell C11 the active cell. Press F2 to enter Edit mode. Excel opens cell C11, and displays the cursor at the right end of the formula.

Type a plus (+) to tell Excel that you're continuing the formula. Click
the mouse pointer inside cell C6. Excel copies the address for cell C6
into the formula, next to the plus sign.

Excel adds
cell address C6
to the formula

The marquee
appears after
you click
inside cell C6

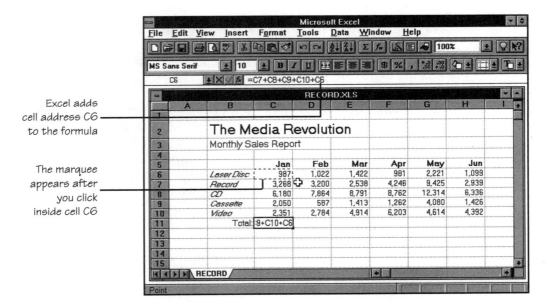

Press Enter. Excel recalculates the formula and shows the new answer in
cell C11. Notice that the cell addresses don't have to be in any particular order in a formula. You can type **C6** at the beginning of this formula
(instead of at the end), and Excel will calculate the correct answer.
Excel doesn't care about the order of appearance of the cell addresses in
most formulas, as long as they're all there. (Actually, order can make a
big difference sometimes, as you'll see in the next section.)

A Formula's Pecking Order

(Basic math rules to remember)

Suppose that you want to add the numbers 50 and 2, and then multiply that answer by the number 100. Doing the math in your head, you quickly come up with the right answer: 5200. But when you type the formula =50+2*100 into a cell, Excel displays 250 as the answer.

What gives? Excel has a strange way of looking at formulas that combine two or more different math operations—in this case, addition and multiplication. It may seem strange, but Excel is actually following a fundamental rule of math. This rule says that certain math operations, like multiplication and division, are always performed before other math operations, like addition and subtraction. The order goes like this:

✔ Math operations in parentheses ( ) are always performed first

✔ Exponentiation (^) operations are performed second

✔ Multiplication (*) and division (/) are performed third

✔ Addition (+) and subtraction () are performed last

You might be wondering how the heck you can enter a formula which, first, is supposed to add some numbers and then, second, multiply the answer by another number? The trick is to use parentheses. You can use parentheses to set apart special math operations. Excel always performs the math inside a pair of parentheses before it does the math outside of the parentheses. If you enter the formula as =(50+2)*100, Excel will do the addition before the multiplication and give the answer as 5200.

Formulas That Go Bump in the Night

(Illuminating fix-it tricks)

Whenever Excel can't make heads or tails of a formula you're trying to type into a cell, it keeps your formula in the formula bar and displays a dialog box that describes the problem. These dialog boxes say things like `Error in formula` and `Parentheses do not match`. When you can see what's wrong in your formula, click the OK button. Excel returns you to the formula cell.

How to fix a formula

✔ If Excel has an idea of what went wrong, it will highlight that part of your formula for you, making it easier to edit the formula. Type the correct part and press Enter.

✔ If Excel can't figure out exactly what's wrong, it highlights the entire formula in the cell. Press the Home key to move the cursor to the beginning of your formula. Now make the necessary corrections in the formula. When you're finished correcting the formula, press Enter to store the formula in the active cell.

✔ When you can't see what's wrong with your formula, try clicking the Help button in the dialog box. Excel displays a Help window that contains a list of the most common kinds of formula entry boo-boos. Hopefully, yours is on this list. When you're finished getting help, open the File menu and choose Exit (or press Alt+F4 to exit quickly). Excel returns you to the error message dialog box. Go ahead and fix the problem.

continues

✔ When you can't spot the problem in the formula and the Help window is no help at all, it's best to start all over again. Click OK in the dialog box and then click the X button in the formula bar or press the Esc key. Excel cancels your formula and returns you to Ready mode. Try writing out the formula on paper before retyping it into the worksheet. This procedure might help you figure out what went wrong.

Error Message Blues

(Read 'em and weep)

Occasionally, Excel still might have problems with a formula you have typed into a cell. When Excel is unable to properly calculate the formula and display an answer for you, it displays a rather odd-looking error message inside the cell. You're most likely to encounter one of the following messages during your formula-entry escapades.

Error Message	What It Means
#DIV/0!	You're attempting to divide by 0, the cardinal sin of mathematics. (Fall to your knees and beg forgiveness from Pythagoras.) To correct the formula, remove the part that divides by zero. If it's a reference to a cell address that contains zero, edit that cell instead of the formula.
#NAME?	No, Excel doesn't want to know what your name is. This message is telling you that you misspelled a function name, or you

Error Message	What It Means
	typed a formula that contains a cell name that Excel doesn't recognize, as in the formula =C4+BOB.
#NUM!	Don't worry. Excel isn't suffering from hypothermia. This message means that the answer to your formula is a monster-sized number that Excel can't handle, like the national debt figure. Or you typed a function with an unacceptable argument. (Arguments are covered in "The Arguments for Using Functions," later in this chapter.)
#REF!	This message means that your formula contains a reference to a cell that has been deleted from the worksheet. (A ten-yard penalty, according to most refs.) Edit your formula by typing a new cell address for the deleted one or by typing the value you want to calculate with.
#VALUE!	It's Excel's half-year clearance sale, and everything's half off! What a value! Actually this message means that you typed a cell range (like C5:C10) when Excel was expecting a single cell address (like C5). Either that or the cell that's being referenced contains text instead of the number Excel was expecting. Edit the formula by typing a single cell address or placing a value in the cell that your formula is referencing.

What's a Function, and What Does It Look Like?

(The physiology of built-in formulas)

Functions are time-saving tools you can use to simplify math in your workbooks. Excel offers hundreds of these built-in formulas, which you can use in place of many of your own worksheet formulas. (See Chapter 13, "Those Fab Functions," for a list of the most popular functions.) Rather than creating a formula that adds the values in five consecutive cells, for example, you can use the SUM function instead.

Here's a formula written the old way: **=45+23+65+90+12**

Here's a better way to write this formula: **=A1+A2+A3+A4+A5**

Here's the best way, using a function: **=SUM(A1:A5)**

The Arguments for Using Functions

Except for the familiar old equal sign, Excel's functions look quite a bit different from the standard formula fare. All that other stuff—the function name, the parentheses, and the stuff inside the parentheses—plays an important part in making your functions work properly.

Parts of a function

✔ The function name is a short (sometimes abbreviated) word that generally describes the function's duty. For example, the SUM function sums things for you, and the AVERAGE function averages things for you.

✔ The parentheses are used to separate the function name from the information you want the function to use in its calculation. In the function =SUM(A1:A5), for example, the stuff in parentheses tells Excel which worksheet cells contain the values to be summed.

✔ The *arguments*, which I just unceremoniously called "the stuff in the parentheses," can be values separated by commas, as in =SUM(250,345,129); cell addresses separated by commas, as in =SUM(A1,A2,A3); or a cell range, as in =SUM(A1:A5).

Entering a Function

Using the sample record store worksheet as an example, you can create a SUM function instead of using the formulas you created in row 11 in the last exercise. Here's how:

1. Click the cell in which you want to enter the function. For example, click cell C11.

2. Type the equal symbol (=) to start the formula.

3. Type **SUM** and then type a left parenthesis.

4. Drag your mouse through the range of cells you want to sum. For example, start by clicking in cell C6 and dragging down to cell C10.

A rotating
outline appears
around the
entire cell range,
and Excel copies
the cell range
into the formula,
next to the left
parenthesis

```
┌─────────────────────────────────────────────────────────────┐
│                      Microsoft Excel                     ▼ ▲ │
│  File  Edit  View  Insert  Format  Tools  Data  Window  Help │
│  ╔══════════════════════════════════════════════╗  100%  ▼ ♀ ▶? │
│  MS Sans Serif  ▼  10  ▼  B I U ▦▤▥▦ $ % , ▒▒ ▦▦▦▦ │
│  C6           ▼ X ✓ ƒ  =SUM(C6:C10                           │
│  ┌─────────────────── RECORD.XLS ──────────────────── ▼ ▲ ── │
│  │   A    B       C      D      E      F       G      H    I  │
│  │ 1                                                          │
│  │ 2      The Media Revolution                               │
│  │ 3      Monthly Sales Report                               │
│  │ 4                                                          │
│  │ 5             Jan    Feb    Mar    Apr    May    Jun      │
│  │ 6  Laser Disc  987   1,022  1,422    981  2,221  1,099    │
│  │ 7  Record    3,268   3,200  2,538  4,246  9,425  2,939    │
│  │ 8  CD        6,180   7,864  8,791  8,762 12,314  6,336    │
│  │ 9  Cassette  2,050     587  1,413  1,262  4,080  1,426    │
│  │ 10 Video     2,351   2,784  4,914  6,203  4,614  4,392    │
│  │ 11      Total: =SUM(C6:C10                                │
│  │ 12                    ⬦                                    │
│  │ 13                                                         │
│  │ 14                                                         │
│  │ 15                                                         │
│  │ ◄ ► ►│ RECORD /                                           │
│  Point                                                        │
└─────────────────────────────────────────────────────────────┘
```

5. Type a right parenthesis to complete the function.

The rotating outline disappears from the cell range. The original cell again becomes the active one.

6. Press Enter.

Excel enters the function into the cell and displays the answer.

TIP

Whenever Excel can't make heads or tails of a function you're trying to type into a cell, it reacts the same way as it does when it doesn't recognize a formula. For help with your functions, refer to the section "Formulas That Go Bump in the Night," earlier in this chapter. It covers formula-entry problems.

Warp Speed Addition with the AutoSum Button

Excel includes a tool that automatically sums a range of cells for you, to save you even more time! To use this feature, select the cell where you'd like the SUM function to appear. Next, click the AutoSum button in the Standard toolbar. It's the one that contains the Greek letter sigma (Σ).

As soon as you click this button, Excel inserts the SUM function into the formula bar and into the active cell. Excel takes a guess at the numbers you want to sum and shows the marquee around that range. To accept that range of cells and store the function in the active cell, click the check mark button in the formula bar or press Enter. If you want to sum a different range of cells, highlight the cell range with your mouse, and then press Enter.

CHAPTER 8

Editing
(Messing with Your Workbook)

IN A NUTSHELL

▼ Repeating workbook operations
▼ Inserting rows, columns, and sheets
▼ Clearing cell entries
▼ Deleting rows, columns, and sheets
▼ Special editing techniques

I HATE EXCEL FOR WINDOWS!

This chapter covers valuable workbook editing techniques. Did you forget one of the lines in your row of figures? See how to insert a row or column. Want to get rid of a cell? Learn how to delete it. Need a new sheet in a workbook? Just insert a new one. Step right up and see all this and more in the amazing workbook editing chapter. Right here. Right now.

Repeating History

(Over, and over, and over again)

You have seen how easy it is to undo mistakes you make in Excel workbooks. Just choose the **Edit Undo** command.

For those who can't get enough of the things you do *right* in your workbooks, there's the **Edit Repeat** command. With this command you can actually repeat the things you have just done in a workbook. Changed the font for a range of cells and now you'd like to add the same font to a different range? You can repeat it quickly. Aligned a whole column of text and now you want to do the same for another column? You can repeat that quickly, too. Made a large deposit into your bank account? Hah, now wouldn't that be a great trick?!

To repeat your last command, move to a place in the sheet where you want the activity repeated; then open the **Edit** menu and choose the **Repeat** command. Suppose, for example, that you have just added a fancy font to range D5:K5. To apply the same font to a different range, say C125:P125, select that range and choose the **Edit Repeat** command.

TIP

You also can quickly repeat a workbook activity by clicking the Repeat button. It's the button in the middle of the Standard toolbar with the arrow that loops over to the right.

Repeating rules to remember

✔ Until you perform some other workbook activity that's repeatable, you can repeat your most recent workbook activity as many times in a row as you want.

✔ The description for the **R**epeat command in the **E**dit menu constantly changes to reflect the action you just took in the workbook. For example, after pressing the Delete key to clear an entry from a cell, the **E**dit menu entry will say **R**epeat Clear. If you used the Format Cells command to change the font for a cell, the **E**dit menu will say **R**epeat Format Cells.

✔ You can't use the **R**epeat command to repeat stuff you've typed into a cell. To accomplish this task, you have to either retype the information elsewhere or copy it. (You learn how to copy in the next chapter, "Moving and Copying Data.")

✔ Excel doesn't warn you about activities that can't be repeated. The only way you will know is when you open the **E**dit menu and see the Can't Repeat message. At this point, unfortunately, you're plum out of luck.

Inserting More Space in a Workbook

Everyone who creates Excel workbooks eventually finds the need to insert blank rows, columns, and sheets in a workbook. Sometimes you just need to add an extra category or two in a report. Rather than type the new information in the bottom row or in the column farthest to the right, you can insert a blank row or column and type the new data exactly where you need it.

Inserting Rows, Columns, and Sheets (Move over)

You have just finished typing the information for a new worksheet report—let's call it the Weekly Production Schedule. As you admire your fine work, you suddenly notice that you left out two important categories of data. You forgot to include a column for the Saturday schedule, and you left out the row where the Gadgets data belongs.

The Weekly Production Schedule worksheet report

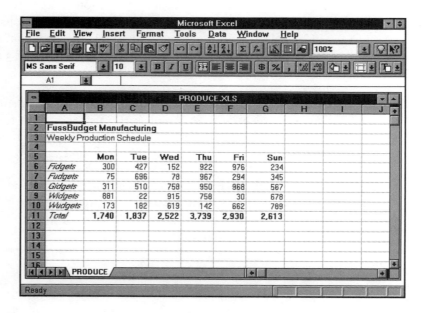

In the sample worksheet, you need to insert a blank column between F and G, and you need to insert a blank row between 7 and 8. This will save you the trouble of having to retype data to make room for the missing categories.

The quickest way to insert a row or column is to select a single cell inside each row or column where you want to insert blank space, and then choose Insert Rows or Insert Columns. When you insert a row, Excel

pushes down the row where the active cell was, leaving a single, blank row in its place. When you insert a column, Excel pushes the active column to the right, leaving a single, blank column in its place.

Inserted column ———

Inserted row ———

	A	B	C	D	E	F	G	H	I	J
1										
2	FussBudget Manufacturing									
3	Weekly Production Schedule									
4										
5		Mon	Tue	Wed	Thu	Fri		Sun		
6	Fidgets	300	427	152	922	976		234		
7	Fudgets	75	696	78	967	294		345		
8										
9	Gidgets	311	510	758	950	968		567		
10	Widgets	881	22	915	758	30		678		
11	Wudgets	173	182	619	142	662		789		
12	Total	1,740	1,837	2,522	3,739	2,930		2,613		
13										
14										
15										

"I HATE THIS!"

I hate it when there are 50 ways to do the same thing!

You also can use the Insert dialog box to insert blank rows and columns wherever you need them in your sheets. Position the active cell anywhere in the row or column where you want to insert new data, then open the Insert menu and choose the Cells command. In the Insert dialog box, click the Entire **R**ow option or the Entire **C**olumn option, and then click OK.

EXPERTS ONLY

I only want to insert part of a row or column!

To insert a partial row, use your mouse to highlight the cell range where you want to insert new data, such as cell range D10:H10. Open the Insert menu and choose the Cells command. In the Insert dialog box, click the Shift Cells Down option and then click OK. Excel pushes down only those cells in the columns you highlighted, leaving a blank partial row in its place. Cell range D10:H10 shifts down to cells D11:H11, D11:H11 shifts down to D12:H12, and so on.

To insert a partial column, use your mouse to highlight the cell range where you want to insert new data, such as cell range G5:G15. Open the Insert menu and choose the Cells command. In the Insert dialog box, click the Shift Cells Right option, and then click OK. Excel pushes to the right only those cells in the rows you highlighted, leaving a blank partial column in its place. Cell range G5:G15 shifts over to cells H5:H15, H5:H15 shifts to I5:I15, and so on.

To insert more than one blank row or column at a time, highlight two or more cells in a row or column before you choose the Insert Rows or Insert Columns command.

"I HATE THIS!"

Hey, I ran out of room in my workbook!

Excel gives you 16 blank sheets in every new workbook, but you need more. You're on a roll creating a cool, complex report but now there's no more room to grow. How can you get more sheets into the current workbook? Open the Insert menu and choose the Worksheet command. In less than a second or two, Excel creates a new sheet for you and places it in the front of your workbook. It's the one named Sheet17.

To undo any insert operation, immediately choose the **Edit Undo** command, press Ctrl+Z, or click the Undo button in the Standard toolbar.

What Happens to Your Formulas?

When it comes to inserting rows and columns, Excel treats your worksheet formulas with kid gloves. That's because your formulas use cell addresses. And when you insert rows or columns, these same formulas might try to use numbers from cells that are now blank. Fortunately, when you do insert rows or columns, Excel generally adjusts all affected formulas so that they continue pointing to the same cells, even though they are at different cell addresses.

Let's see how this works. To help you understand how formulas change when you insert rows and columns, refer to the sample worksheet shown here as you read the following checklist.

Cell B12 is highlighted to show you an example of the formulas in row 12

	A	B	C	D	E	F	G	H	I	J
1										
2	FussBudget Manufacturing									
3	Weekly Production Schedule									
4										
5		Mon	Tue	Wed	Thu	Fri	Sat	Sun		
6	*Fidgets*	300	427	152	922	976	530	234		
7	*Fudgets*	75	696	78	967	294	673	345		
8	*Gadgets*	85	45	677	114	455	120	85		
9	*Gidgets*	311	510	758	950	968	150	567		
10	*Widgets*	881	22	915	758	30	450	678		
11	*Wudgets*	173	182	619	142	662	353	789		
12	*Total*	1,825	1,882	3,199	3,853	3,385	2,276	2,698		
13										
14										
15										
16										

B12 = =SUM(B6:B11)

How inserting stuff affects formulas

✔ Let's say that you insert a new column to the left of column B. Column B now becomes column C. Excel changes all formulas to reflect their new column positions. For example, the formula in B12 moves to C12 and changes from =SUM(B6:B11) to =SUM(C6:C11). All other columns are affected in the same way.

✔ If you insert a new row above row 6, row 6 becomes row 7. Excel changes all formulas to reflect their new row positions. For example, the formula in B12 moves to B13 and changes from =SUM(B6:B11) to =SUM(B7:B12). All other rows are changed in the same way.

Deleting Space from a Workbook

(Shrinking your work down to size)

Once you're comfortable inserting blank rows and columns, you're ready to move on to something much more exhilarating: deleting entire rows and columns! Now before you start haphazardly deleting stuff from a workbook, beware of this one thing: always be cautious when it comes to deleting stuff. When you delete a row, column, or sheet, you delete all the entries in that row, column, or sheet. Are you sure you don't need anything? *Are you sure that you're sure?*

TIP

If you want to rearrange a workbook—move some entries to another spot in a sheet, or move a whole sheet elsewhere in a workbook—you don't have to delete the entries from one spot and reenter them in another. You can move them. Chapter 9, "Moving and Copying Data," explains how to move stuff.

To recover from a delete operation, immediately choose the **Edit Undo** command, press Ctrl+Z, or click the Undo button in the Standard toolbar. Remember, you can undo only the very last thing you did in the workbook, so think quickly if you accidentally delete something you need.

Clearing Cells (To make room for new prisoners)

Let's start small and see the quickest way to delete information from a few cells. Start by selecting a few cells in any sheet in your workbook. Then open the **Edit** menu, choose the Clear command, and then click the **All** option. Poof! Your cell data disappears.

TIP

Here's the easiest way to delete stuff from cells: just select the cells you want to delete and press the Delete key. The cells are cleared.

What about the four mysterious options on the **Edit Clear** menu? Do they mean anything important?

Options on the Edit Clear menu

✔ The **All** option erases the contents, formatting, and notes from the cells you selected.

✔ The **Formats** option erases only the formatting from the cells (like number formats or bold), leaving the contents and notes intact.

continues

✔ The Contents option erases only the contents of the selected cells, leaving the formatting and notes intact. This is what happens when you press the Delete key.

✔ The Notes option removes notes from the cells you selected, leaving the contents and formatting intact.

Deleting Rows, Columns, and Sheets (Out of my way!)

Suppose that it's now six months later. Your supervisor just announced that the manufacturing plant is scaling back production. The Saturday and Sunday shifts have been eliminated. And those geniuses over in marketing have decided to scratch Fudgets and Widgets from the product line. You quickly open your Weekly Production Schedule in Excel and begin assessing the damage.

As usual, there are two ways to proceed. First, you can type the whole darn thing over again. Second, you can selectively delete columns and rows from your sheet. Which sounds quicker?

The quickest way to delete a row or column is to select the entire row or column (click the number in the row heading or the letter in the column heading), and then choose **Edit Delete**. When you delete a row, Excel removes everything in that row from the sheet, pulling up the row beneath that one to fill the empty space. When you delete a column, Excel removes everything in that column and pulls over the column to the right to fill the empty space. If you're worried about what happens to formulas when you delete rows and columns, see the section "What Happens to Formulas?" later in this chapter.

The sample worksheet after deleting the target rows and columns

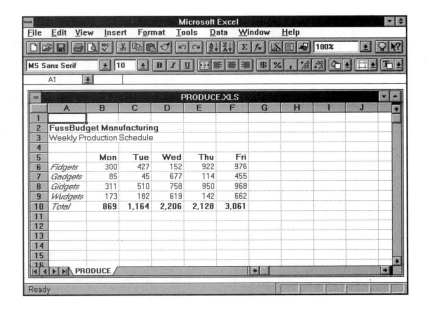

"I HATE THIS!"

You mean there's another way to delete them?

Yes, there are two ways to delete rows and columns. Position the active cell anywhere in the row or column you want to delete, open the **E**dit menu, and choose the **D**elete command. In the Delete dialog box, click the Entire **R**ow option (for rows) or the Entire **C**olumn option (for columns). Then click OK.

EXPERTS ONLY

Getting rid of only part of a row or column

To delete a partial row, use your mouse to highlight the cell range you want to delete, such as cell range D10:H10. Open the **E**dit menu and choose the **D**elete command. In the Delete

continues

Getting rid of only part of a row or column (continued)

dialog box, click the Shift Cells **U**p option, and then click OK. Excel removes the contents of the selected cell range and pulls up only those cells below the ones you highlighted. Cell range D11:H11 shifts up to replace D10:H10, D12:H12 shifts up to replace D11:H11, and so on.

To delete a partial column, use your mouse to highlight the cell range you want to delete, such as cell range G5:G15. Open the **E**dit menu and choose the **D**elete command. In the Delete dialog box, click the Shift Cells **L**eft option, and then click OK. Excel removes the contents of the selected cell range and pulls to the left only those cells to the right of the ones you highlighted. Cell range H5:H15 shifts left to replace G5:G15, I5:I15 shifts left to replace H5:H15, and so on.

To delete more than a single row or column at a time, highlight two or more cells in a row or column before you choose the **E**dit **D**elete command.

EXPERTS ONLY

Chucking out an entire sheet

Sometimes it does make sense to start all over again. When you simply can't do a thing with that rats nest of a sheet, delete it. Before you do, make sure that you really don't need any of the stuff in the sheet. Then, choose the **E**dit **D**elete Sheet command. When Excel displays the dialog box with the ominous-sounding warning, click OK. Your proverbial Excel slate is now clean.

What Happens to Formulas?

As with inserting rows and columns, deleting them might affect worksheet formulas that use cell addresses. But when it comes to deleting, you must pay closer attention to how the formulas might be affected. In many cases, Excel will adjust the affected formulas so that they continue pointing to the same numbers. Other times, deleting rows and columns will put your formulas on the fritz, like when a formula is trying to calculate with numbers in a row you just deleted. (See Chapter 7, "Formulas and Functions," for a list of the most common formula error messages and how to correct the offending formula.)

How deleting stuff affects formulas

✔ If you delete column B, Excel shifts to the left all the data and formulas from columns C on. All formulas are adjusted to reflect their new location. For example, if you had a formula in column C12 that said =SUM(C6:C11), it would move to B12 and change to =SUM(B6:B11). This applies to rows, too.

✔ If you delete a row or column and that row or column is referenced in a formula, the formula is updated. (That value is no longer included in the result.)

✔ If you delete a row or column that contains formulas, the formulas disappear.

Other Exciting Editing Techniques

(To astound your friends and family)

If you run into a special editing circumstance—for instance, you need to select all cells in a workbook that contain a formula, or you have to re-place all instances of the word *Widget* with *Midget*—this section provides the answers. The remainder of this chapter looks at several editing techniques.

Moving Somewhere Fast

Are you in a hurry to edit a sheet, but can't seem to find the cells you're looking for? Do you nod off while scrolling down a sheet with PgDn, only to discover that you passed your stop minutes ago? If this sounds at all like you, you will be happy to know that Excel can get you where you're going. And fast, too.

To move to any single cell in the active sheet, open the Edit menu and choose the Go To command. Keyboard nuts can press F5, the shortcut key for the Edit Go To command. When the Go To dialog box appears, type the address of the cell you would like to visit. Then click OK. Whoosh! Excel moves you there in a flash.

You also can go to a cell quickly by clicking inside the name box, typing the cell address, and then pressing Enter. The name box (you may re-member) is that small box at the left end of the formula bar that shows the address for the active cell.

Selecting Specific Types of Cells (picky, picky)

The boss just handed you a workbook you've never seen before. It takes 35 minutes for Excel to open it. Yep, it's a monster of a workbook. Three thousand lines of numbers, text, and formulas. Your job? Make a list of every cell in the workbook that contains a formula; that way, your boss doesn't have to hunt around each and every sheet every time the workbook needs updating. The active cell is A1, and there's steam rising from the top of your head.

No problem! With the Edit Go To command, you can have Excel instantly highlight areas of the active sheet in your workbook that have unique qualities, like only cells that contain formulas, only cells that contain text, or the last cell in the active sheet, and much more.

To use this editing tool, open the Edit menu, choose the Go To command, and then click the Special button in the Go To dialog box. Check the option in the Go To Special dialog box that describes the type of information you're looking for. Then click OK to turn Excel loose on your workbook.

Options in the Go To Special dialog box

✔ The Constants option selects all cells that contain uncalculated numbers and/or text when the Numbers and/or Text boxes also are checked.

✔ The Formulas option selects all cells that contain formulas.

✔ The Blanks option selects all cells that contain nothing; you know, blank cells.

continues

✔ The Last Cell option selects the last cell in the active sheet that contains data or that's now blank but at one time contained data.

✔ The Objects option selects all graphs you have added to the active sheet. (Graphs are covered in Chapter 15, "You Say Chart, I Say Graph.")

The remaining Go To Special options are designed for more advanced editing tasks, such as when you're calculating the median flight speed of the space shuttle while it's traveling backward through a meteor shower.

Finding Information

If you know that somewhere in your workbook you used the word *noodle* and you want to find it, you can use the **Edit Find** command to find the cell. The **Edit Find** command lets you search through a workbook for specific words, numbers, and formulas.

To use the **Find** command, follow these steps:

1. Open the **Edit** menu and choose the **Find** command.

Excel displays the Find dialog box. It's in here that you can tell Excel all about the stuff you want to find. For most of your find operations, the default settings in this dialog box will work just fine.

BUZZWORDS

> **DEFAULT SETTINGS**
>
> Default settings are the settings that Excel uses unless you tell it otherwise. Most of the time, Excel "guesses" right with the defaults, so you don't need to change any of the options.

2. In the Find What text box, type the text or formula you're searching for, and then click **Find Next**.

Excel selects the first cell that contains a match. Click the Find Next button to find the second occurrence, then again to find the third occurrence, and so on. If the "something" that Excel finds is hidden behind the Find dialog box, just drag the whole dialog box out of the way. Once you find the stuff you're looking for, what do you do with it? Well, you can edit the entry, retype new stuff into the cell, or delete it completely. Before you can do any of that, click the Close button or press the Esc key to get back to your workbook.

When Excel can't find the stuff you're looking for, it will display a dialog box message that says `Could not find matching data`. Click OK to return to the workbook. Try again.

Game rules for finding stuff

✔ You also can press Shift+F5, the shortcut key for the **Edit Find** command, to display the Find dialog box.

✔ To stop the find operation and return to your workbook, click the Close button.

continues

✔ The Look In options search for stuff only in certain types of cell entries. Your cell entry choices are Formulas, Values, and Notes. Use Look In Formulas to find cell references—like to find all formulas that reference C5. Use Look In Values to find the calculated values—like to find all cells that have a value of 6. Use Look In Notes to find information in your notes, which are memos you can add to cells.

✔ The Find Entire Cells Only check box searches for stuff as a whole or as a part of a bigger entry. For instance, if you're searching for the letters *idg*, leaving this check box *unchecked* allows Excel to locate the words *Fidgets, Widgets*, and *Gidgets*. If you are looking for the word *the* by itself, click the Find Entire Cells Only check box, which tells Excel to stop only on the word *the*, not *theater, theme song*, or anything else with the letters *t-h-e*.

✔ The Search options tell Excel how to search through your workbook, either by rows or columns. Using the production schedule as an example, you would use Search By Rows to look for something by product. To look for something by days of the week, use Search By Columns.

✔ Click the Match Case check box to locate exact uppercase and lowercase matches for the search text. If you type **pig**, Excel will find *PIG, pig, Pig, piG*, and so on. If you type **pig** and click on Match Case, Excel will find only *pig*. It won't stop on *PIG, Pig*, or *piG*.

Replacing Information (Tit for tat)

The Edit Replace command can search through a workbook for specific words, numbers, and formulas and then replace each occurrence with

something entirely different. Suppose that your product name has changed from *Widgets* to *Tidbits*; you can change all instances of *Widgets* to *Tidbits* in a flash.

To use the Replace command, follow these steps:

1. Open the Edit menu and choose the Replace command.

Excel displays the Replace dialog box. It's in here that you can tell Excel all about the stuff you want to find and replace. For typical replace operations, the default settings in this dialog box work just fine.

The Match Case, Find Entire Cells Only, and Search options work exactly the same here as they do in a find operation.

2. In the Find What text box, type the stuff you're searching for, such as **Widgets**.

3. In the Replace With text box, type the replacement stuff; for example, type **Tidbits**.

4. Click the Find Next button.

Game rules for replacing stuff

✔ After Excel finds the first occurrence of the stuff you're looking for, click the Replace button to replace the search text with the replacement text.

✔ To find the next occurrence of the search stuff *without* replacing the first occurrence, click the Find Next button. You can click this button for each occurrence of the search text you want to skip.

continues

Game rules for replacing stuff (continued)

✔ Click the Replace **All** button to replace every occurrence of the search stuff with the replacement stuff. Excel does not stop at each occurrence; it blasts through the entire sheet until the job's done.

✔ To stop the replace operation and return to your workbook, click the Close button.

✔ When you accidentally replace something in the workbook, use the **Edit Undo** command as soon as Excel returns you to your workbook.

✔ When Excel can't find the stuff you're looking for, it will display a dialog box message that says `Could not find matching data`. Click OK to return to the workbook. Try again.

TIP

Excel automatically searches the active sheet in the workbook during find and replace operations—that is, unless you want to do otherwise. To tell Excel to search through only a particular cell range, select the cell range before you choose the **Edit Find** or **Edit Replace** command. To tell Excel to search through more than one sheet, hold down the Ctrl key and click the tab for each sheet you wish to search before you choose the **Edit Find** or **Edit Replace** command.

Moving and Copying Data

(Rearranging Your Cells)

IN A NUTSHELL

- ▼ Moving cell data
- ▼ Copying and pasting cell data
- ▼ Copying formulas
- ▼ Filling cells
- ▼ Pasting special data
- ▼ Switching columns and rows around

When you first start pecking away in your workbook, you probably aren't going to remember every little fact and figure. And you probably aren't going to get everything in the right cell without some shuffling.

One way to rearrange a sheet in your workbook is to insert a new row or column. This trick, covered in the preceding chapter, is great if you left out a row or a column. But what if the change isn't so neat and tidy? What if you want column A where column B is and column C where column A is? Do you have to redo the sheet? Nope. You can move cells around so that they're exactly where you want them.

A more powerful companion to moving cells is copying them. For example, Excel allows you to enter a formula once and copy it across the row or column. This chapter focuses on ways to rearrange your data.

Moving Cell Data

(Reorganizing a mess)

Creating workbook reports is an inexact science at best. You type something into one cell, then decide it doesn't belong there. Instead of erasing the cell's contents and retyping the entry elsewhere, just move it. You can move data by dragging and dropping or by using menu commands.

Dragging and Dropping (with your mouse)

One way to move stuff is called "dragging and dropping." You literally drag one or more cells to a different area in the sheet and drop them there. This method requires a keen eye and a steady hand because you have to make precise mouse pointer movements. (No shaky hands allowed.)

Here's how it works. Suppose that you want to move a cell range like B12:E12 up a few rows to B7:E7. Start by highlighting the cell range you want to move. Then position your mouse pointer anywhere on the thick border that surrounds the selected cell range. The pointer changes from a cross to an arrow when you position it correctly. Now drag the cell range to row 7 and drop it there. That's how you use dragging and dropping to move cells from one place to another.

Dragging range B12:E12 up to range B7:E7

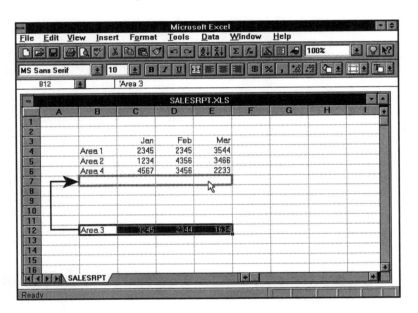

As soon as you release the mouse, the outline border you were dragging disappears, and Excel displays the moved data at its destination.

Things to remember when dragging and dropping

✔ If you are unable to drag and drop in your workbooks, the drag and drop feature is probably turned off. To fix this problem, open the Tools menu and choose the Options command. The Options dialog box opens. Click the Edit tab to display the editing options. Click the Allow Cell Drag and Drop check box (put an x in it) to enable the feature, and then click OK to return to the workbook. You may now drag and drop to your heart's delight.

✔ Be sure that you don't drop the cells onto cells that already contain data. The cells you drop will overwrite any stuff in the "receiving" cells. Excel warns you when this is about to happen.

✔ If you make a mistake, open the Edit menu and choose the Undo command. Or, click the Undo button in the Standard toolbar.

✔ If you move a formula or any cells referenced in a formula, in most cases, all references are adjusted accordingly. You don't have to mess with the formulas at all. Pretty neat, huh?

Cutting and Pasting (with your keyboard)

You also can use your keyboard to move stuff around in a sheet. Excel calls this particular task *cutting and pasting*. The procedure is similar to cutting an article out of a newspaper and taping it onto a piece of paper.

Start by highlighting the cell range you want to move. Next, open the Edit menu and choose the Cut command. Excel displays the marquee around the cell range. Now select the top left cell of the area where you want to move the range. Open the Edit menu and choose the Paste command.

CAUTION

Be sure that you don't paste the new cells over cells that contain data. The pasted cells will overwrite any data in the receiving cells, and you won't get a warning.

Time-saving keystrokes for moving cell data quickly

✔ To select a range of cells, press F8. Then use the arrow keys to highlight the range and press F8 again.

✔ Press Ctrl+X, the shortcut key for the **E**dit C**u**t command, to cut a range of selected cells.

✔ Once you're at the destination spot in the sheet, press Ctrl+V, the shortcut key for the **E**dit **P**aste command. Or you can just select the destination cell and press Enter to paste the cell range.

✔ Press Shift+Delete to delete the contents of the selected range. Immediately move to the destination cell range and press Shift+Insert to restore the deleted information in the new location.

✔ Press Ctrl+Z immediately to reverse a move operation.

Time-saving toolbar buttons for moving cell data quickly

 ✔ Click the Cut button on the Standard toolbar to cut a range of selected cells.

 ✔ Once you're at the destination spot in the sheet, click the Paste button to paste the cell range.

EXPERTS ONLY

Dropping data between the cracks

If you want to cram cells between existing data, you can try a little trick. You can move a range of cells—including its data—between existing cells. Highlight the cell range you want to move, and position the mouse pointer on the range's outline border. Drag the outline border until it's positioned over a row or column, and then press and hold the Shift key. As soon as you press the Shift key, the outline border changes into a thin, horizontal line (for rows) or vertical line (for columns). If the border doesn't change on your screen, slide your mouse around until it does. When the line is properly positioned, release the mouse button. Excel instantly crams the cell range and pushes the other cells up, down, right, or left, depending on where you stuck the new cells.

Copying and Pasting Cell Data

(Creating perfect forgeries)

Copying information is definitely on the list of the top 10 most used Excel features. Copying stuff in a sheet is just like moving it, except that you're actually making a duplicate of something instead of shifting it around the sheet. Copying data, especially formulas, is a great time-saver. You don't have to type the same thing over and over and over.

Excel offers two ways to copy data in your sheets: the drag-and-drop method and the menu method.

Dragging and Dropping (à la mouse)

Yes, this is the same dance step covered earlier in the chapter. Only here it applies to copying stuff, not moving it. With this feature, you can literally drag a copy of a cell range and drop it into a different area in the sheet.

Here's how it works. Suppose that you need to create a table for second-quarter sales data, a table that looks almost exactly like another one in your sheet, except that the numbers and column headings need to change slightly. You can be a total Excel bonehead and type the new information into the existing table, or you can work smart by making a copy of the table and then editing it a little so that you can use it for the second-quarter sales data.

Start by highlighting the cell range you want to copy. Then position your mouse pointer anywhere on the thick border that surrounds the cell range. The pointer changes from a cross to an arrow when you position it correctly. Now press and hold the Ctrl key and drag the cell range to where you want the copy. As soon as you release the mouse and Ctrl key, the outline border you were dragging disappears, and Excel displays the copied data in its new destination.

Copying cell range B3:E7 to range B9:E13

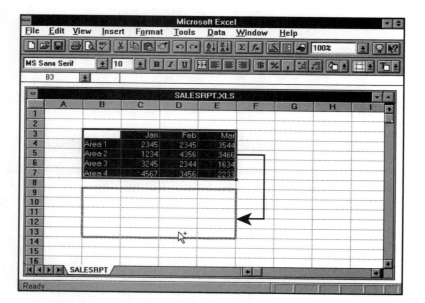

More things to remember when dragging and dropping

✔ There's a tell-tale sign that you're copying a cell range rather than moving one. As soon as you press the Ctrl key and begin dragging a cell range, Excel displays a tiny plus symbol (+) next to the mouse pointer. Whenever you lose track of whether you're moving or copying a cell range, look to see whether the plus symbol is on-screen.

✔ If you drag the copy onto cells that already contain data, the copy overwrites that data, so be careful. Excel *doesn't* warn you when this is about to happen.

Copying and Pasting (à la keyboard)

You also can use your keyboard to copy stuff in a sheet. Excel calls this particular procedure *copying and pasting*. It's like photocopying a newspaper article and taping the copy to a piece of paper.

Start by highlighting the cell range you want to copy. Next, open the Edit menu and choose the Copy command. Excel displays the marquee around the cell range you're copying. Now select the top left cell of the area where you want to copy the range. Open the Edit menu and choose the Paste command. Excel transfers the copy to the cell range. Press Esc to remove the marquee from the original cell range.

CAUTION

Be sure to paste the copy in a blank area. If you select an area of the sheet that contains entries, the copy overwrites those entries without any warning—no messages, hiccups, or loud sirens. Nothing.

Shortcuts you can use when copying cell data

✔ To select a range of cells, press F8. Then use the arrow keys to highlight the range and press F8 again.

✔ Press Ctrl+C—the shortcut key for the Edit Copy command—to copy a range of selected cells.

continues

I HATE EXCEL FOR WINDOWS!

Shortcuts you can use when copying cell data (continued)

✔ Once you're at the destination spot in the sheet, press Ctrl+V—the shortcut key for the **Edit P**aste command—to copy the selected cell range. Or you can move to the destination cell and press Enter to paste the cell range immediately.

✔ Press Ctrl+Insert to copy the contents of a selected cell range. Immediately move to the destination cell range and press Shift+Insert to transfer the copied information to the new location.

✔ Press Ctrl+Z immediately to reverse a copy operation that goes bust or when you accidentally overwrite other cell data that you need.

✔ You also can copy and paste data by using the Copy button and the Paste button in the Standard toolbar. Select the cell range you want to copy, and click the Copy button. Select the top left cell of the area where you want to place the copy, and then click the Paste button; it's located to the right of the Copy button.

EXPERTS ONLY

Making room for the copy

If you want to copy cells and cram them between existing data, you can try a little trick. Select the cell range you want to copy, and position the mouse pointer on the range's border. Drag the outline border until it's positioned over a row or column, and then press and hold the Shift and Ctrl keys. As soon as you press these keys, the outline border changes into a thin, horizontal line (for rows) or vertical line (for columns). If the border doesn't change on your screen, slide your mouse around until it does. Position the line where you want to insert the copied range, and then release the mouse button.

Excel crams the copied cell range and pushes the other cells up, down, right, or left, depending on where you stuck the new cells.

Be sure that you keep holding down the Ctrl and Shift keys until you release the mouse button. If you happen to release both these keys before releasing the mouse button, you will actually be telling Excel to copy your cell range on top of whatever data you happen to be above at the time. Excel displays the message `Overwrite non blank cells in destination?` Click the Cancel button and try again.

Copying Formulas

(Building worksheets the easy way)

Excel is pretty darn smart when it comes to copying formulas. Consider the formula =SUM(C6:C10), which sums numbers in column C. When you copy this formula one cell to the right, Excel changes the copied formula so that it looks like this: =SUM(D6:D10).

Notice that only one thing changed in the copied formula—the column letter. Since you placed the copy of the formula in column D, Excel changed the cell addresses so that the formula adds numbers in column D. If you copied the formula into column G, its column letters would change to G.

Can you see how easy it is to create new formulas simply by copying them from cell to cell? Consider what happens when you copy the formula =SUM(C6:F6) into a cell one row down. Instead of changing the column letter, Excel changes the row number. The copied formula is =SUM(C7:F7).

The reason Excel adjusts the formula is because Excel uses *relative references* for the cells. Suppose that you have a formula in cell B5 that sums the cells in B2:B4. Rather than tell Excel to add the specific cells B2:B4, Excel says, "Sum the three cells above this one." When you copy the formula to C5, Excel still says to itself, "Sum the three cells above this one." It would sum cells C2:C4. You don't have to change the formula.

Sometimes you want the reference to stay the same. In this case you use an *absolute reference*. An absolute reference tells Excel to use the named cell; absolutely and positively accept no substitutes! If you have an interest rate in cell A1, for example, and you have several formulas that refer to that interest rate, you would use an absolute reference.

TIP

To make a reference absolute, type a dollar sign before the row and column indicators, such as $A$1. To edit a formula and change a reference, press F2. Click the insertion point within the reference, and then press F4. Edit the formula, and press Enter to accept the change.

BUZZWORDS

RELATIVE AND ABSOLUTE REFERENCES

When you copy or move a formula, relative references change in relation to where they're placed. Absolute references do not change; they always refer to specific cells.

Filling Cells with Data

(Automatically, the Excel way)

The Fill command on the Edit menu offers a simpler way of copying formulas. Actually, you also can use this method to copy words and numbers, but let's focus on formulas for the moment.

To copy a formula down a column of cells, highlight a cell range so the first cell in the range contains the formula you want to copy and the remaining cells are the blank cells where you would like to place the copies. Open the Edit menu, choose the Fill command, and then choose the Down option. Or, simply press Ctrl+D—the shortcut key for the Fill Down command. Excel immediately fills in the range with copies of your formula.

To copy a formula across a row of cells, do the same thing, but choose the Fill Right command or press Ctrl+R.

More great ways to fill a cell range with words, numbers, and formulas

✔ You also can copy a formula to the left or up by choosing Left or Up from the Edit Fill menu.

✔ Excel can fill a range with an incremental series of words when it recognizes the first word as a date abbreviation like *Jan* or *Qtr1*. To try this technique, locate the cell that contains the first entry and click it once. Next, click the fill handle and drag it in the direction of the range you wish to fill, and then release the mouse. If cell C10 contains the word *Jan*, for example, Excel fills cells D10, E10, and F10 with *Feb*, *Mar*, and *Apr*.

continues

More great ways to fill a cell range with words, numbers, and formulas (continued)

✔ To fill a range with an incremental series of numbers, move to the cell that contains the first number, then hold down the Ctrl key and drag the fill handle to select the target range. Excel increments each new number by 1.

✔ To fill a range with a series of numbers using an increment other than 1, type a second value into a cell next to the first cell. Select both cells, then hold down the Ctrl key and drag the fill handle to select the target range. For example, to enter the series (10, 20, 30, and 40), type **10** in the cell B5 and **20** into cell B6. Then select both cells, hold down the Ctrl key and drag the fill handle until you reach cell B8. Excel fills in the rest of the range for you.

BUZZWORDS

FILL HANDLE

Not to be confused with Excel's love handles, the *fill handle* is the tiny square box that sits in the bottom right corner of the active cell. When you position your mouse pointer on top of a cell's fill handle, the pointer changes from a thick, white cross to a thin, black cross. Drag away, as they say.

This worksheet shows some of the kinds of series you can fill

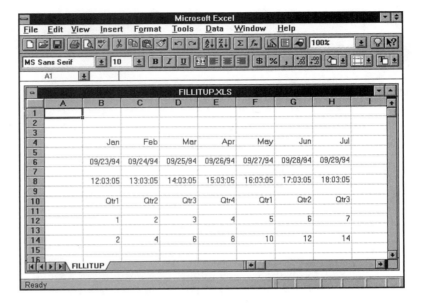

Cool Pasting Techniques

(Going way beyond the call of duty)

Whenever you paste a copy of something into your sheets, Excel places an exact duplicate for you. (Except in the case of formulas, as you saw earlier.) Not only do you get a duplicate of the cell contents, you also get the cells formatting. The Edit menu contains another pasting command: Paste Special. This command lets *you* decide exactly which parts of your cell range Excel copies. With Paste Special, you can achieve copy effects that range from mildly interesting to truly amazing.

CHAPTER 9

TIP

The coolest way to paste only the formatting that's attached to something in a sheet is to use the Format Painter button on the Standard toolbar. Here's how: Click the cell with the formatting you want to copy, and then click the Format Painter button. Now click the cell, or select the cell range, where you want to copy the formatting. Excel copies the formatting instantly.

Suppose that you spend lots of time typing numbers into a summary section at the top of a sheet. The numbers you type are actually formula answers from all around the same sheet. You have tried copying the formula cells directly into the summary section, but their answers keep changing. (All that stuff about relatives, absolutes, and references was too confusing to remember.) Using the Paste Special command, you can quickly copy each formula's answer into the summary section and leave the formula behind.

To use the Paste Special command, select the range you want to copy, open the Edit menu, and choose the Copy command. Select the spot where you want to paste the copied cells, open the Edit menu, and choose the Paste Special command. Select the option you want, and then click OK. You can use only one Paste option at a time with the Paste Special command.

Special ways to paste stuff

✔ The **All** option copies everything from the target cells into the destination cells. But, if your goal is to paste everything, you don't want to do it by using the Paste Special command. Just open the **E**dit menu and choose **P**aste; it's much quicker.

✔ The Values option copies only the numbers and words in your cells. Excel converts all formulas to their answers, and displays these numbers in the copied cell range. For example, maybe you want to create a second table of data that summarizes the totals from a first table. These displayed totals come from formulas, and you don't necessarily want the formulas in the second table. Use this option to paste them as values instead of formulas.

✔ The Formats option copies only the cell formatting into the copy range. All values and formulas stay behind. This is really helpful after you have formatted a sheet and realize that you need to use the format from a particular cell elsewhere in the same sheet. Instead of choosing all the Format commands again, just copy the entire group of formats from one cell to another.

TIP

If your pasting job doesn't go as planned, press Ctrl+Z immediately after using Paste **S**pecial to undo the effects on your workbook. Or, better yet, click the Undo button on the Standard toolbar.

Switching Rows and Columns

If your sheet is topsy-turvy with rows that should be columns and columns that should be rows, you can make a quick switch.

Select the range you want to switch. Open the **E**dit menu and choose the Copy command. Select the spot where you want to put the copied cells, then open the **E**dit menu and choose the Paste **S**pecial command. Click the Transpose option to tell Excel to switch the organization of your rows and columns when it pastes the copied cells into the sheet,

and then click OK. Press Esc to eliminate the marquee. The following figure shows a "before" and "after" view of how a sample worksheet looks if you use this option.

Before switching the rows and columns

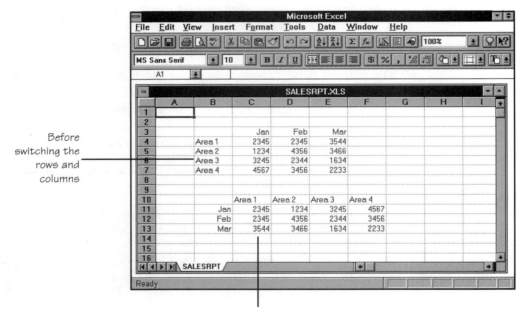

After switching the rows and columns

✔ Notice that the transposed row and column descriptions retain their original alignment setting.

✔ After transposing a cell range, you might have to do some minor reformatting to make things look well laid out once again.

CHAPTER 10

More Workbook Formatting

(Pretty as a Picture)

IN A NUTSHELL

- ▼ Creating titles that really look centered
- ▼ Choosing the right font
- ▼ Adding font effects and colors
- ▼ Adding lines and borders for clarity
- ▼ Shading cells to make them stand out
- ▼ Auto-formatting in the wink of an eye

Excel has lots of tools for transforming basic workbooks into stylish, professional-looking documents—the type of documents usually associated with megabuck marketing departments and Fortune 500 companies.

In an earlier chapter you saw how to use a few of these tools to make some formatting changes to your workbooks. You saw how to add bold and italic style to text and how to align words and numbers so that they make sense. (Chapter 5, "Formatting Your Workbook," remember?) Those few tools represent only a small percentage of what's available in Excel's makeup drawer. Now it's time to create even more attractive and innovative looks for your workbooks.

CAUTION

Excel's formatting tools are great fun to use. You can go hog-wild experimenting with all the different combinations (sort of like reassembling Mr. Potato Head a thousand different ways). Keep in mind that when it comes to formatting workbooks, a well-thought plan of attack brings structure, emphasis, and style to your work. Haphazard formatting usually mangles it. If you don't like what you did, you can use the **E**dit **U**ndo command to undo the change.

What the Heck Is WYSIWYG, Anyway?

(Acronym of the rich and famous)

Great question. WYSIWYG (pronounced "whizzy-wig") is one of the most widely quoted computer terms today. Not to be confused with Don King's coif, this word actually is an acronym for "what you see is what you get."

The term WYSIWYG came into existence a few years back, when some programs had you formatting your work without actually showing the formatting on-screen. I'm not kidding. Can you imagine a hair stylist cutting your hair while wearing a blindfold? Maybe that's what happened to Sinead O'Connor.

Then along came a whole new class of computer programs that touted themselves as being WYSIWYG products. In other words, what you do on-screen with these programs is exactly (more or less) what you get when you print on paper. With WYSIWYG programs, you can easily try different formatting effects, see whether you like the effects, and then tinker some more—all before printing.

Selecting the Makeover Candidate

(Choosing the before model)

When you format a cell, you start by selecting the cell or cell range you want to format. Chapter 2, "Making Changes," covers methods for selecting cells.

TIP

Keep in mind that you can select ranges that aren't next to each other. For example, you might want to change the font in rows 10, 14, 16, and 18. Instead of formatting one row at a time, why not change the font in all four rows at once? Select the first cell range you want to format. Next, hold down the Ctrl key and select the second cell range. Keep holding down the Ctrl key as you select any additional cell ranges. Now format your data. Excel applies your formatting choices to each and every cell you selected.

continues

141

continued

For any of the formatting changes you learn in this chapter, you can use the shortcut menu. After you select the cell or range you want to format, click the right mouse button anywhere in the selected range. When Excel displays the shortcut menu, choose the Format Cells command to display the Format Cells dialog box, and choose the settings you want.

You can use the Format Painter tool to quickly copy any of the workbook formatting options covered in this chapter. Remember, that's formatting without the cell contents.

To use this feature, just click the cell that has the formatting you want to copy, and then click the Format Painter button in the Standard toolbar. Now click the cell, or select the cell range, where you want to copy the formatting. Excel copies the formatting instantly. This trick will save you lots of time that otherwise might be spent re-creating the same formatting over and over again in the same workbook.

Parallel Parking and Other Popular Alignments

(Creating order in your rows and columns)

The easiest way to change the alignment of the data in your workbook is to select the cells you want to change and use one of the alignment buttons on the Formatting toolbar, as you learned in Chapter 5, "Formatting Your Workbook." You have some other options. The three options that are the most fun are centering rows across columns, justifying text, and turning cells topsy-turvy.

To change the alignment of data, select the cell or cell range, open the Format menu and choose the Cells command, and then click the Alignment tab. Excel displays the alignment options in the Format Cells dialog box.

The Alignment dialog box shows a complete list of alignment settings for your data

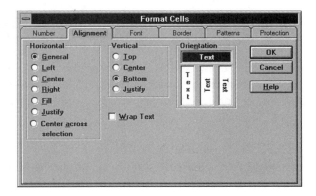

The alignment settings you are most likely to use are discussed next. If you want to experiment, try some of the other choices to see what happens.

Centering Titles

The Center across selection alignment option lets you center text or numbers inside the entire width of a selected range of cells. This alignment option makes it easy to center a report title along the top of the worksheet, without having to move it from cell to cell until it looks just right.

Suppose that you typed a report title into cell C2. Then you entered a table of data that uses columns C, D, E, F, and G. The report title in C2 is short. Although it starts in column C, it only extends over into column D. To center the title over the entire table of data (columns C

through G), you would usually have to move it from cell to cell on row 2 until it looks centered. Many times this method doesn't even really center the title; it just gets the title close enough to call it centered.

To *really* center a title across the top of your sheet, select the range of cells over which you want the title centered. In this case, you would select cells C2 through G2. (Excel assumes that the title is in the leftmost cell of the range you select. You get peculiar results if it's not.) Open the Format menu and choose the Cells command, and then click the Alignment tab inside the Format Cells dialog box. From the list of alignment options that appear, pick the Center **a**cross selection option and click OK.

Excel centers your title exactly over the range of cells you picked. Here's the wild part: your title stays in its original cell. Excel doesn't move the title anywhere, it just *displays* it in the center of the range you selected. (Don't look for hidden mirrors; there aren't any!)

A title centered across columns G through M

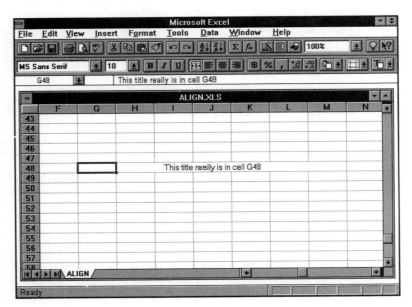

TIP

To quickly center data in a sheet, select the cell range across which you want the data centered, and then click the Center Across Columns button.

It's a Wrap!

The Wrap Text alignment option is useful for counterattacking the text spillover problem. You know, the problem where you type lots of words into a single cell and they spill into the cell to the right.

If you click the **Wrap Text** check box in the Format Cells dialog box (so that an **x** appears in the box), Excel rearranges the words so that they fit the width of the current cell. No, Excel doesn't lop off anything. It just elongates the cell from top to bottom and shuffles the words onto several lines so that everything fits. In other words, Excel increases the row height setting for that cell's row.

Wrapping text in a cell

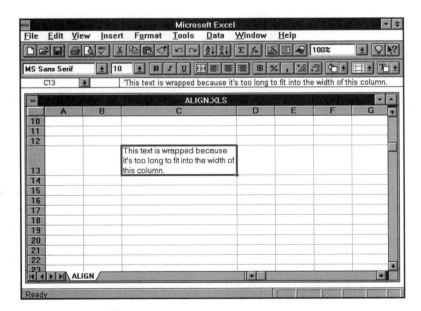

Stacked and Sideways Text

For a cool special effect, you can spin text so that it sits on its side. Open the Format menu and choose the Cells command, and then click the Alignment tab. Take a look at the area labeled Orientation in the Format Cells dialog box. The four boxes with the word *Text* show the different choices. To change the orientation for your data, click the box you want.

Here are some rotated row headings ——

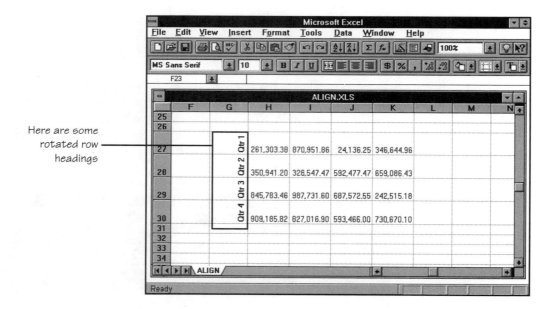

Fonts Are Our Friends

(Bringing feelings to your work)

With Excel, you can easily change the look of numbers and text in your sheets. A good way to grab someone's attention with your sheets is to change the characteristics of its type—the font, the size, the style, or the color.

BUZZWORDS

FONT

A font is a set of characters (like AZ or 19) in a particular typeface, such as Helvetica or Times Roman.

To enhance the appearance of your data, select the cell or cell range you want to change, open the Format menu, choose the Cells command, and then click the Font tab. Excel displays the font formatting options inside the Format Cells dialog box. With these options, you can choose a new font, pick a style, choose a different size, and more! The following sections tell you how to do all this stuff.

The options in the Format Cells dialog box determine how words and numbers look in your workbook

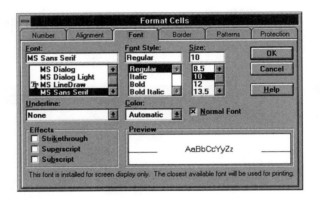

After you're finished making changes in the Format Cells dialog box, click OK to return to your workbook. Excel (being the WYSIWYG wizard that it is) immediately puts your font choices into effect.

Fonts Have Feelings, Too

Different fonts say different things. Some look conservative and businesslike; others feel fun and fanciful. The fonts you choose for your workbooks should convey the right impression to the reader. You can change both the font and the font size.

I HATE EXCEL FOR WINDOWS!

Goudy	**Revue**
Helvetica	𝕱𝖊𝖙𝖙𝖊 𝕱𝖗𝖆𝖐𝖙𝖚𝖗
Hobo	Tekton

The Font box contains a list of all the fonts you have available. Click the up- or down-scroll arrows to check out the list. Notice that the Preview box displays an example of each font as you highlight it. When you find the best-looking font for your purposes, click it to select it.

The Size box contains a list of the point sizes that are available for the current font. Click the up- or down-scroll arrows to see all the available sizes. For most fonts, you can choose sizes from 1 point to 72 points. Keep an eye on the Preview box for examples. Then click the size you want.

HUH?

BUZZWORDS

POINT SIZE

Fonts are measured in *point sizes* from 1 point to 72. There are 72 points per inch.

TIP

Unless you're one of those lucky folks who spent lots of money buying extra fonts, your font choices are limited to the ones that come with the Microsoft Windows package.

When a report needs that extra special something, but you just don't have the right fonts for the job, here's what to do: Ask your favorite computer nerd to help you purchase additional fonts for your computer. Heck, convince him or her to

pay for the fonts. Be sure to pick someone who has both an opinion about different brands of fonts and the desire and time to help you install them. (Keep in mind that the fonts you choose must work with your particular printer.)

BUZZWORDS

TRUETYPE FONTS

Here's another buzzword for the next office party: *TrueType fonts* (as if you'd buy something called FalseType fonts). These kinds of fonts are the current rage if you're running Windows and Excel on your computer. That's because TrueType fonts are versatile (they come in virtually every size you could possibly need), inexpensive (I've seen packages of 100 fonts that sell for about $40), and come in about a billion different flavors (from Astaire to Zorba). The next time you're asked which class of fonts you prefer, just say, "Why, TrueType, of course."

Stylizing a Font

In addition to picking the font and the size, you can change the font *style*. Add bold and italic formatting to your sheet data to make titles and row headings stand out. These font styles help a reader scan a worksheet quickly and find important data—that is, the data *you* think is important. After all, you're the one who's doing the formatting.

TIP

Remember, you can quickly apply a bold or italic style to your data by selecting the cells you want to format and then clicking the Bold **B** or Italic *I* button on the Formatting toolbar.

Special Font FX (spesh-el fänt effects)

In the Effects area of the font formatting options in the Format Cells dialog box, you can choose Strikethrough, Superscript, and Subscript. Just above the Effects area, in the Underline list box, you can choose from among five cool underlining options. The following sample worksheet shows what these effects look like. You decide for yourself whether they're worthwhile. (In the upcoming section, "Headin' for the Borders," you learn how to draw lines under cells.)

Special effects you can create by using the font formatting options in the Format Cells dialog box

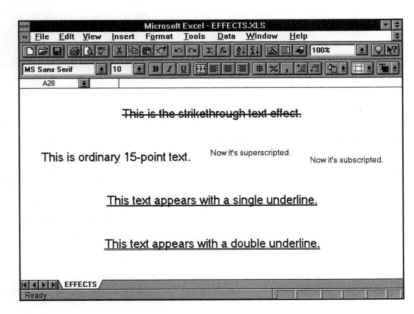

Color Me Blue (Or yellow, or red, or...)

Color can create feelings and convey impressions in ways that simply can't be achieved with other formatting tools. I'm green with envy. The firm's in the black. You're singing the blues. Have fun with color in your Excel workbooks. Remember that too much color can blind your reader, and certain color combinations are guaranteed to cause migraine headaches.

The font formatting section of the Format Cells dialog box has a Color list that shows all the different colors you can use for the text in your workbooks. To activate this list, click the down arrow at the right edge of the list box. Then click the color you want. Keep in mind that unless you have a color printer, or can produce your work on a friend's color printer, colors won't appear in your printouts. You're stuck with black and white.

Headin' for the Borders

(Great treatments for totals and subtotals)

After you have made basic formatting changes to your workbook, you might want to add a few finishing touches. Borders are one effective way to highlight important data. A border can be a single line drawn on one side of a cell, such as the top or left side, or lines surrounding a cell. It's up to you.

TIP

Removing the gridlines from around your cells improves the view of many formatting effects, particularly borders and shading (that's next). To remove gridlines, open the **T**ools menu and choose the **O**ptions command, and then click the View tab. In the Window Options section of the Options dialog box, uncheck the **G**ridlines option by clicking it, and then click OK to return to your workbook. The gridlines disappear.

To add borders to a cell range, select the range, open the Format menu, choose the Cells command, and then click the Border tab in the Format Cells dialog box. Your options are **O**utline (all sides), **L**eft, **R**ight, **T**op, and **B**ottom. Next, choose the style of line you want to use. Your line style options, clockwise from the upper-left corner of the Style block, are the following: Hairline, Double, Dotted, Dashed, None, Thick, Medium, and Thin.

The Border dialog box displays a complete list of border options

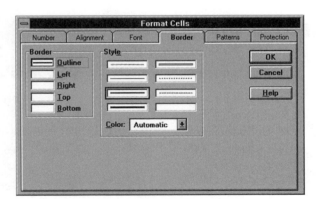

"I HATE THIS!"

The borders aren't turning out the way I want!

In an Excel sheet, cells that sit side by side always share borders. For example, the right edge of cell D4 also is the left edge of cell E4, and the top of cell H6 also is the bottom of cell H5. When you add a border to a cell, keep in mind that you're also adding it to the adjacent cell. You might have to tinker around with the borders to get them just the way you want.

When you choose a line style, a sample of the line style appears to the left of the border position you selected in the Border block. You can use any combination of positions and line styles for the cell or cell range you select. If you select a position and style for the top of the cell, for example, you can select a different line style for the bottom or sides of the cell.

Borders help set apart different groups of data

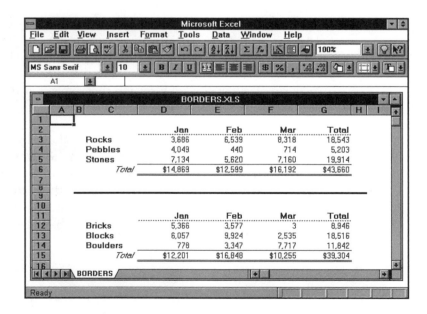

TIP

To quickly apply borders to data in a sheet, select the data and then click the down arrow next to the Borders button in the Formatting toolbar. Now click a choice from the list of 12 border options that Excel displays.

Restin' under a Shady Cell

(Subtle ways of grabbing a viewer's eye)

Another way to call attention to important stuff in your sheet is to "shade" the cells. To do so, select the cell range you want to shade, open the Format menu, choose the Cells command, and then click the Patterns tab. Excel displays the pattern formatting options in the Format Cells dialog box. You can shade your selected cells with a solid color, a pattern, or a combination of both.

To choose a pattern, click the down arrow next to the **Pattern** style box. Choose a pattern from the list that Excel displays. The pattern you pick normally is colored black. To choose a different color for that pattern style, simply click any color swatch that appears at the bottom of the **Pattern** list.

If you choose a color from the **Pattern** list, the color you pick is applied to the pattern, not to the cells background; for example, if you choose a dotted pattern, the dots appear in whatever color you pick from the **Pattern** list. To change the color that's behind the pattern, close the **Pattern** list and then click any color swatch that appears in the **Color** list box. Keep an eye on the Sample box to see how the combination of colors and patterns will look.

A few cell-shading effects you can create with a little practice

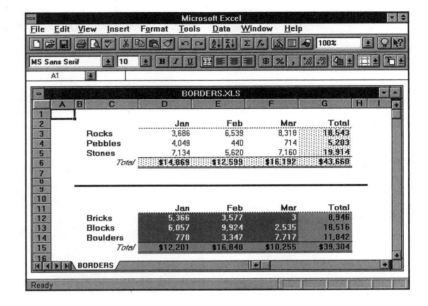

Advice about shading your cells

✔ When you add shading to your cells, use light colors so that you don't obscure the contents of a cell. Or use a bright color for the font and a dark background for the cell to achieve a fun reverse effect.

✔ To return to the standard pattern style and color, open the **Pattern** list and click Automatic, and then click the None option at the top of the **Color** list.

✔ To use no pattern whatsoever, open the **Pattern** list box, and then click the blank box in the upper-left corner of the list.

continues

Advice about shading your cells (continued)

✔ When you return to your workbook, you may see some odd colors in your workbook. Don't worry, that's a result of combining your color choices with black—the color that Excel uses to display a selected range of cells. Just unselect the formatted cell range so you can view your handiwork.

TIP

 To quickly apply color shading to selected cells in a sheet, click the Color button in the Formatting toolbar.

 To quickly apply color to the data in selected cells, click the Font Color button in the Formatting toolbar.

Auto-Formatting Tables of Data

(Painting by numbers)

When the expiration date on your creative juices has long since expired, Excel proudly presents you with the **AutoFormat** command. This feature takes all the hassle of making formatting decisions for tables and places it firmly on the shoulders of Excel. All you have to do is choose from the 17 predefined format styles.

CAUTION

This feature works best on tables—data set up in rows and columns, with row and column headings. If your data is not set up as a table, you should do the formatting by hand.

Select the entire table of data, open the Format menu, and choose the **A**utoFormat command. Excel displays the AutoFormat dialog box, in which you choose a table format from a list of 17 predesigned formats. Just pick the one you want! The Sample box in the middle of the AutoFormat dialog box shows you how the table looks with that format. If you like it, click OK.

In this example, the Sample box shows you what the table format called Colorful 2 looks like

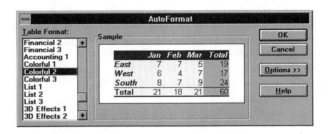

CHAPTER 11

Beyond Basic Printing

IN A NUTSHELL

- ▼ Other ways to start a printer printing
- ▼ Printing more than one copy, and other fun stuff
- ▼ Being selective about what to print
- ▼ Adding print titles for big sheets
- ▼ Controlling the look of the printout
- ▼ Adding headers and footers
- ▼ Using the Print Manager to speed things up

E xcel gives you total control over printing. Now, that may or may not be a good thing. Most folks are comfortable knowing only the bare-bones essentials of printing (like what's covered in Chapter 6, "Printing Basics"). Some people want to understand these same essentials plus a few other features, like how to print parts of a sheet, change margins, and switch between draft-quality and letter-quality printing. The remaining three people are the ones who absolutely have to know every single nuance of printing in Excel, from printing sideways on a three-part carbon to printing sheets in Swahili to disassembling and reassembling a printer in 40 seconds flat while blindfolded.

This chapter is for the middle group of people. If you are in this group, you might want to know how to print a range of selected cells. Or how to print more than one copy of a sheet without having to sit at your desk and choose the **P**rint command over and over again. Or maybe you just want to know how to add a date and page number to the bottom of your printouts.

If you're not in this group, skip this chapter. (But you just might miss something...)

Basic Printing Revisited

(For just a second or two)

Chapter 6, "Printing Basics," shows how easy it is to print in Excel. With a workbook on-screen, and the sheet you wish to print displayed, you simply open the **F**ile menu, choose the **P**rint command, and then click OK inside the Print dialog box. Printing this way requires no special preparation or advanced degrees. Here are some other ways to print in Excel.

✔ Click on the Print button. It's the icon fourth from the left in the Standard toolbar and looks like a little printer. This prints everything in the current sheet.

✔ Press Ctrl+P or Ctrl+Shift+F12, the shortcut keys for the **File Print** command. This displays the Print dialog box. Click OK or press Enter to begin printing everything in the current sheet.

TIP

It's always a good idea to save a workbook before printing it. That way you won't lose any information if your computer suddenly dies on you, if the printer jams or croaks, or if you accidentally flip off the power switch or hit the Reset button while Excel is printing.

Printing More Than One Copy

(and other fun stuff)

When you want to exert just a little bit more control over your printouts, open the Print dialog box and select one of the following options.

Printing only what you need

✔ To choose exactly what part of the workbook you wish Excel to print, choose an option in the Print What block. To print only a group of selected cells in a sheet, click the Selection option. To print the sheet that's displaying on your screen, click the Selected Sheet(s) option. To print an entire workbook, click the Entire Workbook option.

continues

Printing only what you need (continued)

✔ To print more than one copy of your sheet, click the up arrow next to the Copies box until the correct number of copies appears. Or, just type the number of copies into the Copies box.

✔ To display additional options for controlling how Excel prints, click the Page Setup button. The dialog box that appears is the same one you get when you choose the Page Setup command from the File menu. (More on that one later in the chapter.)

✔ To display a printout in the Print Preview window, click the Print Preview button on the Standard toolbar.

✔ To select a new printer to print to, or to change settings for the current printer, click the Printer Setup button. (Again, we'll look at this feature more closely in a few sections.)

Controlling What Excel Prints

(Coaxing a printer to heed your every wish)

When you print a sheet, Excel prints the whole darn thing unless you tell it otherwise. That's fine when your sheet is fairly small. But if the sheet is a worksheet that is 200 columns wide and 5,000 rows long, it would take you a full workday just to churn out that baby. More often than not, you will be selective when it comes to what stuff gets printed from your workbook.

Printing a Range of Pages

If you want to print just certain pages, open the Print dialog box. Click the Page(s) option in the Page Range block. In the **F**rom box, enter the starting page number. In the **T**o box, enter the ending page number. Then click OK. Excel will print the selected pages.

"I HATE THIS!"

How much is a *page*?

Margins, column width, and other things affect what will print on one page.

To figure out where Excel is going to split the pages when you print a sheet, use the Print Preview command (it's on the **F**ile menu). Or, click the Print Preview button inside the Print dialog box, or the Print Preview button on the Standard toolbar.

Printing a Particular Area of a Sheet

If you want to print just a particular area of your sheet, start by selecting the range of cells you want to print. Next, open the **F**ile menu and choose the **P**rint command. In the Print dialog box, choose an option from the Print What block that best describes what you want to print. Click OK to begin printing.

Here's how to be really selective about the information you print. In your worksheet, select several different cell ranges that are not connected. (Remember to hold down Ctrl while you select each disconnected range.) Next, open the **F**ile menu and choose the **P**rint command, then click the

Selection option in the Print What block. When you return to your sheet, you will notice that Excel did not display the dotted lines around your disconnected cell ranges. Don't worry, it's supposed to be that way. When you print a group of disconnected cell ranges, Excel prints each selection on its own page.

TIP

Check out your sheet in a Print Preview window before you print it. That way you'll be sure that you have selected the correct cell ranges.

"I HATE THIS!"

I changed my mind—I want to print the whole thing!

If you print part of a sheet and then want to print the entire sheet, just click the Selected Sheet(s) option inside the Print dialog box. It's the default setting every time you open up the Print dialog box, so that makes it even easier to make the change.

Bestowing Titles upon Your Sheet

(Hey, where's that data heading?)

A *print title* is text that Excel prints at the top and/or left side of each page in a printout. Print titles are the row and column headings, and they're great for sheets that just don't seem to fit on a single printed page. Consider the worksheet on the opposite page. It's so wide that everything to the right of column H has to be printed on another page. The problem is that the second page doesn't show what the rows mean. (A potential disaster if these two pages accidentally get separated at birth.)

Excel printed
this worksheet
on two pages
because it's too
wide to fit on one

	Jan	Feb	Mar	Apr	May	Jun
Rent	10,000	10,000	10,000	10,000	10,000	10,000
Telephone	6,401	5,278	4,217	6,734	4,632	5,050
Utilities	8,067	519	1,154	6,793	8,372	584
Insurance	4,482	5,654	8,232	2,527	6,454	9,804
Contract Labor	6,298	1,400	2,551	9,648	4,219	9,457
Commissions	8,955	2,723	7,298	6,078	2,004	3,723
Accounting	3,110	4,967	1,455	6,539	8,751	2,979
Legal	5,924	4,324	5,485	9,648	7,760	2,535
Furniture	5,525	1,121	947	7,501	9,966	3,538
Hardware	5,570	5,286	4,583	9,831	7,505	5,867
Software	7,123	8,787	7,736	3,529	1,371	1,432
Postage	526	6,174	8,057	3,972	9,670	9,177
TOTAL	$71,981	$56,233	$61,715	$82,800	$80,704	$64,146

Jul	Aug	Sep	Oct	Nov	Dec
10,000	10,000	10,000	10,000	10,000	10,000
387	7,366	7,035	2,878	2,277	9,383
9,688	6,834	350	3,034	8,857	5,879
9,952	5,082	5,755	734	4,102	5,757
748	3,531	8,910	6,303	5,399	2,361
6,008	581	9,864	5,523	9,082	1,881
6,318	1,771	9,518	719	8,672	4,123
2,885	3,294	3,905	558	3,809	5,314
1,414	7,386	4,643	690	490	2,102
6,138	2,648	3,661	1,889	1,273	8,426
2,231	6,239	2,153	9,471	6,597	9,246
4,187	9,988	16	9,173	2,626	3,027
$59,956	$64,720	$65,810	$50,972	$63,184	$67,499

To solve this problem, add some print titles:

1. Open the **F**ile menu and choose the Page Set**u**p command, and then click the Sheet tab inside the Page Setup dialog box.

2. Click inside the **C**olumns to Repeat at Left box. (You want to create row titles for the second page in the printout.)

3. Now click outside the Page Setup dialog box, and click anywhere in the column that contains the row titles you want to display on all pages of the printout. You can select several columns for titles by dragging across the columns you want.

   For the sample worksheet, you would click anywhere in column A. Excel displays a marquee around the entire column range you select. The column letter now appears in the **C**olumns to Repeat at Left box.

4. Click OK to return to the worksheet.

5. Print your worksheet.

More tantalizing title tricks

✔ You also can print titles by using text from the top of a sheet. This is great for narrow sheets that have tons of rows of information. For that situation, click inside the **R**ows to Repeat at Left box in the Page Setup dialog box, and then click in the row that contains the titles you want displayed at the top of each printed page. For example, you might select row 3 in the sample worksheet to display the month headings at the top of each page in the printout. You also can drag across multiple rows to get several rows of titles.

✔ To cancel any sheet titles you have created, simply reopen the Page Setup dialog box, click the Sheet tab, and delete the information from the appropriate box inside the Print Titles block.

Here's what the printout of the sample worksheet looks like now that the row headings from column A have been repeated on the second page in the worksheet.

Now it's easy to see what the rows mean on the second page of the printout

	Jan	Feb	Mar	Apr	May	Jun
Rent	10,000	10,000	10,000	10,000	10,000	10,000
Telephone	6,401	5,278	4,217	6,734	4,632	5,050
Utilities	8,067	519	1,154	6,793	8,372	584
Insurance	4,482	5,654	8,232	2,527	6,454	9,804
Contract Labor	6,298	1,400	2,551	9,648	4,219	9,457
Commissions	8,955	2,723	7,298	6,078	2,004	3,723
Accounting	3,110	4,967	1,455	6,539	8,751	2,979
Legal	5,924	4,324	5,485	9,648	7,760	2,535
Furniture	5,525	1,121	947	7,501	9,966	3,538
Hardware	5,570	5,286	4,583	9,831	7,505	5,867
Software	7,123	8,787	7,736	3,529	1,371	1,432
Postage	526	6,174	8,057	3,972	9,670	9,177
TOTAL	**$71,981**	**$56,233**	**$61,715**	**$82,800**	**$80,704**	**$64,146**

	Jul	Aug	Sep	Oct	Nov	Dec
Rent	10,000	10,000	10,000	10,000	10,000	10,000
Telephone	387	7,366	7,035	2,878	2,277	9,383
Utilities	9,688	6,834	350	3,034	8,857	5,879
Insurance	9,952	5,082	5,755	734	4,102	5,757
Contract Labor	748	3,531	8,910	6,303	5,399	2,361
Commissions	6,008	581	9,864	5,523	9,082	1,881
Accounting	6,318	1,771	9,518	719	8,672	4,123
Legal	2,885	3,294	3,905	558	3,809	5,314
Furniture	1,414	7,386	4,643	690	490	2,102
Hardware	6,138	2,648	3,661	1,889	1,273	8,426
Software	2,231	6,239	2,153	9,471	6,597	9,246
Postage	4,187	9,988	16	9,173	2,626	3,027
TOTAL	**$59,956**	**$64,720**	**$65,810**	**$50,972**	**$63,184**	**$67,499**

Adding Page Breaks

(Divvying up your workbook)

Excel automatically decides where to split the pages of your sheet when you print it; however, Excel also allows you to add *page breaks* to your sheet. A page break tells Excel where to start a new page during printing. To force a page break, select the row above which you want a page break. Then open the Insert menu and choose the Page Break command.

"I HATE THIS!"

> **My Page Break command is dimmed on the Insert menu!**
> If the active cell is A1 when you open the Insert menu, Excel won't allow you to choose the Page Break command. That's because it makes no sense to insert a page break above the first line in a printout.

Tinkering with Printing Special Effects

(Making losses look like profits)

In Excel, the phrase *page setup* is used to describe all the changeable things about the pages in your printouts. It's not the information contained in the sheet itself, but the way stuff is laid out on the printed page. Like whether the sheet prints up and down a page or across a page or whether the row letters and column numbers and gridlines are printed. And other stuff.

For most sheets, you will be happy to use Excel's normal settings. When you want to change these settings for one of your Excel sheets (you masochist, you), open the File menu and choose the Page Setup command.

When Excel displays the Page Setup dialog box, notice that there are four tabs: Page, Margins, Header/Footer, and Sheet. Welcome to the world of desktop publishing for workbooks, where the decisions to be made seem endless.

Reviewing the Page tab options in the Page Setup dialog box

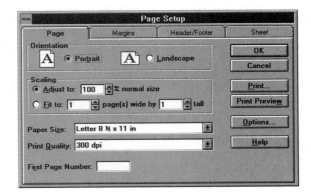

TIP

There are two other ways to get to the Page Setup dialog box: click the Page Setup option in the Print dialog box, or click the **S**etup button in the Print Preview window.

Page tab options

✔ The Orientation options tell Excel which direction to print: the Portrait option is the usual way to print, and the Landscape option prints everything sideways on the paper.

✔ The Scaling options allow you to change the size of information in your printouts. Choose the **F**it to option to automatically scale a sheet (or a selected range of cells) to fit onto a single printed page. The normal settings are 1 page wide by 1 page tall, which tells Excel to fit your data onto a single printed page. Type other numbers to fit your data into more or less space, as desired. To cram a large

continues

block of data onto a single page, click the **A**djust To button and type a percent number between 10 and 400 in the % normal size box. Anything under 100% shrinks the data, and anything over 100% enlarges the data in the printout.

✔ The Paper Size option tells Excel what size paper you're using. The normal setting for this option is `Letter 8 1/2 x 11 in.` That's the size of a typical piece of printer paper. To use a different size (such as legal size), click the down arrow next to the Paper Size option. Then click the size you want. Keep in mind that your printer has to be able to handle these different sizes of paper. You can't ~~jam legal-~~sized paper into the regular printer tray and hope that everything prints okay.

✔ If you want to print a draft of a sheet, click the down arrow next to Print **Q**uality. The list that appears shows you the different qualities your printer can achieve. Printing quality is measured in terms of *dots per inch* (dpi). The more dots, the higher the quality and more professional-looking your printouts will be. The less dots, the quicker the sheet will print.

✔ The First Page Number option tells Excel which page number to print on the first page of your sheet. Normally, this is set to Auto, which numbers pages starting with 1, but if you want to start numbering with a different number, type that number in the entry blank. This can be helpful, for example, when you want to add your workbook data starting on page 20 of a 50 page report.

✔ The **T**op, **B**ottom, **L**eft and **R**ight settings control how many inches of blank space appear between the outside edge of the paper and the printed information. Rather than mess around with typing margin settings, you can use the Horizontally and **V**ertically check boxes in the Center on Page block to center the printed information on the paper, regardless of any margin settings you have selected.

✔ Use the From Edge block options to tell Excel how far from the top and bottom margins it should print a header and footer.

✔ You can keep tabs on the margin settings for the sheet by checking out the page graphic in the Preview block.

Reviewing the Sheet tab options in the Page Setup dialog box

This cell range will be printed

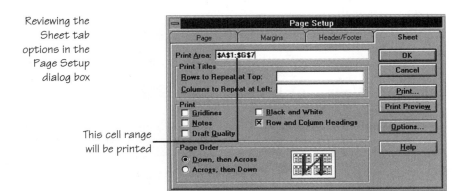

Sheet tab options

✔ The Print **A**rea option stores the cell range for the area of the sheet you are printing. You can update the range information in this box (if you decide to print a different cell range) simply by dragging your mouse pointer in the sheet, behind the Page Setup dialog box.

✔ The Print block settings control what appears on the printed page. Choose **G**ridlines to print data with gridlines; choose Draft **Q**uality to skip printing any presentation-quality formatting you may have added to the sheet; choose **B**lack and White to tell Excel to ignore the colors you have added to your sheet and print it using only black and white; and choose Row and Column Headings to print row numbers and column letters in your printout.

Changing the Headers and Footers

(Reading the small print)

Headers and footers are extra text you can include at the top and bottom, respectively, of each page in a printout. A *header* appears at the top, and a *footer* at the bottom.

To change a header or footer, open the Page Setup dialog box and click the Header/Footer tab. The easiest way to create a header or footer is to click the down arrow next to the Header or **F**ooter box, and then select one of the predesigned styles from the list that Excel displays.

Excel normally shows the sheet name at the top and the page number at the bottom of your printouts. These settings appear at the top and bottom of the Page Setup dialog box (in the sheet preview areas) when you first activate the Header/Footer tab in the Page Setup dialog box.

If for some crazy reason you can't find a style that suits your taste, you can type in your own header or footer text. Just click the **C**ustom Header or **C**ustom Footer button, and Excel displays the Header or Footer dialog box. Notice that Excel uses a special code for the file name and page number (take a look at the next Experts Only box). If you want to change the text to something different, select the text and type something new. Anything you type in the **L**eft Section window appears at the left edge of the printout; anything in the **C**enter Section window appears in the center; and (you guessed it) anything in the **R**ight Section window appears at the right edge of the printout.

The Header dialog box contains three section windows into which you can type text

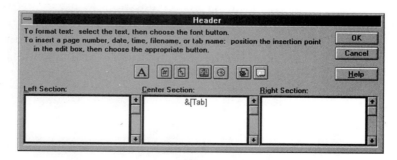

EXPERTS ONLY

Secret codes for headers and footers

Look at the preceding figure closely. Notice that strange-looking thing in the center section? That &[Tab] thing is the code for the sheet tab name. The code for page number is &[Page]. The easiest way to include one of these codes in header or footer text is to click in the window section where you want to show the information and then click one of the special code buttons. Here's what these buttons do:

 Displays the Font dialog box so that you can change fonts for your text

 Inserts the current page number code

 Inserts the code for the total number of pages in a printout

 Inserts the current date code

 Inserts the current time code

 Inserts the workbook file name code

 Inserts the sheet name code

For clarity, you also can type text before or after one of these codes. For instance, if you type **Page**, press the space bar once, and click the button with the number sign (3), the footer on the fifth page would look like this: **Page 5**.

To show where this page is in relation to all the pages in the printout, try this entry: **Page &[Page] of &[Pages]**. On the seventh page of a ten-page printout, this is how the footer would look: **Page 7 of 10**.

I HATE EXCEL FOR WINDOWS!

Help! I Can't Seem To Manage Printing in Excel

(Is there a cure for me?)

Printing can be the most time-consuming aspect of working with computer software. Have you ever had to sit around and wait for your printer to finish printing before you could continue working with Excel? Printing speeds can be different from computer to computer. Some computers can print Excel sheets in the blink of an eye. Others seem to blink a few times, blink a few more, and then blink even more before they start printing a sheet.

When your computer runs more like a Geo than a Porsche, you might be able to soup it up so that your sheets print faster. To do this, turn on the Windows Print Manager program, as explained in the next section. Once on, the Print Manager takes over responsibility for printing your sheets, allowing you to keep working in Excel with a minimum of interruptions. When the Print Manager is off, Excel itself must deal with the printing chores, which means that you will have to wait anywhere from a few seconds to a half hour before you can continue working in Excel.

Turning On the Print Manager

You activate the Print Manager from the Printers utility in the Control Panel. If that last sentence made absolutely no sense to you, remain calm, take a few deep breaths, and follow these steps:

1. From Program Manager (the main Windows screen), double-click the Main group icon to open its window—that is, unless it's already open. Then double-click the Control Panel program icon.

2. In the Control Panel window, double-click the Printers icon. Windows displays the Printers dialog box.

The Printers
dialog box is
where you
activate Print
Manager

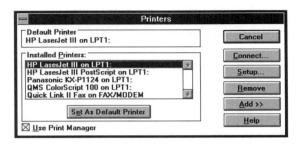

3. Click the Use Print Manager check box (if it isn't already selected).

4. Click the Cancel button to return to the Control Panel window.

5. Press Alt+F4 to close Control Panel and return to Program Manager.

Nothing spectacular will happen on your screen after you activate Print Manager. Just keep printing the same old way you have been. You'll continue to see the same Printing dialog box that appears while you're printing. The only noticeable difference will be that the Printing dialog box disappears much more quickly with Print Manager on the job! The faster that box goes away, the faster you can get back to your Excel work.

Choosing a Printer

Excel prints to the default printer (the one that's selected) in Print Manager every time you choose the Print command from the File menu. You're allowed to have only one default printer at a time, so be sure to pick the one you use most often. Here's how to select a new default printer from within Excel:

1. Open the File menu and choose Print. Excel displays the Print dialog box.

I HATE EXCEL FOR WINDOWS!

2. Click the Printer Setup button. Excel displays the Printer Setup dialog box.

3. In the Printer Setup dialog box, click the name you want to use as the default printer.

4. Click OK to return to the Print dialog box.

You're now done choosing a new default printer. The next time you choose the **Print** command on the **File** menu, Excel will print to the printer you selected above.

CHAPTER 12
Excel Does Windows

IN A NUTSHELL

▼ Resizing your workbook window
▼ Viewing the same workbook in two different windows
▼ Hiding workbook windows
▼ Splitting workbook windows
▼ Freezing window panes
▼ Zooming in and out

CHAPTER 12

Excel's Window menu is the loneliest menu of all. It sits way down at the right end of the menu bar, next to the **Help** menu. It's easy to forget that there's a **Window** menu in Excel because, well, when we think of windows, it's usually Microsoft Windows (the graphical program) that comes to mind.

The **Window** menu is a wallflower because, frankly, its commands just aren't the nuts and bolts of the program. You don't add or subtract with the **Window** menu commands. You can't print with them either. You can't even insert a row or save your workbook from this menu.

So what the heck is the **Window** menu for? This chapter shows you. You will learn some truly unique ways of looking at your workbooks—ways that make entering and updating data easier.

Controlling Your Workbook Window

(Look into my panes, you are getting sleepy)

Have you noticed that every time you create a new workbook, its window fills up most—but not all—of your Excel screen? There's always a white or gray area behind the workbook. You can enlarge a workbook so that it fills up this space. You also can move it around inside this space. You can accomplish these feats and many other, similar appearance-altering tricks using the **Window** menu commands.

"I HATE THIS!"

A window is a window is a window...

When you start Excel, the program is displayed in a window—known as the *program window*. Each Excel workbook you create sits in its own window, which somebody at Microsoft once decided should be officially known as a *document window*.

> But that sounds pretty formal, so the rest of us have always called it exactly what it is: a *workbook window*. The area behind the workbook window is called the workspace, or the space in which you *do* your work in Excel.

The easiest way to work with the window is with a mouse, using the following checklist.

Mousing around in a window

✔ To move a workbook, drag its title bar around the workspace.

✔ To resize a workbook, drag one of its window borders.

✔ To *minimize* the workbook (turn it into an icon), click the Minimize button. Be sure to click the Minimize button in the workbook window, not in the Excel window, which also has a Minimize button. (The easiest way to figure out which is which is to remember that the workbook window Minimize button is *always* below the Excel window button.) To go from the icon back to the workbook, double-click the minimized icon.

✔ To *maximize* the workbook (zoom it to full-screen), click the Maximize button. When a workbook is fully enlarged in the workspace, you can't resize the window, and the Restore button replaces the workbook window's Minimize and Maximize buttons. Click the Restore button to return to the original workbook size.

✔ To close a workbook, double-click the Control menu icon. You will be reminded to save your workbook, if you haven't already.

I HATE EXCEL FOR WINDOWS!

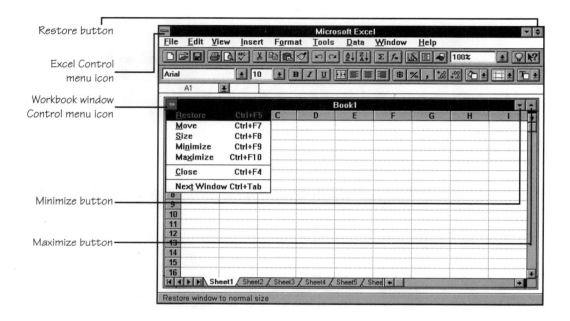

Restore button

Excel Control
menu icon

Workbook window
Control menu icon

Minimize button

Maximize button

TIP

You also can use the commands on a workbook's Control menu. (Don't look for the word "Control" in the menu bar; it's not there.) To get to a workbook's Control menu, click the Control menu icon once. It's the one that looks like a hyphen in the upper left corner of the workbook. Don't confuse the workbook window's Control menu icon (a short dash) with Excel's Control menu icon (a long dash). Once the menu is open, choose the command you want.

TIP

Another way to control your windows is by using the keyboard shortcuts for the Control menu commands:

Ctrl+F5	Restore a window
Ctrl+F7, arrow keys	Move a window
Ctrl+F8, arrow keys	Resize a window
Ctrl+F9	Minimize a window
Ctrl+F10	Maximize a window
Ctrl+F4	Close a window
Ctrl+F6	Select the next window

Looking at the Same Workbook Twice

(Double vision)

Excel allows you to create a copy of the active workbook and place the copy in its own window. Then you can rearrange both windows on your screen so that you see different parts of each, just like if you could look through a microscope and see two different parts of the same slide.

TIP

Even if you create a million copies of a window, you can always tell which one's active by locating the window with the different-colored title bar. It's dark blue on most color screens.

There are several good reasons why you want to do something like this. ("Because it's there," isn't one of them. Really.) The truth is, as you work more and more in Excel, you will become comfortable creating wider and longer sheets in your workbooks. It's inevitable. Creating a new window for a large sheet makes it easier to quickly move around and find stuff.

Suppose you have a workbook with a really wide sheet open in Excel. The formulas are in column BB, but the data you're changing is in column C. You're updating your payroll-budget report, and it's important that you keep an eye on the bottom-line figure as you enter each new number into the workbook. After all, heads will roll if you go over budget.

Opening a Second Window

First, create a new window by opening the **Window** menu and choosing the New Window command. Excel opens a second window that overlays the first. It looks almost exactly the same as the first one. The only difference is that at the end of the workbook name in the title bar, there's a colon followed by a number. That's the window number. Your original window is window 1, and the new window is window 2.

Working with your windows

✔ Excel allows you to create as many windows as your computer's memory can handle. It's easiest when you stick to a maximum of four to five windows. Any more than that, and your screen will feel overcrowded. This makes it difficult to work effectively with the open windows.

✔ You can move back and forth between windows by pointing and clicking inside a window or by pressing Ctrl+F6.

✔ When a workbook has more than one window, information that you enter or edit in one window also appears in the other.

✔ The names of all open workbooks and workbook windows appear in the bottom of the **Window** menu. The one that's currently

active will have a check mark next to it. You can choose a name from this list (just as if you were choosing a command) to make that one the active workbook or window.

✔ If you use the **F**ile **S**ave command to save a workbook you're displaying in two or more windows, Excel saves the original workbook file with all its windows. You don't need to save each window separately.

Arranging the Windows

You should arrange the windows on-screen so that you can see both of them because chances are that one window covers up part of the other. Ideally, you want them displayed in such a way that it's easy to watch your formula answers change as you type in new numbers. To do so, open the **W**indow menu and choose the **A**rrange command. When the Arrange Windows dialog box appears, click the **V**ertical button, and then click OK. Here's what your screen should look like:

Two windows arranged vertically next to each other. The one on the right is the active window.

	Microsoft Excel		
File Edit View Insert Format Tools Data Window Help			

PAYROLL.XLS:1					PAYROLL.XLS:2			
	A	B	C	D		AZ	BA	BB	BC
1	Payroll Budget Report				1				
2	Fiscal 1994				2				
3					3				
4		Week1	Week2	Week3	4	Week51	Week52	Totals	
5	Bob	1,588	1,724	1,552	5	1,631	1,710	85,352	
6	Carol	1,729	1,736	1,504	6	1,683	1,586	84,881	
7	Ted	1,681	1,649	1,559	7	1,566	1,718	84,592	
8	Alice	1,609	1,653	1,658	8	1,647	1,722	85,702	
9	Pat	1,634	1,556	1,651	9	1,728	1,532	83,539	
10	Cathy	1,652	1,533	1,525	10	1,704	1,565	83,361	
11	John	1,706	1,649	1,707	11	1,516	1,728	85,376	
12	Gary	2,651	2,558	2,565	12	2,730	2,735	136,625	
13	Michelle	2,510	2,553	2,663	13	2,654	2,584	135,695	
14	Jim	2,503	2,513	2,505	14	2,748	2,621	136,087	
15	Frank	2,531	2,596	2,726	15	2,693	2,508	136,348	
16	Barbara	2,613	2,588	2,558	16	2,708	2,699	136,599	

PAYROLL / Sheet2 / Sheet3 / Sheet4 / Sh   PAYROLL / Sheet2

Ready

A vertical window arrangement is ideal for this workbook. That's because the active sheet in this workbook has plenty of information in columns. (It's only 24 rows long.) Other workbook layouts might require a different arrangement of windows. Here's what the other window-arranging options do:

Arranging your windows

✔ The **T**iled option lays out all windows in a tile fashion.

✔ The Horizontal option arranges windows one above the other, so they look short and very wide. This layout is useful when your workbooks have lots of rows of information.

✔ The **C**ascade option arranges windows in a one-on-top-of-the-other fashion. This layout is useful when you have several workbooks open in Excel and need to quickly scan their title bars for names.

✔ The **W**indows of Active Workbook option allows you to arrange only the windows for a particular workbook when there is more than one workbook open in Excel's memory. This means, for example, that if you have workbooks named Frank and Stein open, and Frank has a second window (Frank:2), checking this option tells Excel to arrange only the windows for the Frank workbook. Excel ignores the Stein workbook and leaves it hidden in the background.

✔ For a different angle on how to arrange two windows, see the upcoming section "Splitting a Window in Two."

To close a window after you're finished working with it, make the window active, open its Control menu, and choose the **C**lose command.

Keyboarders can simply press Ctrl+F4. When there's only one open window left on your screen, you're back to the original window.

TIP

When you create several windows for a workbook, each one looks exactly the same as the next window. You can create unique display views for different windows. For example, you might want to remove the display of cell gridlines from one window but not the other. To accomplish these display effects, click the window you want to change, choose the **Op**tions command from the **T**ools menu, and then click the View tab. See Chapter 18, "Excel, Made To Order," for more information about changing the display settings for a workbook.

Hiding and Unhiding Windows (Peekaboo with panes)

Has anyone ever tiptoed up behind you and peered over your shoulder to see what you're doing in Excel? It's almost as if this nosy intruder expects to see your personal statement of net worth or a payroll register listing everyone's salary. Well, it's annoying enough to be tiptoed upon. But when you really *are* working on a personal financial report or the company payroll register, these sneaks can really irritate you. To keep the sneaks from peeking, hide the window.

When you choose the **H**ide command from the **W**indow menu, Excel immediately removes the active workbook from your screen. To redisplay the workbook, open the **W**indow menu and choose **U**nhide. When the Unhide dialog box appears, click the name of the workbook you want to redisplay and click OK. Poof! It's back in an instant. That's pretty much all there is to hiding and unhiding your private workbooks.

"I HATE THIS!"

Hey! Where'd my Window menu disappear to?

When the workbook you just hid was the only one open in Excel, all the menus except File and Help will disappear from the menu bar. This is normal, so don't panic. Open the File menu and you will see the Unhide command. Choose the Unhide command, click the name of the workbook in the Unhide dialog box, and click OK to get everything back to normal.

Working on Two Files at Once

(Double duty)

Some of the more adventurous Excel users enjoy working with more than one workbook at a time. This is easy enough to accomplish; you just use the File Open command to open as many as you would like. With two different workbooks open, you can see key figures in one workbook, and copy data from one to the other.

Arranging your workbooks

✔ When you have several workbooks open at once, but the active workbook isn't the one you want to work in, you can select the one you want. To do this, open the Window menu. The names of all open workbooks are listed at the bottom of the menu. Click the name of the one you want. A quicker method is to click the open workbook, if you can see it on your screen.

✔ To arrange all the workbooks you are working on, go back and read the section "Arranging the Windows."

✔ To close a workbook, save it and then either double-click the Control menu icon for that window or open the File menu and choose Close.

TIP

Because this several-files-open-at-once tactic has a tendency to fill up the workspace, you might want to try this trick: minimize all workbooks you're not using at the moment, so that they're displayed as icons at the bottom of the workspace. To do this, open the Control menu and choose Minimize. Whenever your icons get messy in the workspace, open the **Window** menu and choose **Arrange Icons**. Yes, I know that it wasn't on your **Window** menu when you looked before. In fact, the only time the Arrange Icons command does appear on the **Window** menu is when (...drum roll please...) you have minimized a workbook to the size of an icon and that icon is active.

Splitting a Window in Two

(Panes, that is)

The Split command on the Window menu works a lot like the Arrange command. You use it to check out two distant parts of the same workbook. The difference is that you don't create a second window when you use the Split command. You actually create two *panes* in the same workbook window. Heres how: Position the active cell in the area of a sheet in the workbook where you would like the split to occur. To create two horizontal panes, for example, you might select cell A9 on Sheet1. To create two vertical panes, try cell E1 on Sheet1. Now open the Window menu and choose Split. As soon as you choose Split, Excel divides Sheet1 in the workbook into two panes.

Creating two
horizontal panes
in a workbook
window

Split bar —————

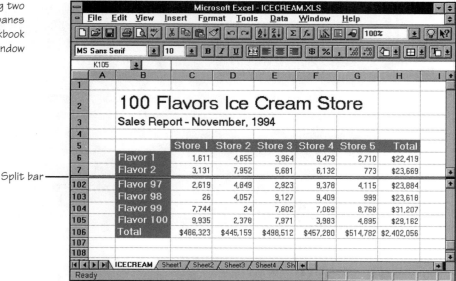

What to do once you've split a workbook into panes

✔ When you use the Split command, Excel creates panes for the active sheet only. To create panes for another sheet in the workbook, move to that sheet and choose the Split command again.

✔ If cell A1 is the active cell when you choose the Split command, or if the active cell is not in column A and not in row 1 (if it's in cell E9, for example), Excel will display four panes. To create a two-pane horizontal view, drag the vertical split bar to the far left side of the active sheet in the workbook and release it. It will disappear from the workbook. To create a two-pane vertical view, drag the horizontal split bar to the top of the active sheet in the workbook and release it. It will disappear from the workbook.

✔ The scroll bars at the bottom of the workbook window scroll only the sheet you are displaying in the active window pane. This way, you can scroll panes independently to see different parts of the active sheet in the workbook.

✔ To move back and forth between panes, point and click inside a pane. Or, using the keyboard, press Shift+F6 to move the active cell back and forth between panes.

✔ When you create two horizontal panes, the panes scroll together horizontally but not vertically. That's because Excel assumes that you've created two horizontal panes so that you can simultaneously display stuff from the top and bottom of the workbook.

✔ When you create two vertical panes, the panes scroll together vertically but not horizontally. That's so you can simultaneously see information from the very left and very right sides of a workbook.

✔ To remove split panes from a workbook, open the Window menu and choose Remove Split.

✔ To split a workbook into panes using the split boxes, drag a split box until the panes are correctly sized, then release your mouse.

✔ To remove split panes from a workbook using the split boxes, either drag the split boxes back off your screen, or just double-click on the split bar.

Freezing Windows

(Don't put your tongue on 'em)

The Window Freeze Panes command is extremely effective for fixing titles so that they don't go off screen when you scroll through your workbook window. For example, you can freeze the titles in rows 1 through 5 of the active sheet in the sample workbook. That way, when you scroll down to see more information, the titles stay in place, but the information below the frozen rows scrolls up toward the top of the workbook window as usual. This will help you remember what goes in what row as you enter data.

Here's how it works. Position the active cell in column A in the row just below where you want to freeze the titles. (That's cell A6 in the ICECREAM sheet of the sample workbook.) Open the **W**indow menu and choose **F**reeze Panes. Excel splits the window into two panes, and displays a thin black line between the panes. The first pane includes rows 1 through 5; the second pane includes everything else.

Now try scrolling through the active sheet in the workbook. The titles don't move, and the information that appears below the titles scrolls below row 5.

Rows 1-5 are frozen and will always appear at the top of the active sheet in your workbook, even if you're in row 99

		Microsoft Excel - ICECREAM.XLS						

File Edit View Insert Format Tools Data Window Help

K105

	A	B	C	D	E	F	G	H	I
1									
2		**100 Flavors Ice Cream Store**							
3		Sales Report - November, 1994							
4									
5			Store 1	Store 2	Store 3	Store 4	Store 5	Total	
99		Flavor 94	4,094	4,684	7,250	2,221	3,578	$21,827	
100		Flavor 95	5,079	2,159	3,342	9,473	7,662	$27,715	
101		Flavor 96	496	3,964	9,620	8,338	4,852	$27,270	
102		Flavor 97	2,619	4,849	2,923	9,378	4,115	$23,884	
103		Flavor 98	26	4,057	9,127	9,409	999	$23,618	
104		Flavor 99	7,744	24	7,602	7,069	8,768	$31,207	
105		Flavor 100	9,935	2,378	7,971	3,983	4,895	$29,162	
106		Total	$486,323	$445,159	$498,512	$457,280	$514,782	$2,402,056	
107									

ICECREAM Sheet1 Sheet2 Sheet3 Sheet4 Sh

Ready

Other ways of working with frozen panes

✔ You also can freeze column titles at the left edge of the active sheet in the workbook. To do so, position the active cell in the first column to the right of where you want to freeze titles in row 1, and then choose the **F**reeze Panes command.

190

✔ You can freeze column titles and row titles in the same sheet. It doesn't matter which you create first. Or you can create them at the same time by selecting a cell that's not in column A and not in row 1, and then choose the Freeze Panes command.

✔ You can split a workbook window into panes with the Split command and then freeze the top pane, the left pane, or both by choosing the Freeze Panes command.

✔ Unlike the panes created with the Split command, those that Excel creates when you freeze titles do not have their own scroll bars.

✔ To move back into the area that contains the frozen titles, click anywhere in that area or use the arrow keys to move there.

✔ To remove frozen titles from the active sheet in a workbook, open the Window menu and choose the Unfreeze Panes command.

"I HATE THIS!"

Hey! Where did it go?

If you have scrolled text off the screen and *then* you freeze the window, you can't *ever* see the stuff that's above or to the left. Even using File Go To doesn't get you there. The cell pointer goes, but it's not on-screen, so you can only tell what's in the cell by looking at the formula bar (not helpful if the cell contains a formula and you want to know the value).

Who's Zooming Who?

(Magnifying and shrinking your workbook view)

The View Zoom command. Okay, so it's not on the Window menu. I've still never been able to figure out if by selecting this command I'm actually enlarging my workbook, or simply shrinking myself, my computer, my desk, and everything else in my office. In any case, the choices you have when it comes to shrinking and enlarging your view with the Zoom command follows.

Za-zoom zettings

✔ The 200% option doubles the size of your workbook.

✔ The 100% option displays the normal workbook size.

✔ The 75% option shows your workbook at 75% of its normal size. (Of course, this also can mean that you have been enlarged to 125% of your normal size. Do your pants feel tight?)

✔ The 50% option shows your workbook at 50% of its normal size.

✔ The 25% option shows your workbook at 25% of its normal size.

✔ The Fit Selection option allows Excel to calculate the optimal zoom factor for a selected workbook area so that it fits the current window size.

✔ The Custom option allows you to make the choice. Type any value from 10 to 400 into the box.

When the boss gripes to you about how small sales have been lately, you can zoom in on the bottom line so that it looks like this

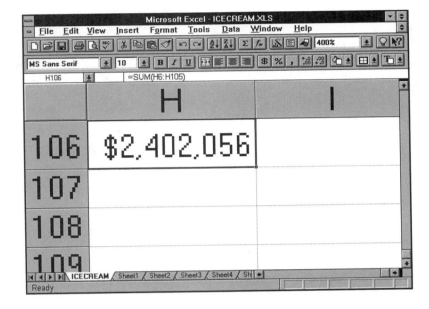

TIP

Want to get more book for the buck in a workbook window? Do you ever get tired of all those toolbars and scroll doohickies in the Excel window? If so, open the **V**iew menu, choose **F**ull Screen, and watch as Excel stashes all that stuff away, leaving only your workbook in all its glory and splendor (well, whatever can fit onto your screen anyway). To get out of full-screen view and return all those bars, click the little Full Screen button that Excel sneaked onto the upper left corner of your screen when you weren't looking.

PART III

Formulas for Success

Includes:

13: Those Fab Functions

14: Functions You'll Profit From

CHAPTER 13

Those Fab Functions

IN A NUTSHELL

▼ Why you need functions

▼ Functions that total a range

▼ Functions that can average and count

▼ Functions that display dates and tell time

▼ Functions that make decisions for you

▼ Functions that display the N/A message

▼ Functions that round off your numbers

▼ Functions that change the case of letters

▼ Functions that use a 360-day calendar

I HATE EXCEL FOR WINDOWS!

n Chapter 7, "Formulas and Functions," you figured out how to type basic formulas into a worksheet. These were great for doing things like adding, subtracting, multiplying, and dividing groups of numbers. As your calculation needs get more involved, though, so must your formulas.

The reality of crunching numbers in Excel is that your workbook is only as smart as you. When you type a formula correctly, you always get the correct answer. And when you don't, well, you don't. That's the nature of formulas in Excel.

But let's face it, we're not mathematicians. That's why Excel offers a whole slew of built-in formulas, called *functions*. I like to call them the "fabulous functions." In this chapter we take a look at the most fabulous ones around.

TIP

> Chapter 14, "Functions You'll Profit From," covers financial functions—functions that calculate a home loan or car loan payment and other fun things. Don't forget to look at that chapter for other useful functions.

Why Functions?

Functions are invaluable because some workbook calculations can't be done easily with those other, basic formulas. Like calculating the sum of the differences of squares of corresponding values in two arrays. (Why would anyone ever want to do that?)

And when it comes to typing them into cells, Excel's functions tend to be more forgiving than the formulas you create on your own. If Excel doesn't recognize the function you're typing into a cell, Excel will

display a rather impersonal message on your screen—something like "Error in your formula." This means, "Nice try, but give it another shot."

Excel catches any typos you make in functions, because each function is designed to do a very specific calculation. When you type a function into a cell, Excel expects to see things in a very specific order—things such as the *arguments*.

BUZZWORDS

ARGUMENT

Arguments are the extra things (characters and numbers) you type with the function, things that tell Excel which numbers to crunch.

The basics of entering a function are covered in Chapter 7, "Formulas and Functions." Here are the major parts of a function:

✔ The equal sign (=) is the must-have part of the function. Without it, Excel has no way of regonizing that you're about to enter a function.

✔ The function name is a short—sometimes abbreviated—word that generally describes the function's duty.

✔ The two parentheses are used to separate the function name from the information that you want the function to use in its calculation. You have to type the parentheses.

✔ The arguments—the stuff in parentheses—can be values separated by commas, or cell addresses separated by commas, or a cell range.

TIP

Here's an easy way to let Excel type your function arguments for you. For any function, type everything up to and including the last letter in the function name into the formula bar. Then press Ctrl+A or click the Function Wizard button on the Standard toolbar. Excel displays the Function Wizard—Step 2 of 2 dialog box. Don't worry too much about what this dialog box is for. For now, click the **F**inish button. Excel automatically types the necessary argument descriptions for you into the formula bar. The insertion point appears in the active cell next to the first of these. Now edit each description, replacing the text with the number needed to complete the function. When you're finished doing this, press Enter to display the answer in your worksheet.

Using Function
Wizard to sum
up cell range
C5:C7

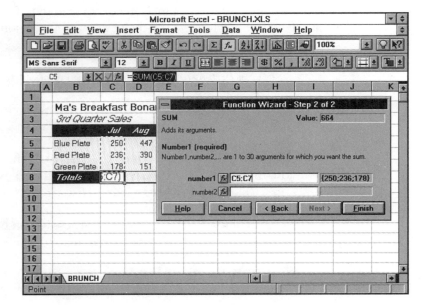

SUM Day It'll All Add Up

The SUM function calculates the sum of a group of numbers. It's great to use when you have run out of toes and fingers.

The SUM function looks like this:

=SUM(*number1,number2,...*)

Things to remember about using SUM

✔ *number1* and *number2* are the arguments.

✔ You can include up to 30 arguments in a SUM function. That's 30 separate entries separated by commas.

✔ Arguments can be numbers, addresses of individual cells that contain numbers, or cell range addresses that describe where the numbers are.

Table 13.1 Examples of SUM

The Function	The Result
=SUM(1,2,3)	6
=SUM(C1:C3)	**25**, when C1, C2, and C3 contain 10, 5, and 10
=SUM(C1,D3,F4)	**35**, when C1, D3, and F4 contain 5, 20, and 10

TIP

Σ Don't forget that the AutoSum button in the Standard toolbar is the quickest way to sum numbers in your worksheets. Just move into a blank cell next to the range you want to sum, click the AutoSum button, and then press Enter.

Just Your AVERAGE Run-of-the-Mill Function

The AVERAGE function calculates the average of a group of numbers, like the average of six sales figures, the average salary earnings for ten employees, or the average air speed velocity of an African swallow flying into a 30-mph head wind. It's up to you to decide what you want to average.

The AVERAGE function looks like this:

=AVERAGE(*number1,number2,...*)

Things to remember about using AVERAGE

✔ *number1* and *number2* are the arguments.

✔ You can include up to 30 arguments in an AVERAGE function. That's 30 separate entries separated by commas.

✔ Arguments can be numbers, addresses of individual cells that contain numbers, or cell range addresses that describe where the numbers are.

✔ When figuring out an average, Excel first adds up all the numbers you give to it and then divides that answer by the total number of items you have included in the function.

✔ Excel treats blank cells and zero values differently when it averages numbers. When you include a blank cell as an argument, Excel does not count it as an item when calculating an average. When you include 0—or a cell that contains 0—as an argument, Excel does count it as an item when calculating an average.

Table 13.2 Examples of AVERAGE

The Function	The Result
=AVERAGE(2,4,6)	4
=AVERAGE(A1:A3)	7, when A1, A2, and A3 contain 10, 3, and 8

The following worksheet is an example of using AVERAGE in a worksheet. Notice the different answers Excel comes up with when the cell range contains a blank cell, as opposed to containing the value 0.

Figuring out
the average
for ranges of
numbers in a
worksheet

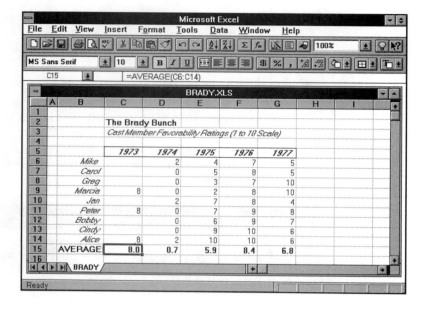

You Can COUNT on It

The COUNT function counts how many numbers there are in a cell range. This function is helpful for double-checking your work. Suppose you have just entered today's invoices into a worksheet. You know that there are 282 invoices, but you're not sure whether you actually entered all of them. Use the COUNT function to check it out.

The COUNT function looks like this:

=COUNT(*value1*,*value2*,...)

✔ *value1* and *value2* are the arguments.

✔ You can include up to 30 arguments in a COUNT function. That's 30 different entries separated by commas.

✔ Arguments can be numbers, addresses of individual cells that contain numbers, or cell range addresses that describe where the numbers are.

✔ If you select a cell range, Excel doesn't count cells that contain text or formula errors.

✔ Excel doesn't count blank cells if they're in a cell range you're using as an argument. (But it does count zeros.)

The following worksheet is an example of using COUNT in a worksheet. Notice that Excel ignores the three blank cells and the formula error message when it counts the entries in column C.

Counting the number of entries in a worksheet

```
┌─────────────────────────────────────────────────────────────────────┐
│ ─                        Microsoft Excel                      ▼ ▲    │
│ File  Edit  View  Insert  Format  Tools  Data  Window  Help          │
├─────────────────────────────────────────────────────────────────────┤
│ [toolbar]                                              100%   ▼ 💡 ▶?│
├─────────────────────────────────────────────────────────────────────┤
│ MS Sans Serif   ▼ 10 ▼  B I U ...                            $ % ... │
├─────────────────────────────────────────────────────────────────────┤
│ C15      ▼        =COUNT(C4:C13)                                     │
├─────────────────────────────────────────────────────────────────────┤
│ ─                        COUNT.XLS                           ▼ ▲    │
│     A   B      C      D       E      F       G      H      I     J   │
│  1                                                                   │
│  2          Invoice Register                                         │
│  3             #      Date    Acct #   Net    Tax    Gross           │
│  4            234   10/16/94   234    770.06  57.75  827.81          │
│  5                  10/16/94   444    942.02  70.65  1012.67         │
│  6            236   10/16/94   212    54.14   4.06   58.2            │
│  7            237   10/16/94   778    886.15  66.46  952.61          │
│  8                  10/16/94   566    706.41  52.98  759.39          │
│  9            239   10/16/94   455    10.13   0.76   10.89           │
│ 10                  10/16/94   534    953.45  71.51  1024.96         │
│ 11          #NAME?  10/16/94   99     765.78  57.43  823.21          │
│ 12            242   10/16/94   122    158.09  11.86  169.95          │
│ 13            243   10/16/94   677    496.89  37.27  534.16          │
│ 14                                                                   │
│ 15   COUNT    6                                                      │
│ ◄ ◄ ► ►│ COUNT                                                       │
├─────────────────────────────────────────────────────────────────────┤
│ Ready                                                                │
└─────────────────────────────────────────────────────────────────────┘
```

How 'bout a DATE?

Every worksheet wants one; every worksheet needs one. The DATE function is most useful in workbooks that keep track of things by date, but don't necessarily show the parts of the date in a single cell. For example, an inventory tracking report may show the month, the day, and the year in three different cells. To use the dates in a calculation—say to determine how long an item has been sitting idly in your inventory—you could use the DATE function to join the three.

The DATE function looks like this:

=DATE(*year,month,day*)

Things to remember about using DATE

✔ *year*, *month*, and *day* are the arguments.

✔ The arguments can be numbers or the addresses of individual cells that contain numbers.

✔ Don't use cell ranges as arguments in the DATE function; Excel will display the #VALUE error message in the cell.

The following worksheet is an example of using DATE in a worksheet. In this particular version, the function is used to show the expiration date for a perishable inventory item. The expiration date is ten days from the date of purchase.

Keeping track of time with the DATE function

	Microsoft Excel
File Edit View Insert Format Tools Data Window Help	

MS Sans Serif · 10 · B *I* U

H7 · =DATE(F7,D7,E7)+G7

DATE.XLS

	A	B	C	D	E	F	G	H	I
1									
2		Inventory Tracking Report							
3									
4				Date Purchased			Max Days	Toss Out	
5		Item #	Description	Month	Day	Year	On Hand	Date	
6		1	Rose, Samantha	6	3	93	7	06/10	
7		2	Rose, Sterling	6	3	93	10	06/13	
8		3	Freesia, Mixed	6	4	93	4	06/08	
9		4	Alstromeria	6	6	93	5	06/11	
10		5	Bells of Ireland	6	7	93	5	06/12	
11		6	Gloriosa Lily	6	9	93	3	06/12	
12		7	Carnations	6	12	93	12	06/24	
13		8	Mixed Poms	6	2	93	12	06/14	
14		9	Mini Carnations	6	1	93	12	06/13	
15		10	Gyp	6	12	93	14	06/26	

DATE

Ready

The Date and Time Is NOW

The NOW function displays the current date and time in the following format in any worksheet cell: 10/28/94 12:25. This is useful for folks (like me) who have three calendars on their desk, one wrist watch, and two wall clocks, but never seem to remember what time or day it is.

The NOW function looks like this:

=NOW()

Things to remember about using NOW

✔ When you enter this function into a cell, you may see that annoying ######## stuff instead of an actual date and time. Choose For-mat Column AutoFit Selection so that Excel increases the width of the column containing the function just enough to show the date and time.

✔ This function has no arguments, but you must always include the empty parentheses () after it.

✔ If you don't include the empty parentheses, Excel displays the #NAME? error message. Press F2 to edit the entry, type (), and press Enter.

✔ The day and time Excel displays is for the exact moment you typed the NOW function into the cell. Every time you enter or edit stuff in the same worksheet, Excel updates the NOW function so that it shows the current date and time. If this doesn't happen in your worksheets and you see Calculate in the status bar, press F9 to recalculate all worksheets in your workbook.

✔ The date and time that Excel displays when you use the NOW function comes from your computer's internal clock. Be sure that your computer's clock is correctly set.

✔ Use the NOW function in formulas to figure out things like how many days have gone by between now and when you last paid a vendor, or between now and when a client purchased something from you.

Collect $200 Only IF You Pass Go

The IF function is one of the most useful Excel functions. It lets you ask questions about things and then take different courses of action, depending on the answer you get. The power of the IF function is extended when you combine it with other functions, like the SUM function.

The IF function looks like this:

=IF(*logical_test*,*value_if_true*,*value_if_false*)

Things to remember about using IF

✔ *logical_test*, *value_if_true*, and *value_if_false* are the arguments.

✔ The *logical_test* argument is a value or a question that has a true or false answer. For example, if you want to ask the question, "Is the value in cell C5 greater than or equal to 450?" you would type **C5>=450** for this argument. Or you can ask the question, "Is 500 equal to the value in cell B9?" by typing **500=B9** as the argument. The questions you ask in the IF function can include any of the following *comparison operators:*

This operator	*Means…*
=	Equal to
>	Greater than
<	Less than
>=	Greater than or equal to
<=	Less than or equal to
<>	Not equal to

✔ The *value_if_true* argument tells Excel what to do if the answer to the question is TRUE.

✔ The *value_if_false* argument tells Excel what to do if the answer to the question is FALSE.

✔ The "what to do" aspect to using the IF function means many things. To tell Excel to calculate a formula and display the result, type the formula as you normally would. To display a few descriptive words in a cell, type the text within quotation marks.

In the following sample worksheet, notice the IF function that appears in the formula bar when you highlight cell D3. The function looks at the number in B3. If it is equal to 100, Excel displays Perfect Score (the *value_if_true* argument). If B3 doesn't equal 100, Excel displays Good Try (the *value_if_false* argument). As you can see, the score that appears in cell D4 belongs to the class curve-buster. (Don't you just hate those people?)

Use the IF function to ask questions and then give direct answers about information in your worksheets

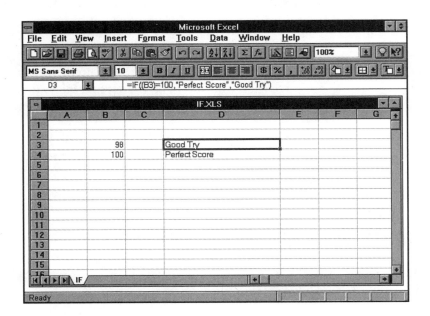

Sorry, I'm NA Quite Ready

Use the NA function to display #N/A in any cell (that is, any cell used in a formula) that doesn't currently contain information, but soon will. This message means no value available. Any formulas that reference this function will display #N/A rather than a zero. This would alert your workbook readers that the information is a coming attraction.

The NA function looks like this:

    =NA()

Things to remember about using NA

✔ This function has no arguments, but you must always include the () after it.

✔ When you forget to place the () after the function, Excel can't recognize the entry and therefore displays the #NAME? error message. Press F2 to edit the entry, type (), and press Enter.

✔ You can type **#N/A** directly into a cell. Excel treats this entry exactly as if you had typed in the NA function.

Let's Just ROUND It Off a Bit

The ROUND function gets rid of all those unsightly numbers to the right of a decimal place. In some workbook reports, it's just not politically correct to show decimal-place values; for example, imagine how a Fortune 500 sales figure like $283,451,229.02 would look in an annual report. Not kosher.

With the ROUND function, you can round a number to a certain amount of digits. Rounded numbers do not change in their cells; the original numbers are still used in all the calculations. Only what's displayed on your screen changes.

The ROUND function looks like this:

=ROUND(*number,num_digits*)

Things to remember about using ROUND

✔ *number* and *num_digits* are the arguments.

✔ The *number* argument is the number you want to round.

✔ Arguments can be numbers or the addresses of individual cells that contain numbers.

✔ The *num_digits* argument is the number of digits to round by. If this value is greater than 0, Excel rounds to that many digits to the right of the decimal point. If this value is equal to 0, Excel rounds to the nearest integer. If this value is less than 0, Excel rounds to that many digits to the left of the decimal point.

Table 13.3 Examples of ROUND

The Function	The Result
=ROUND(567.891,2)	567.89
=ROUND(567.891,0)	568

continues

Table 13.3 (Continued)	
The Function	The Result
=ROUND(A1,A2)	570, when cell A1 contains the number 567.891 and cell A2 contains the number 1

UPPER-Case Appeal

The UPPER function converts text characters to all uppercase characters. At first glance, you might look at a feature like this and say to yourself, "Oh, come on! Why not just retype it?" Good point. But when your boss asks you to change a 27-word report title, the UPPER function's appeal will suddenly dawn on you.

The UPPER function looks like this:

=UPPER(*text*)

Things to remember about using UPPER

✔ *text* is the only argument.

✔ The argument can be text, enclosed in quotation marks, that you type as part of the function, or it can be the address of an individual cell that contains text. Cell ranges will not work with this function.

Table 13.4 Examples of UPPER

The Function	The Result
=UPPER("stuff")	STUFF
=UPPER(C5)	STUFF, when cell C5 contains the word *stuff*

TIP

Once you have converted text with UPPER, you may want to get rid of the function itself, leaving the appropriately cased text behind. Here's how. Select the cell that contains the UPPER function. Click the Copy button in the Standard toolbar. Now open the **E**dit menu and choose the Paste **S**pecial command. In the Paste Special dialog box, click the **V**alues option and then click OK. Once Excel returns you to the worksheet (the marquee should still be showing around the cell), press Enter. Excel converts the UPPER function into its displayed value (even though the "value" really is text).

I'm How Many DAYS Late on That Payment?

Bankers, financiers, and accountants often use a 360-day calendar. Where did those extra five days disappear to? The fact is, this calendar was invented because no one likes dividing by 365 or having to remember the leap years. This shorter calendar assumes that there are 30 days per month and 12 months per year, for a total of 360 days per year.

Excel uses a 365-day calendar whenever you perform calculations on dates in a workbook. When your business reports and accounting system are based on a 360-day calendar, you can use the DAYS360 function to determine the "actual" number of days between two points in time.

The DAYS360 function looks like this:

=DAYS360(*start_date,end_date*)

Things to remember about using DAYS360

✔ *start_date* and *end_date* are the two arguments.

✔ The arguments can be date numbers or the addresses of individual cells that contain date numbers.

✔ You also can type the arguments as dates surrounded by quotation marks, as in **"12/09/94"** and **"5/01/95"**. But when you use DAYS360 this way, don't use cell addresses to refer to the cells that contain the arguments; type the text, surrounded by quotation marks, directly into the cell with DAYS360. If you use cell ranges as arguments, Excel will display the #VALUE error message in the cell.

✔ You can enter a formula as an argument. For instance, if you type **5** as the start date and **7+8** as the end date, Excel treats the end date as 15 and displays the answer 10.

✔ When *start_date* is after *end_date*, the DAYS360 function gives you a negative answer.

✔ The DAYS360 function is particularly useful for computing the number of days late a customer's payment is. Many businesses use "aging" reports to organize late payment information according to the number of days late: 0 to 30 days late, 31 to 60 days late, and 61 to 90 days late.

 I HATE EXCEL FOR WINDOWS!

Table 13.5 Examples of DAYS360

The Function	The Result
DAYS360(C1,D1)	**31**, when cell C1 contains the date 09/23/94 and cell D1 contains the date 10/24/94
DAYS360(C1,D1)	**360**, when cell C1 contains the date 09/23/94 and cell D1 contains the date 09/23/95

TIP

If you're worried about the negative impact on your finances of using a 360-day calendar, don't worry too much. Unless you're computing the interest that's due you on a $5,000,000 loan you gave to a friend, the difference between computing with a 365-day and a 360-day calendar is negligible.

CHAPTER 14

Functions You'll Profit From

IN A NUTSHELL

▼ "If I borrow x amount of money at x interest rate for x number of years, what will my monthly payments be?"

▼ "If I can afford to pay x amount of money each month at x interest rate for x number of years, how much can I borrow?"

▼ "If I owe x amount of money at x interest rate, how many payments of x amount do I have to make?"

▼ "How much interest did I pay on that loan?"

▼ "If I save x amount of money at x interest rate, how much money will I have in x years?"

▼ "If I want to have x amount of money in x years, how much do I have to save each month at x interest rate?"

I HATE EXCEL FOR WINDOWS!

In the last chapter we came to grips with the fact that we aren't mathematicians, which is exactly why those fabulous functions are so handy. In this chapter we make another startling revelation: we're not stockbrokers either.

Even so, with a little background material and your fine typing skills, you can learn how to produce some useful information about your finances by using Excel's financial functions. You can get answers to questions like these: "How long should I invest this money to end up with a billion dollars?" and "What's the total interest paid on my yacht loan last year?" and "How can I buy real estate with no money down?"

CAUTION

Your worksheet is only as smart as you are. Typing the right numbers into your financial functions can mean the difference between making money and losing it—in your worksheet, anyway. (Now for the disclaimer.) That's the nature of investing. Just be sure that you understand the information that the financial functions give you, always triple-check your numbers, and don't ever bet your life savings on a sure thing. Finally, never forget the first rule of investing: you can always bury the cash in your backyard.

If you can't remember how to enter a function, turn to Chapter 7, "Formulas and Functions," for a quick review. Or check out the section on using the Function Wizard in Chapter 13, "Those Fab Functions."

Why Financial Functions Are Special

There are three important rules to understand about financial functions before you use them in your own worksheets. Here they are, spelled out for you in plain, non-technical English sentences.

The three cardinal rules of using financial functions

✔ Don't mix year units with month units with day units. For example, to figure out the monthly payment on a mortgage, be sure to type the *monthly* interest rate and the total *months* for the loan.

✔ Any money amount that goes out of your pocket must be typed as a negative number. That includes things like deposits you make in a bank, payments you make on a loan, and checks you write to buy stocks and bonds. Money that comes back into your pocket (that's the best kind) are positive numbers.

✔ Any argument called "optional" is just that—optional. You don't have to enter a value for the function to return a correct answer. So don't make up numbers just for the heck of it.

Financial Arguments

Excel's financial functions use pretty much the same arguments. This makes it easy to work with them. You don't have to learn a whole new set of arguments for each one. Here's the hit list:

Arguments for investing wisely

✔ *fv* is the future value of the investment. When somebody offers to pay you an amount of money ten years from now if you invest today, that future amount is the investment's future value.

✔ *nper* is the total number of payment periods. A 30-year home mortgage, for instance, has 30 annual payments or 360 monthly payments. (Don't get this one confused with *per*.)

continues

Arguments for investing wisely (continued)

✔ *per* is a number that corresponds to a particular payment period. For example, to get principal and interest information for the fifth year in a 10-year loan, you would use the number 5 for this argument. (Don't get this one confused with *nper*.)

✔ *pmt* is the payment you make each period. This amount typically includes principal and interest, but does not include fees like documentation charges or taxes. When you're the one who's making the payments, use a negative number to show that the money is going out of your pocket. When someone else is making the payments to you, use a positive number to show that the money is flowing into your pocket.

✔ *pv* is the value of an investment at this very moment. When someone asks you to deposit a lump sum of money into a bank today, that sum would be considered the present value of the investment.

✔ *rate* is the interest rate earned or paid per period. When you enter the rate, you have to match the rate term to the number of payments in the period. Usually, you do this by dividing the rate by the payment term. For example, for an annual interest rate of 12% and 12 monthly payments, you'd enter **.12/12**. That's the same as a monthly interest rate of 1%.

✔ *type* is an optional argument that describes when payments are made. Use the number 1 for payments you make at the beginning of the period, or the number 0 for payments you make at the end of the period. If your payments are due at some other interval, omit this argument. Excel will assume that it's an end-of-period payment.

✔ *guess* is an optional argument. It's your best guess of the per-period interest rate. I know, it sounds funny that you should guess about anything that has to do with money. Don't worry. Excel simply uses the guess to make a calculation go quicker. It has to do with the way some financial calculations work. In any case, the value you type will in no way impair the function's accuracy.

✔ If you want to skip an optional argument that's in the middle of the argument list, you must enter the comma to let Excel know that you're skipping it.

How Much Is That Loan Payment?

The PMT function is most commonly used to figure out what your payment will be on a loan. You can, for example, use this function for home or car loans.

The PMT function looks like this:

=PMT(*rate,nper,pv,fv,type*)

Things to remember about using PMT

✔ *rate*, *nper*, and *pv* are the required arguments.

✔ *fv* and *type* are optional arguments. If you leave out *fv*, Excel assumes a value of 0. If you leave out *type*, Excel assumes that you're making end-of-period payments.

✔ Arguments can be numbers or the addresses of individual cells that contain numbers.

Suppose that you want to purchase your dream house with a loan amount of $250,000 and a flat-rate mortgage of 30 years at 10%. Here's the formula:

=PMT(.1/12,30*12,250000)

Because you are making monthly payments, you have to convert the interest rate and term to months. The monthly interest rate, for example, is equal to 10 percent-per-year divided by 12 months-per-year (.10/12). The actual number of payments you'll make is 360 (12 payments per year for 30 years). The result is $–2,193.93.

TIP

The best way to work with the function is to type the variables (the stuff that can change) into cells and then use cell references in the function. That way you can change the interest rate or the amount of the loan and see the effect on the payment. Here's an example:

Cell	Enter	What it means
A1	.1	rate
B1	30	nper (term)
C1	250,000	pv (amount of loan)
D1	=PMT(A1/12,B1*12,C1)	function

TIP

Another way to figure loan payments is to ask yourself, "If I can afford car payments of $300 a month at 9% interest for 4 years, how much can I afford to borrow?" The next section helps you with this one.

A different twist on this function is to figure out how much money you need to save to reach a certain amount. For example, suppose that you want to save $12,000 in eight years at an interest rate of 6% annually. How much should you save a month? Use a different set of arguments, like this:

=PMT(.06/12,12*8,,12000)

The extra comma between the *pv* and *type* arguments tells Excel that there's no entry for the *fv* argument. Without this extra comma, Excel would not be able to return the correct answer of $–97.70. (A negative number indicates that the money comes out of your pocket, remember?)

How Much Money Can I Borrow?

Another way to figure a loan payment is to start with the amount of money you can afford to spend each month and then work backward to the amount you can afford to borrow. To do this, use the PV function.

Here's what the PV function looks like:

=PV(*rate,nper,pmt,fv,type*)

Things to remember about using PV

✔ *rate*, *nper*, and *pmt* are the required arguments.

✔ *fv* and *type* are optional arguments. If you leave out *fv*, Excel assumes a value of 0. If you leave out *type*, Excel assumes that you're making end-of-period payments.

✔ Arguments can be numbers or the addresses of individual cells that contain numbers.

Suppose that you can afford car payments of $300 a month, and the current annual interest rate is 9%. You want a four-year loan. Use this function:

$$=PV(.09/12,4*12,-300)$$

The answer is $12,055.43.

If you want to enter the rate, term, and payments in cells, you might have something like this:

Cell	Enter	What it means
A1	.09	*rate*
B1	4	*nper* (term)
C1	−300	*pmt* (payment)
D1	=PV(A1/12,B1*12,C1)	function

EXPERTS ONLY

Read this if you have money to invest

If you are big on investments, use the PV function in a different way to figure out the present value of an investment. This function can evaluate the worth of an investment in terms of today's dollars. If the investment payoff is worth more than $0 in terms of today's dollars, then the investment is worth it. However, if the worth of the investment today is less than $0, it's a money loser. You're better off investing in something else.

Suppose that you're looking into purchasing a life insurance policy that offers an investment feature. You can buy the policy today for $25,000. The policy earns an annual interest rate of 8% and returns to you a $250 monthly payment for the next 15 years. Is this a good investment?

The function you would type into the worksheet looks like this:

=PV(.08/12,15*12,250)

The answer you get is $26,160.15. This means that the value in terms of today's dollars of receiving $250 per month for 15 years is $26,160.15. Since you can buy that "worth" today for only $25,000, it's a good deal.

How Many Payments Do I Have To Make?

The NPER function tells you how many payments you have to make on a given loan. Here's what the NPER function looks like:

=NPER(*rate,pmt,pv,fv,type*)

Things to remember about using NPER

✔ *rate*, *pmt*, and *pv* are the required arguments.

✔ *fv* and *type* are optional arguments. If you leave out *fv*, Excel assumes a value of 0. If you leave out *type*, Excel assumes that you're making end-of-period payments.

✔ Arguments can be numbers or the addresses of individual cells that contain numbers.

Suppose that you're considering borrowing some money to buy a car. A friend has offered to loan you $15,000 at an annual interest rate of 15%. (What a pal, huh?) The friend wants you to make monthly payments of $557.51. How long will it take you to pay off the loan?

The function you'd type into the worksheet looks like this:

=NPER(.15/12,–557.51,15000)

It would take you exactly 33 months to pay off the loan.

What's the Interest Rate I Need?

The RATE function calculates the periodic interest rate for a loan or investment. Here's what the RATE function looks like:

=RATE(*nper,pmt,pv,fv,type,guess*)

Things to remember about using RATE

✔ *nper*, *pmt*, and *pv* are the required arguments.

✔ *fv*, *type*, and *guess* are optional arguments. If you leave out *fv*, Excel assumes a value of 0. If you leave out *type*, Excel assumes that you're making end-of-period payments. If you leave out *guess*, it may take Excel a bit longer to figure out your rate for you.

✔ Arguments can be numbers or the addresses of individual cells that contain numbers.

Let's fantasize that your local yacht dealer offers you a five-year, $40,000 loan with monthly payments of $899. You go across town to the competition to price-shop, but you forget to bring the other quote along. You can't remember what interest rate you were quoted on the other loan. (Loan people are great at giving you the monthly amount, but they sometimes don't tell you the interest rate, unless you ask. This function will come in handy in these cases, too.) The second dealer will give you the same $40,000 loan at an annual interest rate of 13%. Which loan is better?

The function you type into the worksheet to find out the first dealer's interest rate looks like this:

=RATE(5*12,_899,40000)

The answer you get is 1.04%. This is the *monthly* interest rate because the period is monthly. You must multiply this by 12 to get the annual rate of 12.45%.

Here's What I'm Really Interested In

The IPMT function tells you how much interest you paid during a single period of a loan. At tax time, for example, your accountant will ask you how much interest you paid on your mortgage during the previous year. This function will tell you:

=IPMT(*rate,per,nper,pv,fv,type*)

✔ *rate*, *per*, *nper*, and *pv* are the required arguments.

✔ *fv* and *type* are optional arguments. If you leave out *fv*, Excel assumes a value of 0. If you leave out *type*, Excel assumes that you're making end-of-period payments.

✔ Arguments can be numbers or the addresses of individual cells that contain numbers.

Here's an example of how to use IPMT. Suppose that you need to determine how much interest you paid during the third year of a five-year loan. The loan is structured so that you make one loan payment per year, at the beginning of the year. The annual interest rate for this $100,000 loan is 12%. What's the interest amount you paid for year number three?

The function you'd type into the worksheet looks like this:

=IPMT(.12,3,5,100000,,1)

The extra comma between the *pv* and *type* arguments tells Excel that there's no entry for the *fv* argument. Without this extra comma, Excel would not be able to return the correct answer of $-7,138.84 (the negative sign means that the money's going out of your pocket).

Now imagine you would like to figure out the interest you paid during the last month of a $50,000 five-year loan. For this loan, you make 12 end-of-month payments each year. The annual interest rate is 10%. The function you'd type into the worksheet looks like this:

=IPMT(.10/12,60,5*12,50000)

The *per* argument value comes from the fact that the number of the last month in a 5-year loan would be 60 (5*12). The correct answer is $–8.78.

Here's the Principal Thing I'm Interested In

The PPMT function tells you how much principal you paid during a single period of a loan. This is a handy figure to know should you ever want to pay off a loan early. Just figure out how much you have paid on the principal, then subtract that amount from the original loan and that's what's still due on the loan. (Be sure to check with your loan shark about pre-payment penalties on the loan. You might decide to keep both the loan and your fingers for a while longer.)

Here's the function:

> =PPMT(*rate,per,nper,pv,fv,type*)

Things to remember about using PPMT

✔ *rate*, *per*, *nper*, and *pv* are the required arguments.

✔ *fv* and *type* are optional arguments. If you leave out *fv*, Excel assumes a value of 0. If you leave out *type*, Excel assumes you're making end-of-period payments.

✔ Arguments can be numbers or the addresses of individual cells that contain numbers.

TIP

You also can use the IPMT function, discussed earlier in this chapter. The IPMT and PPMT functions use the same arguments. When you're evaluating the same period (that means the *per* argument must be the same for both), you place these two functions side-by-side in a worksheet. One will show the interest paid for that period; the other shows the paid principal. Now add them together and you get the total loan payment for that period.

Here's an example of how to use PPMT. Suppose that you need to determine how much principal you paid during the third year of a five-year loan. The loan is structured so that you make one loan payment per year, at the beginning of the year. The annual interest rate for this $100,000 loan is 12%. What's the principal amount you paid for year number three?

The function you would type into the worksheet looks like this:

=PPMT(.12,3,5,100000,,1)

The extra comma between the *pv* and *type* arguments tells Excel that there's no entry for the *fv* argument. Without this extra comma, Excel would not be able to return the correct answer of –$17,629.89.

Now add this value to the one you got from the IPMT example presented earlier in this chapter:

Principal	–17,629.89
Interest	–7,138.84
Total loan payment, year 3	$–24,768.73

EXPERTS ONLY

Creating a loan payment schedule with IPMT and PPMT

With home mortgages and other amortized loans, the amount of the loan payment each period is the same. That means your payment amount in year 1 is exactly the same as in year 2, year 3, and so on. But lenders love to get their money as soon as possible. That's why when they chop up the loan payments into principal and interest, the interest portion is always much higher than the principal portion in the earlier years. The IPMT and PPMT functions show exactly how things are chopped up for any period during the life of the loan. You therefore can create a table of amounts that shows how principal and interest are distributed over the life of the loan. (Take a look at the following sample worksheet.)

Creating a loan amortization schedule for your mortgage

	Microsoft Excel
File Edit View Insert Format Tools Data Window Help	

MS Sans Serif 14 B I U
D8 =IPMT(C3,C8,C4,-C2,,1)

AMORTIZE.XLS

	A	B	C	D	E	F	G
1							
2		Loan Amount	$100,000				
3		Interest Rate	12.00%				
4		# of Years	5				
5							
6							
7			Yr.	Interest	Principal	Balance	
8			1	$0.00	$24,768.73	$75,231	
9			2	$9,027.75	$15,740.97	$59,490	
10			3	$7,138.84	$17,629.89	$41,860	
11			4	$5,023.25	$19,745.48	$22,115	
12			5	$2,653.79	$22,114.93	$0	

AMORTIZE

Ready

What'll It Be Worth Tomorrow?

The FV function tells you what an investment will be worth some day in the future. This is the type of investment where you make equal monthly deposits into an account for a fixed period of time. The FV function looks like this:

=FV(*rate,nper,pmt,pv,type*)

Things to remember about using FV

✔ *rate*, *nper*, and *pmt* are the required arguments.

✔ *pv* and *type* are optional arguments. If you leave out *pv*, Excel assumes a value of 0. If you leave out *type*, Excel assumes that you're making end-of-period payments.

✔ Arguments can be numbers or the addresses of individual cells that contain numbers.

Here's an example of how to use FV. Suppose that you're saving for your child's college education. He is expected to start college (hopefully) in eight years. You can afford to take $100 out of your paycheck each month and deposit it into a savings account. The account pays 6% interest annually. What's the amount in the account at the end of eight years?

The function you would type into the worksheet looks like this:

=FV(.06/12,8*12,-100)

Because you are making monthly payments into the account, you will have to convert some units to months. The monthly interest rate, for example, is equal to .06/12. The actual number of deposits you will make into this bank account over eight years is equal to 96 (8*12).

At the end of eight years, the account will be worth $12,282.85. (You might have to send Junior to a state school.) But suppose that the savings account already contains $5,000 when you start making the monthly deposits. What will it be worth in 8 years? Here's how the function should look:

> **=FV(.06/12,8*12,–100,–5000)**

The answer you get is $20,353.57. That extra $5,000 in the account at the beginning sure makes a big difference!

TIP

If you want to tinker with the figures (the interest rate, the payments, and so on), enter the arguments into cells and then use cell references in the formula. For instance, you can enter the following:

Cell	Enter	What it means
A1	.06	*rate*
B1	8	*nper* (term)
C1	–100	*pmt* (payment)
D1	=FV(A1/12,B1*12,C1)	function

Then you can change the values in A1, B1, and C1 to see how the changes affect the formula's results in D1.

Will I Really Make Any Money?

The NPV tells you what the net present value is for an investment. Net present value is a tool you can use to evaluate the worth of an investment in terms of today's dollars. Here's the rationale. If the investment payoff is worth more than $0 in terms of today's dollars, then the investment's worth it. However, if the worth of the investment today is less than $0, it's a money loser. You're better off investing in something else.

Here's what the NPV function looks like:

$$=NPV(rate, value1, value2, \dots)$$

Things to remember about using NPV

✔ *rate* and *value1* are the required arguments.

✔ The *value1* argument generally is a cell range that contains the series of cash flows (the money you pay out and the money you get back over the life of the investment).

✔ *value2* is the optional argument. It is used as payment and income, like *value1*.

✔ The NPV calculation is for future cash flows. If your first cash flow occurs at the beginning of the first period, the first value must be added to the NPV result, not included in the values argument.

✔ Arguments can be numbers or the addresses of individual cells that contain numbers. The *value1* argument usually is a cell range address.

The easiest way to get a feel for the NPV function is to look at a worksheet that lays out three investment scenarios. In this example, the competing rate of interest on the projects is 13%. But as you can see, the flow of money back to you differs greatly from project to project.

Evaluating the worth of three different investments by comparing their net present values

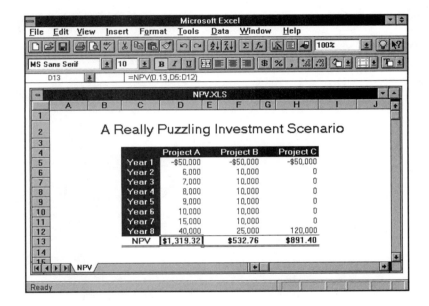

The final decision is made by choosing the project that has the greatest net present value. That's the one (in terms of today's dollars) that will put more money in your pocket over the long haul. Looks like Project A is the winner.

PART IV

Graphs and Data Lists

Includes:

15: You Say Chart, I Say Graph

16: Dynamic Data Lists

CHAPTER 15

You Say Chart, I Say Graph

IN A NUTSHELL

▼ Creating a chart with the ChartWizard
▼ Editing a chart
▼ Saving a chart
▼ Formatting a chart
▼ Printing a chart

E very time you open a newspaper or flip through a magazine, you see all sorts of graphic images. These images are trying to tell you something. They're trying to "inform" you visually without forcing you to read tables full of words and numbers.

Excel charts present your workbook numbers graphically. Charts usually make numbers easier to understand. Sometimes they even uncover trends and patterns that aren't obvious by looking at the numbers themselves. The bottom line is, given the choice between viewing a chart or reading a text report, people will take charts every time.

This chapter shows you the quickest way to turn any group of workbook numbers into an appealing and informative chart.

All You Really Need to Know about Charts

(But were afraid to ask)

There are several ways to create charts in Excel, and each one gets you to the same end result. Of all the methods, only one has enough appeal that you will use it over and over again: the ChartWizard button on the Standard toolbar. (The ChartWizard button is the one with the magic wand waving over the bar chart. I know, it looks like a bunch of smokestacks.)

Creating charts with ChartWizard is painless and effortless because you don't have to memorize lots of confusing steps. ChartWizard takes you by the hand and leads you step-by-step through the chart-creating jungle (lions and tigers and bears, oh my).

Most people don't know the difference between a chart and a graph. I'm one of them. Every software program I've ever worked with uses the term *graph* to describe any colorful picture that's based on numbers. But for some strange reason, Excel uses the term *chart* to describe what we call a graph.

Chart Magic with the ChartWizard

(Nothing up my sleeve)

You can't use the ChartWizard button unless you have a mouse. If you have a mouse but are reluctant to use it, now's the time to get over your bashfulness.

Although there are several ways of creating an Excel chart, the best way to get a feel for charting is to create one next to your data in a worksheet. This cool presentation trick makes it easy to print a worksheet report and chart together.

Here's how to create a chart in a worksheet by using the ChartWizard:

1. Highlight the cell range in your worksheet that contains the numbers you want to include in your chart. Be sure to include the column headings and row headings if you want to show them as well.

I HATE EXCEL FOR WINDOWS!

The highlighted cell range in this worksheet is the one that's going to be charted

			Microsoft Excel - INVEST.XLS				

Invest In Your Future

Portfolio Breakdown

	Jan	Feb	Mar	Apr	May	Jun
Stocks	6,026	2,714	2,681	5,032	4,209	6,856
Bonds	164	1,411	8,673	9,137	4,872	5,007
Money Market	446	9,229	5,283	6,802	9,663	5,065
Commodities	2,169	1,705	8,095	622	3,972	7,610
Market Value:	$8,805	$15,059	$24,732	$21,593	$22,716	$24,538

2. Click the ChartWizard button in the Standard toolbar.

The familiar marquee appears around the worksheet range you selected.

3. Drag your mouse to select the worksheet area where you want Excel to put the chart. The size of the area you drag through determines how big the chart will be. Don't worry, Excel won't overwrite any cell information with the chart. Later, Excel will stack the chart on top of your worksheet. You can easily move the chart aside (perhaps to reveal data underneath it) by dragging it aside.

As soon as you select the worksheet area, Excel displays a dialog box called "ChartWizard Step 1 of 5" and shows the address of the cell range you selected in step 1.

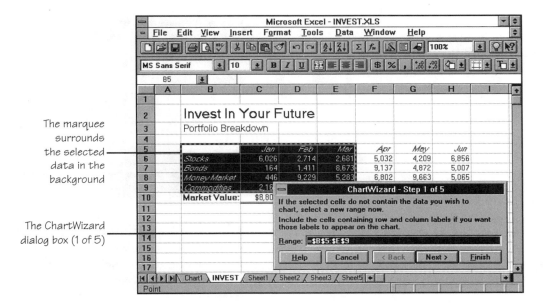

The marquee surrounds the selected data in the background

The ChartWizard dialog box (1 of 5)

4. If you need to change the cell range you selected (maybe you forgot to include a row or column of numbers in step 1), type the new cell range address into the **R**ange box. To be sure that you're typing in the correct cell range, you might have to drag the ChartWizard dialog box out of the way.

5. When the range is OK, click the Next> button.

A dialog box with Excel's 15 chart categories appears. This is ChartWizard Step 2 of 5.

Excel offers
15 different
categories of
charts, from pie
to column to 3-D

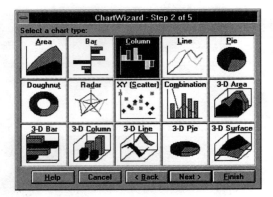

6. Click the chart category that looks closest to the one you want to create. Don't worry if it's not exactly what you're looking for. You can customize it or even change your mind and pick a new category later. If you're not sure, don't pick anything. Keep the chart that Excel has picked for you (it's the one that's flashing). When you're finished, click the Next> button.

A dialog box appears with the various formats for the chart category you selected. This is ChartWizard Step 3 of 5.

7. Click the chart format that looks closest to what you want to create. If you're not sure, don't pick any of them. Excel picks one for you (yep, it's flashing). When you're done, click the Next> button.

The next dialog box displays a sample of your chart. This is ChartWizard Step 4 of 5. For the most part, everything in this dialog box can stay as is. Excel is pretty good at choosing the right settings for you.

8. At this point, you might decide to use a different chart format or chart category. To do so, click the <Back button until you get back to the correct dialog box (you're looking for ChartWizard Step 2 of

5 or Step 3 of 5). Make the change; then click the Next> button until you're back in ChartWizard Step 4 of 5.

When you're happy with how your sample chart looks, click the Next> button to continue. The next dialog box, ChartWizard Step 5 of 5, displays the same sample of your chart and gives you a chance to add a title.

9. To add a title to your chart, click inside the Chart Title box and type the title you want to show at the top of your chart. When you're happy with how your chart looks, click the Finish button.

Handles

A chart embedded in a worksheet

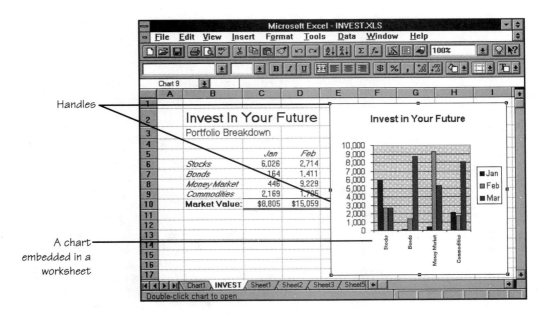

After completing the final ChartWizard step, Excel sends you back to the worksheet. The chart you created now appears as an embedded object. Its size should match up exactly to the size of the cell range you selected in step 3. Notice the small boxes that appear all around the

perimeter of the chart object; these are *handles*. Whenever the handles appear, it means that the object has been selected and that Excel is ready for you to do something to it.

BUZZWORDS

OBJECT

Excel allows you to create and then insert *objects* into a worksheet. These objects range from simple geometric shapes to fully detailed charts. (You just learned how to create and insert a chart, which is an object.) When you insert an object into a worksheet, you're *embedding* that object, also called an *embedded object*.

"I HATE THIS!"

My chart is all smunched! What gives?

If your chart is all squished up, don't worry. You didn't select a large enough area for your chart. You will find out how to fix it later in the section, "Tinkering with the Chart."

CAUTION

You can quickly delete an embedded chart from any worksheet by clicking the chart once and then pressing the Delete key. But be careful. When you delete a chart this way, you can get it back if you choose the Edit Undo command before doing anything else. When that doesn't work, you must re-create the chart with the ChartWizard to display it again.

As you begin looking at your workbooks to figure out what data you want to chart, keep the following range-selecting tips in mind:

Excel's range charting rules

✔ When highlighting the cell range you want to chart, always include the row and/or column containing the words that describe your data. When you do this, Excel creates a legend box for your chart and adds text descriptions to the chart's horizontal axis.

✔ If rows and columns contain SUM functions or any other formulas or functions that calculate totals-type data, leave them out of your cell range selection. Excel charts are designed to help a viewer get a visual feel for the totals represented in your numbers. You don't need to chart your totals data to do that.

Here are some navigational techniques you can use while you work in the ChartWizard:

Roaming around in ChartWizard

✔ The Next> button advances you to the next step in the process. Once you make a selection inside a dialog box, click this button to continue the process.

✔ The <Back button backs up a single step in the process. This is useful for returning to a previous step so that you can review a selection you made there. Whenever a chart you have created is too bizarre-looking for words, you might want to click this button several times to start the process over again.

continues

Roaming around in ChartWizard (continued)

✔ The **F**inish button immediately creates a chart using whatever options you have selected up to that point in time. (This button is for impatient chart-makers.)

✔ The Cancel button stops the current ChartWizard sequence and sends you back to your workbook. This is useful if you suddenly realize that you're working in the wrong worksheet. Cancel the process, click the tab of the other worksheet to activate it, and start over again.

EXPERTS ONLY

Read this if you wanna know what goes where, and why

After you play around a bit, you'll notice that Excel will chart some cell ranges differently than others. Sometimes Excel deals with your cell range in terms of rows of data, so that each row of numbers appears as one data grouping in the chart. Other times, Excel uses columns of data as individual groupings. In both cases, it's easiest to think of these data groupings as data series. That's the term Excel likes to use.

The choice that Excel makes about how to create the data series from your cell range determines what goes where on your chart. In the sample chart, for example, there are three different data series. The data series names appear in the legend box and are color-coded to help you see which bars in each investment grouping belong to the Jan data series, the Feb data series, and the Mar data series.

The easiest way to identify the data series in an Excel chart is to look at the names in the legend box. For a ChartWizard chart that doesn't have a legend, just look under the Data Series In heading in the ChartWizard Step 4 of 5 dialog box. Whichever button is selected shows you how Excel created the data series for your chart.

Creating Chart Sheets

(Just another place to stick it)

Like everything else in Excel, there are a couple ways of placing charts in your workbooks. Allowing ChartWizard to lead you along the chart-creating path will always be the smartest way to go. But if you're the "I-have-to-know-all-the-options" type, Excel also allows you to display charts on their own sheets in your workbooks.

Start by following the first two ChartWizard steps from above. Then, at step 3, open the **Insert** menu and choose the **Chart** command. From the cascading menu that Excel displays, choose the **As** New Sheet option.

Excel inserts a new chart sheet (named Chart1) in front of the sheet that contains your data. Then Excel displays a dialog box called "ChartWizard Step 1 of 5" and shows the address of the cell range you selected in step 1.

After completing the final ChartWizard step, Excel sends you back to the newly created chart sheet. Now you are ready to polish up the chart.

Excel sticks the
chart in a chart
sheet

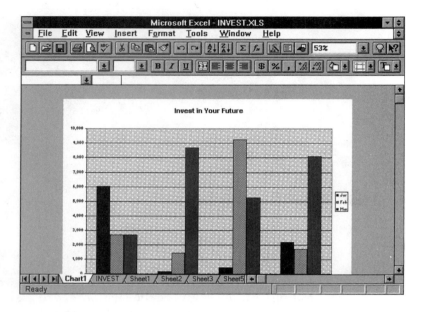

Tinkering with the Chart

(Adding the finishing touch)

ChartWizard inserts its chart into your workbook. Now that it's embedded, what do you do with it?

Working with chart objects

✔ To select a chart object so that handles (those teensy boxes) appear around its perimeter, click once anywhere inside the chart.

✔ Click anywhere outside a selected object to *deselect* it. The handles will disappear.

✔ To move the chart, select it and then drag it with your mouse. Click anywhere inside the chart object and hold down the mouse button; then drag the mouse in the direction you want to move the chart. When you're there, release the mouse to reposition the object.

✔ To resize the chart, drag any of its handles in the direction you want to resize.

✔ To change the data used in the chart, just edit the worksheet. When you change the worksheet numbers in an embedded chart, Excel quickly redraws the chart to show the new numbers. This means that you can actually watch Excel update an embedded chart the second after you change a number in the worksheet.

Changing the Chart

(Into an object of art)

Unless your last name is da Vinci, rarely will your chart's start out looking like the Mona Lisa. That means you'll want to make changes. Perhaps you want to delete numbers from the chart. Or maybe you'd like to use a more descriptive title.

To edit a chart, click it once to select it. Then click the ChartWizard button. Excel displays the familiar ChartWizard dialog box and offers you the opportunity to edit your chart in two easy steps.

"I HATE THIS!"

I thought there were five steps in ChartWizard!

Just when you figured out how to do the ChartWizard 5-Step, you edit a chart and discover the ChartWizard 2-Step. It's not as complicated as it first seems. Just remember that whenever you're editing an embedded chart (or a chart that's displayed on a chart sheet) this way, Excel shows only two of the five dialog boxes you see when you're creating a chart by using the ChartWizard.

Editing a chart with ChartWizard

✔ In ChartWizard Step 1 of 2, you can chart a different set of data: either type a new cell range in the **R**ange box or use your mouse to select the new range in the worksheet (the cell range address automatically appears in the **R**ange box). When you're finished, click the Next> button.

✔ In ChartWizard Step 2 of 2, you can change how your chart numbers are organized. For example, click the **R**ows option under "Data Series in" so that each row of worksheet numbers gets grouped together in a series; or click the **C**olumns option so that each column of numbers gets grouped together in a series. Feel free to experiment on your own graphs by clicking these two options.

✔ When you're finished editing the chart, click **F**inish or OK to return to the chart sheet or the worksheet. Your changes will be reflected in the chart.

Saving Your Chart

(For another day)

Once you have created a chart, or shortly after you have made a few changes, you'll want to make a permanent copy of it.

Saving and opening charts

✔ When you save a workbook that contains an embedded chart, Excel saves both the worksheet data and the chart data in a workbook file.

✔ When you save a workbook that contains a chart sheet, Excel saves both the worksheet data and the chart sheet in a workbook file.

✔ When you use the Open command from the **F**ile menu to open a workbook that contains a chart, both the worksheet, the chart sheet, and/or the embedded chart appear together.

Formatting a Chart

(Clarifying your purpose)

Formatting a chart is similar to formatting a worksheet. You can make a chart look glamorous, or you can keep it simple. The two most common formatting activities are changing the chart type and customizing the look of your chart. You also can add a legend and title to your chart, if the ChartWizard didn't add them already. The title(s) and legend help orient a reader to the information in your chart.

Things to keep in mind when formatting a chart

✔ To start, click the tab of the chart sheet containing the chart you wish to format. Or, double-click the chart object embedded in your worksheet. This activates the chart for editing and formatting.

✔ Whenever a chart is activated, the commands on the menus change. The Format menu contains commands that work specifically with charts.

✔ The commands you use to add objects to your charts (stuff like legends, titles, and arrows) are located on the Insert menu.

✔ Whenever you make a mistake or change your mind about a feature you just added to a chart, you can choose the Edit Undo command, press Ctrl+Z, or click the Undo button in the Standard toolbar to undo it.

Changing the Chart Type

What if you want to change your chart's type, such as changing a column chart to a 3-D bar chart? You can. Open the Format menu and choose the Chart Type command, which displays the names and examples of all the 2-D chart categories available to you. Click the 3-D button in the Chart Dimension block, and Excel displays a list and examples of the 3-D chart types in the gallery area. When you find the one you want to use, click it, and then click OK.

Another way to change the chart type is to right-click your mouse on the chart, and then select the Chart Type command from the shortcut menu that Excel displays. This displays the same dialog box you get when you use the menu approach.

You also can change the chart type from the Chart toolbar. This toolbar usually appears on your screen when you first create the chart. If the Chart toolbar didn't appear on your screen, choose the **View Toolbars** command, click the Chart check box in the **T**oolbars list, then click OK.

The Chart Type button displays a drop-down list with all 15 major chart styles.

The Default Chart button redisplays the active chart using Excel's default chart type, the Column chart.

The ChartWizard button displays the familiar ChartWizard dialog box so you can edit the active chart.

Bestowing Titles (And other meaningful text)

A chart title is just like a worksheet report title. You show it at the top of your chart. People who read the chart can get a good idea about its contents simply by scanning your title. When you're not sure that one title is enough to get the point across, add another one. In Excel, the first title is known as the chart title. The second title is just called text. (Hey, some titles are official-sounding, others aren't.)

If you didn't add a chart title when you created the chart, you can add one now. Open the **I**nsert menu and choose the **T**itles command. When Excel displays the Titles dialog box, click the Chart **T**itle check box (it may already be selected), and then click OK. Excel displays a title marker (with the word Title in it) at the top of the chart. At this point you can begin typing the title. When you're finished, press Enter and Excel will enter the title into the chart. Press Esc to remove the marker from around the title text.

Now suppose you want to add a second title to the chart. This time you won't choose a command from a menu. Instead, just start typing the text. When you're finished, press Enter. Excel shows the text you typed inside a marker somewhere within the boundaries of the chart. But that's probably not the greatest place to show the title, so move it just below the chart title by dragging it there with your mouse. When you're finished, press Esc to remove the marker from around the text.

"I HATE THIS!"

Everytime I try to drag a title, I end up selecting the title text!

Dragging a chart title can be a tricky thing, because your mouse pointer serves two different purposes. First, you can use the pointer to select title text for editing. Second, you can use the pointer to drag the title in the chart. To be absolutely sure which function you're about to perform, keep an eye on the mouse pointer. Whenever the pointer resembles an arrow—and the arrow is positioned somewhere in the title—Excel knows you're about to drag the title. When you move the arrow far enough into the title, however, it will change to an I-beam. This tells Excel that you're about to select text.

A Legend in Its Own Mind

A *legend* is a color-coded (or pattern-coded) visual object that's designed to help a reader understand the information in your chart. If the worksheet cell range you charted contains row headings and columns, Excel automatically shows a legend at the right side of a chart. But if you didn't include headings in the selected range, you might want to add a legend later.

To add a legend to the chart, click the Legend button in the Chart toolbar. If you can't see a Chart toolbar on your screen, open the Insert menu and choose the Legend command. Excel creates a legend—complete with dummy descriptions, like Series1 and Series2, or "guesses"—and inserts it into your chart. To make the dummy series names into more descriptive legend text, you have to follow a second set of steps.

Double-click a series in the chart to select it and display the Format Data Series dialog box. (For example, in a line chart you would double-click one of the lines; in a bar chart, you would double-click one of the bars.) Click the Name and Values tab in the Format Data Series dialog box. Type a name inside the Name text box for the current series, and then click OK. Continue this process until a legend name has been added to each series in you graph. When you're finished, click OK to return to the chart. Press Esc to remove the marker from around the newly edited legend.

Now, to reposition the legend in the chart, double-click the legend to select it and display the Format Legend dialog box. In the Format Legend dialog box, click the Placement tab to activate the legend placement options. Click the button next to the position you want to use. Excel offers five choices: Bottom, Corner, Top, Right, and Left. Normally, Excel places the legend on the right side of the chart. When you have selected a position button, click OK to move the legend.

TIP

An easier way to reposition the legend is simply to drag it to the exact spot in the chart where you want it to appear.

Objects of Desire (Making chart objects pretty)

Anything you can do to text in a worksheet can be done to text in a chart. Need to make the font bigger? Simple enough. Want to choose a new typeface? No problem. You'd love to align stuff differently? Go right ahead.

The great part about formatting a chart is that you can change the appearance of just about anything. This includes stuff like bar colors, pie slice patterns, legend boxes, and much more. Just remember, always start by selecting the object you want to format. When the handles appear around the object, you can do one of the following two things.

Formatting selected chart objects

✔ Open the Format menu. Any commands you can use for formatting the object are black; those that don't apply are dimmed (gray). While inside a formatting dialog box, choose your options; then click OK to apply your selections to the chart.

✔ Right-click the object with your mouse. This displays the shortcut menu. Only the commands you can use to format that particular object are on this menu. While inside a formatting dialog box, choose your options; then click OK to apply your selections to the chart.

The final,
formatted
version of a
chart in a chart
sheet

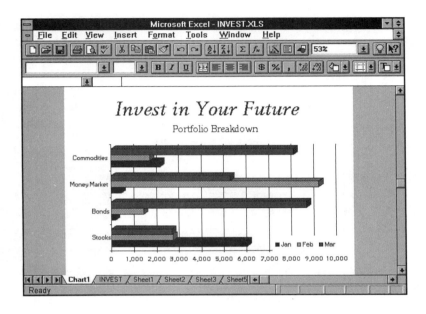

TIP

Double-clicking on most objects inside the chart displays a
Format *objectname* dialog box for that object. The word
objectname here refers to the part of the chart you selected.
For example, when you double-click in the area surrounding a
chart, Excel displays the Format Chart Area dialog box. These
formatting dialog boxes contain option tabs for each type of
format setting that you can change.

Printing a Chart

(For posterity's sake)

Printing a chart is just as easy as printing a worksheet. In fact, you use
the same command: File Print. What actually appears on the printout,
however, will depend on where in Excel you are when you choose the
File Print command.

To print only the chart sheet, first activate the chart sheet. Now open the **File** menu and choose the **Print** command. Click OK to print the chart.

To print an embedded chart alongside its worksheet data, make sure that the worksheet is active. (Click the worksheet to make it active.) Now open the **File** menu and choose the **Print** command. Click OK to print the worksheet and the chart.

TIP

To exert a bit more control over the printing process, you can play around with the dialog box options in the Print dialog box. You also can change the page layout for your chart by using the settings in the Page Setup dialog box. For more information about both of these dialog boxes, go back and read Chapters 6 and 11.

CHAPTER 16

Dynamic Data Lists

IN A NUTSHELL

- ▼ Creating a list
- ▼ Editing a list
- ▼ Sorting information
- ▼ Managing a list with the Data Form
- ▼ Searching for specific types of information

E xcel has an alter ego. You're already familiar with the Excel that lets you analyze facts and figures—the one that makes it easy to spiff up a workbook, save it, and then print it out. All really cool, useful features.

The "other" Excel allows you to organize data like a database program. What if you want to create a list of business contacts? Or perhaps you want to organize your daily invoices. Maybe you would like to create a mailing list for your company's telemarketing division. You don't have to spend gobs of money on complex database programs like dBASE or Paradox. You can gather, store, and reorganize monster-sized collections of information in a list inside an Excel workbook.

BUZZWORDS

DATABASE PROGRAM

A *database program* is a program designed to work with related sets of data. Using the database program, you can enter, sort, find, and list data in many different ways.

This chapter exposes Excel's alter ego. You'll discover that working with a list is just like working with a worksheet. (Hey, they're the same thing!)

A Few Terms To Gnaw On

(Sinking your teeth into a list)

Terminology, buzzwords, and ominous acronyms. I hate them, and maybe you do, too. But before we begin adding data to our bases, let's go over a few of the important terms. As you read each one, keep one eye glued to the sample list shown in the following figure. Things will make a lot more sense to you while you read.

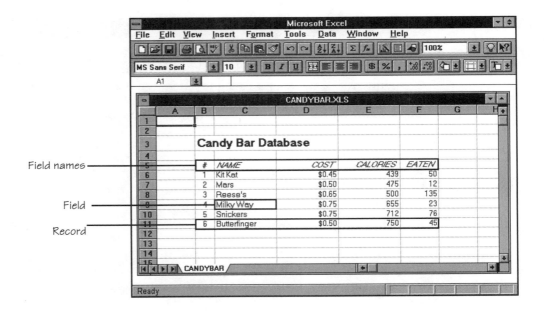

Field names ⎯⎯⎯

Field ⎯⎯⎯

Record ⎯⎯⎯

Stuffy-sounding terms

✔ A *database* is an electronic file. You can type information into it, shuffle the information around, and then pull things back out in lots of different ways. Excel uses the term *lists* to describe databases, so for the remainder of this chapter we will too.

✔ In a worksheet, a *list range* is the cell range where you actually keep your information.

✔ A *record* is everything that's on one row in a list. A record contains one set of information about a person, place, or event. For example, a record in an address list might show a person's first and last name, address, city, state, ZIP code, and phone number.

✔ A *field* is one little chunk of information in a record. Each chunk, such as a last name, an address, or an invoice number, sits in its own cell.

continues

265

✔ A *field name* is the name that sits atop each column in your list. It describes the chunks of data in that column. A column that contains first names, for example, might use the word FIRST for its field name.

Making Out a List

(And checking it twice)

What kind of facts and figures do you want to collect in your list? How do you want to be able to get that information back out? These are the two most meaningful questions to ponder as you sit down to create your first list.

In terms of what information your list will contain, ask yourself some questions: "Do I want to store the names and addresses of my business contacts?" "Do I need to keep track of how many different brands of candy bars I eat each week?" Whatever your ideas, you might want to sketch them out on a piece of paper. (Believe me, it will help to preserve your sanity later on.) You don't have to write down all the individual entries for your list. Just jot down some words that you think would work well as field names.

As for what you want to get back, be sure that each piece of information you want to manipulate is in its own field. If you want to be able to sort by state, for example, be sure to enter the state as a separate field (in its own cell), rather than use one field for both city and state.

Typing into a List

Type your field names into the worksheet. Do so in an order that makes sense to you. In a candy bar list, for example, the first field name might be NAME, the second COST, the third CALORIES, and the fourth EATEN. You're simply typing words into a worksheet, so feel free to use anything you've remembered from earlier chapters to edit or change your entries. Continue doing this until you have entered all your field names.

Then move one row down and start typing the bits and pieces of data that belong to the first record. Move down another row to type in the second record, another row for the third record, and so on. Typing records into a list is exactly the same as typing words and numbers into a worksheet. Use the same common sense you normally follow for entering text, numbers, dates, and times.

Good things to remember when you're building a list

✔ The first row in a list always contains the field names.

✔ For worksheets that contain more than one list, leave at least one blank row and/or column between lists. That way Excel can tell what's what.

✔ When you type a field name into the worksheet, be sure that Excel recognizes it as text (as opposed to a number, a formula, or a pterodactyl). The entries NAME, PHONE#, and TOTAL1 are good examples of words that meet this requirement. The entries 500, 01/25/95, and 8:00 are examples of the kinds of entries to avoid. Also, avoid using formulas or function names for your field names.

✔ Keep your field names short and sweet. Shorter field names are easier to work with and easier to remember.

continues

I HATE EXCEL FOR WINDOWS!

Good things to remember when you're building a list (continued)

✔ The number of field names at the top of the list should always match the number of individual chunks of information in a record. Four field names, four chunks per record. Thirty field names, thirty chunks.

✔ It's okay to enter incomplete records into a list. Just leave the cell blank where that missing chunk of information belongs.

✔ Don't enter records that have more chunks of information than there are field names. Either reduce the number of chunks for that record, or add new field names for the extra chunks.

✔ Except when sorting, Excel's not particular about how you capitalize words in your records or in the field names at the top of the list. As far as Excel's concerned, the entry **SMITH** and **smith** are the exact same thing. Even so, it's a good idea to follow normal capitalization rules for records that contain names and addresses—particularly when you intend to print your records on mailing labels or form letters.

Putting on the List Hat

Typing records is the most time-consuming aspect to working with a list. But once it's full of useful information, you're ready to go. The next thing to do is tell Excel that it's a list. (This is where you unleash Excel's alter ego.)

Here's all you need to do to tell an Excel worksheet that it's now a list: Using your mouse, click inside any cell that's inside the list range. (Hey, that wasn't so bad, now was it?) Nothing special happens, so you don't

need to watch for omens or special signs. Excel is smart enough to recognize list data when it sees it. So as soon as you begin selecting commands to reorganize and search through your list, Excel knows to take off its worksheet hat and put on its list hat. (It's one of those Jekyll and Hyde things.) As long as you followed all those rules for creating and organizing information in a list (back in the Typing into a List section), Excel always knows where your list begins and ends in the worksheet.

TIP

The coolest thing about Excel and lists is that the program's smart enough to know when there's a list nearby in a worksheet. As long as you pick a cell that's in a row or column near your list, for example, Excel usually can figure out that it's there.

Changing Your List

(Who's hot, and who's not)

Your lists will need to change. You can count on that because information changes. People relocate to new addresses, business contacts get promoted, new candy bars hit the market, and so on. Once you create a list and enter records, be prepared to make a few changes in the future. The most typical change is when you want to add a new record or change a chunk of information in an existing record. Another kind of change is when you want to add more chunks of information to what's already available in the list. Both are easy to do.

Changing a list is exactly like changing a worksheet. There aren't any special tricks to learn.

✔ To add new records to your list, just type them, starting in the first blank row at the bottom of the list. As long as they're attached to the original list, Excel is smart enough to include those records the next time you do something to the list.

✔ When you need to squeeze a new record in between two other records, use the **Insert R**ows command.

✔ Want to delete a record that's no longer needed? Use the **E**dit **D**elete command to delete the row.

✔ You can use any of the formatting commands to format a list so that it looks more presentable when you include it in a report.

The A to Z's of Arranging Records

(Cassette tapes, CD's, and videos too)

The one thing you can do in a list that can't be done easily in other programs is quickly rearrange things in different ways. When you rearrange records in a list, you are *sorting* information. You might want to list your address list in alphabetical order. Or, if you are doing a mailing, you might want to sort the list by ZIP code. There are plenty of ways to sort your data with Excel.

TIP

Sorting records changes your list. It's a handy feature if you're going to print mailing labels or inventory sheets that need to be in a particular order. If you just want to find records for all the Smiths in Utah, though, you might try using the AutoFilter feature—it's much faster and doesn't alter the list at all. See "12 Cool Things Nobody Knows You Can Do with Excel" in the Quick & Dirty Dozens section of this book for details.

The Key to the Sort

To sort a list, you need to choose a *sort key*. You can select any cell in the column you want to use for the sort key. In your list, for example, column B might contain the last name, column C the address, column D the ZIP code, and so on. To sort by last name first, you choose column B as your sort key.

BUZZWORDS

SORT KEY

A *sort key* is a fancy way of referring to a cell address that identifies the column that contains the information you want to sort. It is not a key on your keyboard, nor are you likely to find a sort key on your key chain.

Excel allows you to pick as many as three sort keys at a time. This is really helpful when the first field you are sorting contains the same entry for more than one record. Say you know a lot of Smiths. Let's imagine that the address list contains 200 records, and you want a list of all the Smiths that live in Utah. If you sort just by last name, there might be quite a few records for Smith. Even when they're all sorted together in a group of rows, it will take quite a long time to locate the information you want.

So what you do is choose a second sort key—the column that contains the state. Then you tell Excel to sort first by last name, second by state.

Sorting

Here's how to sort an Excel list for the first time:

1. Select a single cell in the list.

2. Open the **D**ata menu and choose the **S**ort command.

Excel displays the Sort dialog box. Notice that your list now appears highlighted in the worksheet behind the Sort dialog box. Also, the name at the top of the column containing the selected cell now appears in the Sort By list. Excel starts by assuming that you want to use that column as your first sort key.

Clicking any cell in column C identifies column C's field name as the first sort key, as shown in the Sort By box in the Sort dialog box

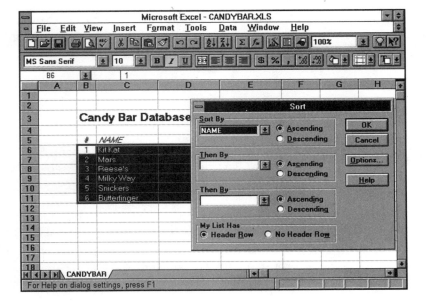

3. Choose the column you want to use as the second sort key. To do this, click the down arrow next to the Then By list box. Excel pops down the list. Notice that the names in the list match your field names in the first row of your list. Select a name from this list as your second sort key.

4. If you want, choose a third sort key. Click once inside the second Then By list box (just under the first Then By box), drop down the list, and then select the one you want. If you don't want a third sort key, skip to the next step.

5. Click the Ascending option next to any sort key box to sort stuff in a top-to-bottom fashion. This sorts letters in an A-B-C order and sorts numbers in a 1-2-3 order.

   Or click the Descending option next to any sort key box to sort stuff in a bottom-to-top fashion. This sorts letters in a C-B-A order and sorts numbers in a 3-2-1 order.

6. If you remembered to create a field names row in your list, click the Header **R**ow option in the My List Has block. Otherwise, click No Header Row.

   It's really important to click the right option here. If you don't have a header row but you select the Header **R**ow option, Excel won't sort the first record. On the other hand, if you have a header row but click No Header Row, Excel thinks the header row is a record. You don't want to sort this row into your list, as if it were just another record.

7. Click OK to sort the list.

   Excel sorts the list according to the sort keys you chose in the Sort dialog box.

"I HATE THIS!"

I added new records, and now everything is all out of sorts again!

If you add records after you have sorted your list, you have to re-sort it to get the new records in the right places. To do this, repeat the preceding steps. Sorry.

Undoing a Sort Operation

If you don't like what you see after Excel sorts your list, you can undo the sort operation. Just open the **E**dit menu and choose the **U**ndo command or click the Undo button in the Standard toolbar. Keyboard nuts can press Ctrl+Z. Remember, you have to do this immediately after you sort the list, or you won't be able to return it to its original order.

TIP

Remember, in order for the Undo feature to work, you must select the Edit Undo command, press Ctrl+Z, or click the Undo button on the Standard toolbar immediately after Excel sends you back to your workbook. Otherwise, you'll get stuck between a list and a hard place.

As a final option, use the **F**ile **C**lose command to close the workbook (but DON'T save your changes); then use **F**ile **O**pen to reopen it. This last-ditch, drastic measure will bring back the list in the same order it was in the last time you saved it by using the **F**ile **S**ave command.

EXPERTS ONLY

Order in the database! Order in the database!

If you need to keep track of the order in which you entered records into the list, you should insert a column to add a field for record numbers. In this field, enter 1 for the first record, 2 for the second record, and so on. Then, if you sort a list lots of different ways and want to get back the original entry order for the records, you can use the record number column as the first sort key.

continues

275

I HATE EXCEL FOR WINDOWS!

> ## Order in the database! Order in the database! (continued)
> This trick also is handy for lists that store any numbers in order: invoices, checks, employee numbers, etc. To quickly enter incremented numbers into a list, try using Excel's Fill Down command. Enter the starting number in a cell, select that cell and drag through the target cell range, then choose the Edit Fill Down command.

Cruising Your List with Data Form

(The nicest ride in town)

Excel allows you to use something called the *Data Form* to manage the data in your list. The Data Form makes it a breeze to work with any list, simplifying its uses in ways you will truly appreciate. When you display the Data Form for a list, you can view one record at a time, edit a bunch of records, and add or delete records. You also can tell Excel to show only the records that have similar characteristics.

To use the Data Form, you first must be sure to tell Excel where your list is located. To do this, just point and click inside any cell in the list. Now open the Data menu and choose the Form command. Excel displays the Data Form for your list. You will recognize the information that Excel shows in the Data Form, because it comes right from your list.

Here's the Data
Form for the
candy bar list

✔ The Data Form shows one record at a time and each field within that record. In the upper right corner of the Data Form, Excel displays the current record number and the total number of records in the list. This is called the *record number indicator*.

✔ The Data Form can work with any size list you create in a worksheet. When your list range contains five fields, for example, the Data Form is fairly small on your screen. When your list range has 15 fields, Excel stretches the size of the Data Form to show as many of the fields as possible.

✔ Click the scroll bar to move from record to record in your list.

✔ Click the Find Prev or Find Next button to show the previous or next record, respectively, in the list.

continues

✔ To edit the contents of any record, display it as the current record in the Data Form. You can press the Tab key to move forward from field to field, and Shift+Tab to move backward from field to field, in a record. Each time you move to a new field, Excel highlights the information in that field. You can either type over the existing entry or edit it. When you're finished editing in a field, press Enter to store the new information in that field.

✔ Click the **Restore** button to cancel any changes you have made to the current record. Excel goes back out into your list and retrieves the original information. Once you have pressed Enter to make a change in a field, you can't use **Restore** to get the original field entry back. Sorry.

✔ Click the New button to add a new record to the list. Type in each entry, and press Tab to move from field to field. When you're finished creating the new record, Excel adds it to your list.

✔ Click the **Delete** button to delete the current record. Excel will display this message: `Displayed record will be deleted permanently`. Click OK to delete the record, or Cancel to keep it.

✔ The Criteria button allows you to search for records that share unique qualities. We'll cover this one in the next section, "Finding Records."

✔ Click the Close button to close the current Data Form and return to the worksheet.

✔ Click the **Help** button to get help with using the Data Form.

CAUTION

Be extremely careful when you use the **Delete** button. Once you delete a record from your list, it can't be restored. Not even with the **Edit Undo** command.

Finding Records

(Giving PgDn and PgUp a breather)

You can be really picky about which records are shown in a Data Form. This makes it easier to work with large lists. You won't have to scroll through thousands of records to find information in just a few. Just tell Excel the rules, or *criteria*, and Excel will do the matching.

BUZZWORDS

CRITERIA

Criteria are the scientifically formal (or formally scientific) descriptions for what the rest of us call "rules." These rules tell Excel how to find stuff in a list. You could concoct a rule that says, "Find every record in the list that has the word Elvis in the NAME field." Excel would immediately look inside your list and locate every occurrence of Elvis.

Match-Maker, Match-Maker, Make Me a Match

First, open the **Data** menu and choose the **Form** command to display the Data Form for your list. To create your rules, click the **Criteria** button. Excel displays what looks like a blank record. But look closely. Notice that the word *Criteria* appears where you usually see the record

number indicator, in the top right corner of the Data Form. At this point you can begin typing your rules into the boxes. If you want to search for a particular name in your list, for example, just type that name into the NAME field. Or, if you want to search for a particular age, type that number into the AGE field.

When you're finished typing your criteria, click the Find **N**ext button to locate the first record that meets your conditions. If more than one record meets the profile, click the Find **N**ext and Find **P**rev buttons to go back and forth between each matching record. Whenever you're in the Criteria area, you can click the **F**orm button to return to the Data Form. When there is only one matching record in Criteria search, Excel automatically sends you back to Data Form.

Close Enough

You also can find matches that fall within a certain range or category. For example, let's say that you want to find all records with a sale price less than $50. In the PRICE field, type **<50** and then click the Find **N**ext button. You also can use comparison criteria with dates and times.

Comparison symbols you can use to search through a database

✔ Use **>** to search for numbers that are greater than some number.

✔ Use **<** to search for numbers that are less than some number.

✔ Use **>=** to search for numbers that are greater than or equal to some number.

✔ Use **<=** to search for numbers that are less than or equal to some number.

✔ Use **<>** to search for numbers that are not equal to some number.

PART V

That's the Way I Like It

(Customizing Excel)

Includes:

17: The Miracle of Macros

18: Excel, Made To Order

CHAPTER 17

The Miracle of Macros

IN A NUTSHELL

▼ Demystifying macros
▼ Recording a macro
▼ Playing back a macro
▼ Changing a macro
▼ Saving a macro
▼ Thinking about some macro ideas

Macro. This seemingly innocuous word is the most menacing of all computer terms. The second that someone suggests that you use a macro or (gasp!) create one, dark clouds begin to form overhead and lightning bolts fall from the sky. By the time the smoke clears away from the top of your computer, you feel like you just survived a week full of Friday the 13th's.

Look, it's really not that dramatic. Maybe you haven't heard, but a macro is supposed to make using Excel easier—not harder. A macro is a tool you use to automate your favorite worksheet activities; it's not the ultimate computer jinx. So if creating and using a macro even remotely resembled black magic, I'd be the first one to warn you. Heck, I'd be the first one out the door.

This chapter shows you how easy it is to create and use macros. If you have ever used a tape recorder before, you already understand about 50% of what Excel macros are all about.

Demystifying Macros

(Looking up the magician's sleeve)

The mysterious macro. What exactly does it do? What does one look like? Do you need an IQ over 200 to create one or to use one? The fact of the matter is that a macro is just a list of instructions. You give the instructions to Excel, and Excel follows them. In most cases, the instructions are no more complicated than those you give to a buddy who's driving across town to visit you. Go to the first light and turn left; it's the third house on the right side of the street. Starting from cell A1 go three rows down and four columns to the right; then draw an outline border.

BUZZWORDS

MACRO

The word *macro* has been around for about 35 years. This term actually is an abbreviation of *macro instruction*, which refers to a single computer instruction that stands for a sequence of operations. In Excel, this sequence of operations can mean a whole set of formatting steps, printing steps, or even database sorting steps. You get to decide which operations are included in your macros.

Let's take a look at some of the most often-asked questions about macros. After reading these, you will be ready to make a little magic macro of your own.

What's So Special about a Macro?

A macro's instructions guide Excel to perform many of the same tasks that you normally do by hand—stuff like typing data into a cell, moving around sheets and workbooks, changing fonts, drawing lines, and so on. It's like having a maid around to take care of your workbooks for you.

The real benefit to using a macro is that it saves you time. Let's face it, most of the stuff you do in Excel takes more than a step or two to do. Every time you want to format something, you have to go through the same old routine of opening the Format menu, choosing a command, clicking option buttons, and typing in text boxes. All this before you even get to click OK to actually accomplish something. A macro can do all that stuff for you.

Where Do Macros Live?

Macros live in one of two places. First, you can keep a macro on any sheet in a workbook of your choosing. When you store a macro in a workbook, Excel places it in a Visual Basic module, affectionately called a *module sheet*. These sheets are just like worksheets or chart sheets—they have names like Module1, Module2, and so on—except they're designed to store macros. To run a macro that's on a module sheet in a workbook, that workbook has to be open. You take care of opening and saving the workbooks you need.

The instructions in an Excel macro are strange-looking words that belong to a bizarre language called Visual Basic. Hence the name Visual Basic module sheet. Macro-nerds like to call macro instructions *code* (as in something to be deciphered).

BUZZWORDS

VISUAL BASIC CODE

Each Visual Basic instruction in a macro is called *macro code*. That's because they look a lot like codes that the spies used during World War II. Depending on what you need the macro to do for you in a worksheet, the code can look quite different. Here's the code that applies the Currency format to a cell, with no decimal places:

```
Selection.NumberFormat = "$#,##0;-$#,##0"
```

But don't worry. You don't have to type all that garble. Because you're on the side of the good guys, Excel does it for you.

The other place that a macro can live is in the *personal macro workbook*. This workbook is just like a regular workbook, except that the macros you store in the personal macro workbook are available in all workbooks. Excel takes care of opening and saving this workbook. Normally, this workbook is hidden.

What Can My Macros Do?

Normally, you wouldn't create a macro to perform an activity that's already easy to do, such as adding bold or italic style to text. You can use toolbar buttons to do this type of thing. But suppose that you have a particular color shading pattern that you use in many of your worksheets. Every time you want to use this pattern in a worksheet, you have to perform the same seven steps:

1. Select the cells to be formatted.

2. Open the Format menu.

3. Choose the Cells command.

4. Click the Patterns tab.

5. Select the pattern style from the **Pattern** list.

6. Select the color from the **Color** list.

7. Click OK to add the color and pattern to the selected cells.

Wouldn't you like to be able to highlight a range of cells and press only two keys to accomplish the same thing? In this case, a macro lets you do in two steps what normally would take seven steps to do!

Macros are ideal for storing instructions for your favorite Excel activities. These are the ones that you find yourself using over and over again. You can create macros that help you move around and edit your worksheets, format data, print a cell range, sort a database, and more.

Your First Recording Session

(Jamming with Fleetwood Macros)

There are two ways to create a macro. Assuming that you speak the Visual Basic macro language fluently, you can create a macro by inserting a module sheet into a workbook and then typing the instructions into the module sheet. But that's not likely.

By far the easiest way to create a macro is to record it. And no, you don't have to speak macro-ese to do it. Excel has a recording feature that, when turned on, keeps a record of every keyboard tap and mouse click you make. You can store this recording in your personal macro workbook and then play it back.

TIP

If you're not certain about which choices you might make, hold a dress rehearsal. Open a new, blank workbook and perform the exact steps that you want to automate. As you go through this dry run, write down the menu and command names.

Starting the Recorder (Lights, Camera...)

To record a macro, start by opening a new, blank workbook in Excel. Now open the **T**ools menu and choose the **R**ecord Macro command.

From the next menu, choose the **R**ecord New Macro option. As soon as you do, Excel displays the Record New Macro dialog box. To personalize your macro, you can change the settings in the dialog box: you can type a new macro name, and you can enter a description about the macro you are about to create.

First, type the name of your macro into the **M**acro Name box. Excel starts by suggesting the name *Macro1* here, but you can use any name you want. Be inventive and descriptive. Come up with a name that's sure to always remind you of what the macro's designed to do. For example, use the name *Pattern* for a macro that shades cells in a sheet.

Second, check out the description that Excel creates for you in the **D**escription box. If you want, replace Excel's description with your own description. (Even though Excel gives you a lot of room, avoid the temptation to write a novel.)

TIP

Try and limit the **M**acro Name and **D**escription box text to under 38 and 123 characters, respectively. Those are the exact number of characters that Excel can display in each box without you having to scroll around looking for the end of a word or sentence.

At this point, you could just click OK and go straight to recording your macro. But it's a good idea to specify more options, so click the **O**ptions button as the third step in the recording process. Excel displays an expanded version of the Record New Macro dialog box. Inside the Ctrl box that appears under the Shortcut **K**ey check box, type the letter you want to use as the shortcut key. The shortcut key is the one you'll press later to run the macro. Excel starts by displaying the letter *e* here, but you can use any letter you want. Capitalization DOES NOT matter to Excel! For example, Ctrl+P and Ctrl+p are the exact same shortcut keys. The letter *p* would make sense for the pattern macro.

CHAPTER 17

Fourth, click the **P**ersonal Macro Workbook button in the Store In block.

The expanded Record New Macro dialog box

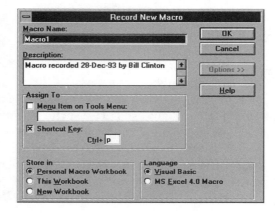

EXPERTS ONLY

Personal vs. regular ol' workbook

The personal macro workbook is a hidden macro workbook that opens every time you start Excel on your computer. Its name is PERSONAL.XLS. The advantage to storing macros in the personal macro workbook is that they're always available to you—regardless of the workbook that's open in Excel. Some macros are ideal for the personal macro workbook, such as the ones you think you will use on any workbook. The most common kinds are editing and formatting macros. A database sorting macro may not be a great candidate for the personal macro workbook, simply because not every workbook you create has a database that needs to be sorted. You might want to store this type of macro in the workbook that contains the database.

If you store a macro on a sheet in a regular workbook, you have to be sure to save and name the workbook. When you want to use or edit the macro, you have to open the workbook first.

Finally, click OK to turn on the recorder. Excel returns to the active sheet in the workbook, ready for you to begin opening the menus and choosing the commands you want to record in the macro. The word *Recording* appears in the status bar at the bottom of your screen, and a tiny, little Stop toolbar with a single button appears at the top of your screen. Both of these features remain on-screen until you turn off the recorder, which you learn next.

Recording Your Actions (...Action!)

Next, complete the steps you want in your macro. Just choose the menu commands and options as you normally would. Excel records each choice you make. Don't worry if you make mistakes while you're recording—you can always go back later and edit the macro.

Using the Pattern macro as an example, let's say that you want to add a colored pattern to the active cell in your worksheet. Open the Format menu and choose the Cells command, then click the Patterns tab. Now click the down arrow next to the Pattern list box to open it. Click a pattern in this list, such as the sixth style. Next, click a color in the Color list, perhaps red. Finally, click OK to return to your workbook and apply the colored pattern.

When you are finished recording your selections, open the Tools menu, choose the Record Macro command, and then choose the Stop Recording command. Excel turns off the macro recorder and removes the *Recording* message from the status bar.

TIP

An even easier way to stop recording is to click the Stop Macro button on the Stop toolbar. Don't worry too much about how to find that button. It's the only one on the Stop toolbar, and depending on how your copy of Excel has been set up, you'll either see this single-button toolbar floating on your screen, or it'll be docked just below your Formatting toolbar at the top of your screen.

This sample recording session shows you how to record a macro that adds a colored pattern to any group of cells, but you literally can record anything you want. Instead of cell shading, how about the steps for changing a font typeface and point size? Or the steps for drawing a double-line under a cell? Or the steps that do all three of these things at once? It's completely up to you, and that's the beauty of the miraculous macro.

Playing Back the Macro

(Rewind and hit the Play button)

Now you're ready to test out the macro you just recorded. Just move to a different cell in the active sheet in your workbook and press Ctrl+p. Excel immediately adds the same pattern to that cell. You can continue moving to other cells in the same sheet and pressing Ctrl+p to add the pattern there. Now try selecting a range of cells and pressing Ctrl+p. The shading appears in every cell in that range.

TIP

If you can't remember your macros shortcut key, you can choose the macro name from a list. Open the **T**ools menu and choose the **M**acro command. In the Macro dialog box, click the name of the macro you want to run. The name is listed in the Macro Name/Reference box. Then click **R**un to run the macro.

```
┌─────────────────────────────────────────────────┐
│ ─                      Macro                      │
├─────────────────────────────────────────────────┤
│ Macro Name/Reference:                 ┌────────┐ │
│ PERSONAL.XLS!HealthCareReformMacro    │  Run   │ │
│ ┌───────────────────────────────────┐ └────────┘ │
│ │ PERSONAL.XLS!HealthCareReformMacro│ ┌────────┐ │
│ │                                   │ │ Close  │ │
│ │                                   │ └────────┘ │
│ │                                   │ ┌────────┐ │
│ │                                   │ │ Step   │ │
│ │                                   │ └────────┘ │
│ │                                   │ ┌────────┐ │
│ │                                   │ │ Edit   │ │
│ │                                   │ └────────┘ │
│ │                                   │ ┌────────┐ │
│ │                                   │ │ Delete │ │
│ │                                   │ └────────┘ │
│ │                                   │ ┌────────┐ │
│ │                                   │ │Options.│ │
│ │                                   │ └────────┘ │
│ │                                   │ ┌────────┐ │
│ │                                   │ │ Help   │ │
│ └───────────────────────────────────┘ └────────┘ │
│ ┌─Description───────────────────────────────────┐ │
│ │ Macro recorded 25-Dec-93 by Bill Clinton      │ │
│ └───────────────────────────────────────────────┘ │
└─────────────────────────────────────────────────┘
```

Changing Instructions in a Macro

(Rewind and record again)

You will occasionally press the wrong keyboard key or misclick your mouse while you're recording a macro. It happens to all of us at one time or another. When you record things in a macro that really don't belong there, you can simply re-record the macro.

Follow the same steps you did when you began creating the macro. Be sure to type the same name in the Record New Macro dialog box. When you click OK, Excel will warn you that a macro with that name already exists and will ask whether you want to overwrite the macro. Click **Yes** and then re-record the steps. Go slow this time and get it right!

CHAPTER 17

EXPERTS ONLY

Cracking the Visual Basic code

If you're one of those people who can pick up a foreign language after only three days in a new country, you may wish to try your hand at Visual Basic, Excel's own foreign (macro) language. You can doctor an existing macro by editing any of the Visual Basic code in that macro. On the other hand, if you have difficulty identifying nouns and verbs in your own language, it's probably best that you avoid editing macros at all. Well, at least for now.

Before you begin, open up the workbook that contains the macro you wish to edit. Then activate the sheet that contains the macros. If your macros are stored in a personal macro workbook, you will have to first unhide the workbook using the **W**indow **U**nhide command.

Excel displays the Visual Basic macro inside a module sheet. When you're finished editing, be sure and choose **F**ile **S**ave to save your changes. Also be sure to rehide your personal macro workbook using **W**indow **U**nhide if your macros are stored there.

Creating Additional Macros

(More fun!)

To record another macro, just follow the same steps you did to create the first one. Excel will add the macro to the personal macro workbook.

TIP

Although Excel is pretty good with macro names, it's not too good with shortcut keys. Suppose that you record another macro and give it the same shortcut key you gave the other one. Guess what happens? Excel goes along happily as if nothing's wrong.

When more than one macro uses the same shortcut key, the macro whose name appears first alphabetically will run when you press that shortcut key. So a macro named FORMAT would run before a macro named WIDEN. Be sure to use a different shortcut key.

To dispose of (delete, zap, terminate) a duplicate or unneeded macro, choose the **T**ools **M**acro command. In the Macro dialog box, click the name of the unwanted macro in the **M**acro Name/Reference list box, and then click **D**elete. It's as easy as that.

Saving the Personal Macro Workbook

(So your macros are there forever)

You don't have to do anything special to save the personal macro workbook. When you try to exit Excel after recording a macro in the personal macro workbook, you will be prompted to save your changes. Be sure to click OK so that Excel saves your macro in the personal macro workbook. It will automatically be there the next time you start Excel on your computer.

Some Macro Recording Ideas

(To get you out of the starting block)

Here are some macro ideas to ponder as you begin experimenting with Excel's macro recording feature. These suggestions are for creating the kinds of macros you're likely to use every time you work in Excel.

Sample macro ideas

✔ Record a macro that applies your favorite combination of formats to any cell in a sheet. This could include your favorite alignment setting, favorite font typeface and point size, favorite pattern, and favorite number format.

✔ Record a macro that prints multiple copies of a document, one for each department head in your company. (Use the **File Print** command and specify the number of copies in the **C**opies text box.)

✔ Record a macro that automatically sorts database records back to their original entry order. Be sure to use the record number column as the first sort key when you're recording. See Chapter 16, "Dynamic Data Lists," for details.

CHAPTER 18

Excel, Made To Order

IN A NUTSHELL

▼ Controlling the look of your workbooks

▼ Changing the appearance of the Excel screen

▼ Displaying more toolbars

▼ Customizing toolbars

▼ Attaching a macro to a toolbar

T he first hundred hours you spend working in Excel are usually devoted to getting cozy with the program's most-often used features. Once you get by your initial infatuation, certain aspects of working with the program become, well, less exhilarating. When you're ready to put a little spice back into your relationship, you'll be happy to learn that Excel can evolve to suit your changing needs.

In this chapter, you see how to add new tools to your screen and how to remove those that you really don't use much. You'll also learn how to control the way data is displayed in your workbooks. When you're finished reading this chapter, you'll be able to forge a new and exciting look for Excel on your computer—a look that's tailored to your own tastes and preferences.

Changing Appearances

(Removing the plain brown wrapper)

Customizing Excel is a lot like driving a new car. At first you're happy using just a few basic features, such as adjusting the seat and rear view mirror. The more time you spend with your car, though, the more interested you become in the other amenities, like the side mirrors and the air conditioning vents and the cruise control. It's exactly the same with Excel. Once you're comfortable creating, editing, and printing worksheets and charts, you'll want to start tinkering with other things.

Maybe you're a devoted keyboard user who rarely uses a mouse. In that case, remove the toolbar and the scroll bars from your screen. (You never use them anyhow.) Doing this will free up more screen room for your workbook window. Or try adding a splash of color to the gridlines in a sheet. Maybe you would like to get rid of the gridlines altogether. You can do all of these things and more.

Déjà View All Over Again

Open the Tools menu and choose the Options command. Excel displays the Options dialog box, which is full of plenty of interesting check boxes. Now click the View tab. You can use these settings to control how Excel displays stuff in a workbook.

The normal View tab settings in the Options dialog box

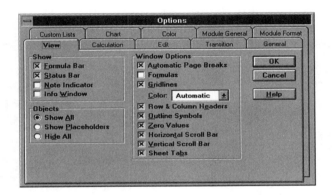

Notice how the View options are separated into three groups. Don't look for any hidden meanings behind this arrangement, there aren't any. Some of the viewing options aren't worth learning at this point—or maybe even ever—so let's concentrate only on the ones you can use immediately and will benefit from. Don't be afraid to experiment a little. Nothing will explode.

The really useful Show options

✔ All the options in the Show grouping affect every workbook you open in Excel. These settings are not peculiar to (nor are they peculiar from) any one workbook.

✔ Click the Formula Bar check box to turn off the display of the formula bar. This box is normally checked. When you uncheck it and then start typing in a sheet, you only see your typing in the cell.

continues

I HATE EXCEL FOR WINDOWS!

The really useful Show options (continued)

✔ Click the **S**tatus Bar check box to turn off the display of the status bar. This box is normally checked, which means that you can see all those cool messages at the bottom of your screen. When you don't feel like taking any messages, uncheck it.

✔ The other settings have nothing to do with displaying and undisplaying bars. Who needs 'em?

"I HATE THIS!"

The Undo button won't undo the mess I just made in the Options dialog box!

The **E**dit **U**ndo command, the Ctrl+Z shortcut keystroke, and the Undo button on the Standard toolbar cannot reverse any changes you make in the Options dialog box. So if you need to fix a mess you just made, you'll have to go back to the Options dialog box and recheck all the boxes you unchecked, or uncheck all the boxes you checked. Check your work carefully.

The really useful Window Options options

✔ All the options in the Window Options grouping (except Automatic Page Breaks, which you don't care about anyway) are saved with the active workbook only. In some cases, a setting may only affect the current sheet inside a workbook. Don't worry, I'll tell you which is which.

✔ Click the Formulas check box to show formulas instead of their answers in every cell that contains one. This box is normally unchecked, and the feature is therefore turned off. When you turn it on, Excel doubles the size of the columns *in the active sheet*, so that your formulas have a little more breathing room to reveal themselves. This feature is useful when you want to know what stupid things you typed in which formulas. Being able to compare a bunch of formulas side-by-side in a row makes it easier to spot your mistakes.

✔ Click the Gridlines check box to turn off the display of gridlines *in the active sheet*. This box is normally checked. This display effect is great when you want your report to look more like a word processing document and less like a workbook. It's the "anti-workbook" workbook setting.

✔ The Color setting actually is a drop-down list. Click its down arrow to reveal a list of really vibrant colors. You can click any of these colors to change the look of your gridlines. Here's a tip: If you use the color white, your gridlines will be invisible against the white background of the workbook window. Tricky, huh? Oh yeah, this setting works only *in the active sheet* too.

✔ Click the Row & Column Headers check box to remove the row numbers and column letters from *the active sheet* in a workbook. This box normally is checked. This feature is another one of those "anti-workbook" workbook settings. Try using it in combination with the Gridlines option. Remember, though, that without row and column headings, you won't be able to use the mouse-clicking shortcuts for column width, row height, and the AutoFit feature.

continues

The really useful Window Options options (continued)

✔ Click the **Z**ero Values box to turn off the display of zero values for *the active sheet.* Normally, this feature is turned on (the box is checked) so that each time you type a zero value into a cell, the value appears as 0. How convenient! But when you turn it off, any cell that contains the number zero by itself, or any formula whose answer is zero, displays as a blank cell. This setting is great for worksheet templates that contain lots of zero values (that is, until someone starts typing in numbers). Warning! Banks, big corporations, and accountants hate to see any financial document that has lots of zeros (unless they're attached to the end of a bigger number, like 10 or 11). Don't worry; Excel will continue to do its math correctly, regardless of whether you can see the zeros.

✔ The **H**orizontal Scroll Bar and **V**ertical Scroll Bar check boxes are another in that long line of "anti-workbook" workbook settings. These boxes determine whether Excel displays the scroll bars around the perimeter of the workbook window. (That means for every sheet in *the active workbook.*) Be forewarned: If you turn these settings off, your mouse may get lonely.

✔ The Sheet Tabs check box is the final installment in that seemingly endless line of "anti-workbook" workbook settings. This box determines whether Excel displays the tabs at the bottom of every sheet in the *active workbook.* (Without sheet tabs, you have to use Ctrl+PgUp and Ctrl+PgDn to navigate your workbook.) Be forewarned again: If you turn this setting off, your mouse may seek counseling.

✔ The other settings are of no use to most Excel users. (But they're great for designing space shuttle warp engines.) Feel free to leave these settings alone and move on to more useful stuff.

This sheet's gridlines and row and column headings have been removed, and it has been designated a Show Formulas zone

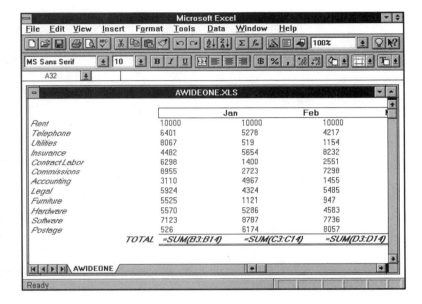

	Jan	Feb	
Rent	10000	10000	10000
Telephone	6401	5278	4217
Utilities	8067	519	1154
Insurance	4482	5654	8232
Contract Labor	6298	1400	2551
Commissions	8955	2723	7298
Accounting	3110	4967	1455
Legal	5924	4324	5485
Furniture	5525	1121	947
Hardware	5570	5286	4583
Software	7123	8787	7736
Postage	526	6174	8057
TOTAL	=SUM(B3:B14)	=SUM(C3:C14)	=SUM(D3:D14)

"I HATE THIS!"

I changed the settings, but the other sheets in my workbook are back to the ugly old style!

Most of the settings in the Window Options grouping change the view only for the active sheet in a workbook. You have to adjust each sheet individually. When you save the workbook, the settings are saved for the next time you work with that workbook.

EXPERTS ONLY

Changing settings for several sheets at once

Well, you didn't have to go too far to find a solution to that last problem, did you? Whenever you need to change options for several consecutive sheets, select the sheets as a group so you can do it all at the same time.

To select three consecutive sheets, for example, click the tab for the first sheet, hold down the Shift key, and then click the tab for the last sheet. Or, to select three nonconsecutive sheets, hold down the Ctrl key and click each sheet's tab in succession. Excel shows all the sheet tabs in the same color so you know that they're a group. Now you can simultaneously change options for all three sheet's. When you're finished working with the sheet group, click a tab for any other sheet that's not a part of the group. Excel disassembles your sheet group, returning them to their normal state.

Organizing Your Workspace

Had enough of the View options? Then try Excel's sheet editing options. Open the **T**ools menu and choose **O**ptions, and then click the Edit tab. When Excel displays the Edit options, you will be struck by how much this tab looks like the one from the previous section. Lots and lots of little check boxes. Don't worry if your dialog box looks different. Anything that's been checked can be unchecked. Really, I've checked.

The normal Edit
tab settings in
the Options
dialog box

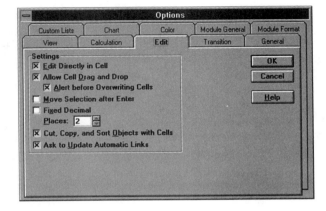

The Edit options are distant cousins of the View options. They affect how editing activity takes places in every Excel workbook—even the ones you haven't even opened yet. In fact, what these settings really control is the look and feel of Excel's workspace.

BUZZWORDS

WORKSPACE

The word *workspace*—you may or may not care to know— refers to the area where Excel displays its workbooks. The View tab options control where the stuff on your workbook is displayed, while the Edit tab options control how certain things work inside your workbook. (Hey, I don't make these rules up; I just ignore them.)

As with any dialog box that looks like a presidential election ballot, only some of the candidates are worthy of your consideration. Let's concentrate on the ones that hold the best hope for the future (of your workbook, that is). And don't be afraid to experiment a little. Nothing will explode, and impeachment is always an option.

The really useful Edit settings

✔ The **E**dit Directly in Cell option tells Excel whether you want to be able to edit text and formulas in their cells. Editing in a cell (as you know by now) is a lot like editing in the formula bar, only it places you a lot closer to the source. Normally checked to allow in-cell editing, click this box to disable the feature.

✔ Click the Allow Cell **D**rag and Drop option to turn this feature off. Once off, you will no longer be able to drag and drop things in your workbook. (What a drag!) But don't do it, because it's one of the coolest and most useful features around. Go back and reread Chapter 9, "Moving and Copying Data," if you don't believe me.

✔ The **A**lert before Overwriting Cells box is normally checked, which allows Excel to display an ominous-sounding message when you try to drop cells onto other cells that contain data. This feature is a safety net for the drag-and-drop feature, so you should leave it checked as well.

✔ Click the **M**ove Selection After Enter box so that Excel automatically advances the active cell down one row each time you press Enter or click the Enter box to complete a cell entry. Also known in worksheet circles as "Excel's Little Helper," this feature normally is turned off.

✔ The **F**ixed Decimal box selects where you want the decimal point to appear in your numbers. By clicking this box and then typing a value in the **P**laces box, you can increase or decrease the precision

of decimal values in your cells. Whenever you type a decimal number, Excel places the decimal where you want it, but by setting this option to 2, for example, any number you type *without* a decimal will show a decimal point two digits to the left. Excel would therefore display the number 456 as 4.56 and the number 21 as 0.21. This feature is helpful when you're using your numeric keypad to type lots of currency numbers and would prefer not to have to type that darn decimal point again and again and again.

✔ The remaining two settings are, well, obscure to say the least. If you really are interested in what they do, look for my upcoming books *I Hate Cutting, Copying, and Sorting Objects with Cells* and *I Hate It When No One Asks To Update My Automatic Links*.

Hanging Out in Your Favorite Toolbar

(Looking for Mr. Goodbutton)

Throughout this book you have been looking at figures that show two toolbars at the top of the screen. They're called the *Standard toolbar* and the *Formatting toolbar*, and by now they have probably become your close personal friends. But the Standard and Formatting toolbars are by no means the only bars in town. In fact, they come from a rather large and talented family of Excel productivity tools.

The Toolbar Family

To visit the toolbar family, open the View menu and choose the Toolbars command. Excel shows you the Toolbars dialog box. It's where the toolbar family lives. All 13 of them!

There are 13
different
toolbars in Excel

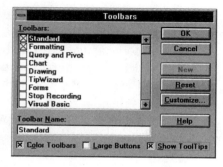

TIP

Here's an easier way to get at the Excel toolbars. Right-click your mouse anywhere in an active toolbar to display its shortcut menu. Click the name of any toolbar on this menu to add it to your screen. Or, click the Toolbars option to display the Toolbars dialog box, where you can visit all the members of the toolbar family.

Each toolbar's name (for the most part) describes what it does. Do you want to look at one more closely? Click its name in the **T**oolbars list, and then click OK. Excel pops the toolbar onto your screen, somewhere in the workbook window. Double-click the toolbar's title bar to slide it into a slot just underneath the Formatting toolbar or, just drag the toolbar up above the formula bar and let 'er go. You can continue adding other toolbars this same way.

The most useful toolbars and their buttons

✔ The Chart toolbar is explicitly devoted to helping you chart your numbers. With these buttons, you can build a chart, change the current chart, or access the ChartWizard.

✔ The Drawing toolbar contains buttons that help you draw graphic images in your workbook. These buttons draw lines, arrows, squiggles, and transparent or filled geometric shapes. They also let you edit the shape or color of any embedded object.

✔ The TipWizard toolbar displays the tip of the day in a scroll list on the toolbar. Fun at first, but it will soon grate on your nerves. You will have to experience it for yourself before you'll be able to hate it.

✔ The Stop Recording toolbar displays whenever you are recording a macro. See Chapter 17, "The Miracle of Macros," for full details.

✔ The Auditing toolbar works only when the IRS pays you a surprise visit. Then it suddenly begins spewing out your most confidential financial information with complete details about all those "business" lunches. Hmmm. I'd avoid that one if I were you.

✔ The Microsoft toolbar displays button icons for seven popular (ta-dah!) Microsoft programs. If you own a copy of Word, PowerPoint, Access, FoxPro, Project, Schedule+, or Mail, you can launch these programs from within Excel by clicking the appropriate icon.

✔ The Full Screen toolbar displays whenever you choose the **Full Screen** command from the **View** menu. Click the (only) button on this toolbar to return to normal view.

✔ The remaining toolbars are of little practical use to Excel users like you and me. Although the Query and Pivot toolbar did come in handy once when I was working on a Mayan dance ritual calculation, I'd recommend waiting until you're in the middle of a really boring workday before experimenting with the rest.

TIP

Here's the best way to figure out which button does what. Place your mouse pointer on the button that's making you curious, and then read the button's description in the status bar. Excel also can display a button's name in a yellow ToolTips flag whenever your mouse pointer is near a button. The **S**how ToolTips check box inside the Toolbars dialog box must be checked for this feature to work.

Organizing Your Toolbars

There's lots of stuff you can do with toolbars besides displaying them on-screen. One thing you can do is move them around Excel's workspace by dragging and dropping them. When you drop a toolbar in the middle of a workbook, it actually floats there in space. You want to get rid of a toolbar that's floating in your workbook? Click that tiny little Close icon in the top left corner of the toolbar.

Tinkering around with the toolbars

✔ To float a toolbar in the active workbook window, click anywhere on the outer perimeter of the toolbar; then drag it and drop it. You also can double-click between any two buttons in the toolbar; Excel will immediately float it in your workbook.

✔ To move a floating toolbar back on top of the formula bar, drag it there and drop it. Excel will do its best to make the toolbar fit correctly. You also can double-click between any two buttons in the toolbar, and Excel will immediately reposition the toolbar above the formula bar.

✔ A floating toolbar actually sits in its own window, just like a workbook sits in its own window. You can resize a floating toolbar by dragging its window border in the direction you want to size it. This makes for some interesting-looking toolbars.

✔ Every toolbar has a shortcut menu. You can display this menu by pointing at a toolbar and right-clicking your mouse. From the shortcut menu, you can display another toolbar by clicking its name in the list. Excel places a check mark by the toolbar name and displays the toolbar on your screen.

✔ Click Toolbars near the bottom of the shortcut menu to display the Toolbars dialog box. This is the same dialog box you get when you choose the **View Toolbars** command.

✔ There are three ways to remove a toolbar from your screen: one, click its Close icon (top left corner) if the toolbar is floating in your workbook; two, uncheck its name on any toolbar shortcut menu; and three, uncheck the check box next to its name in the Toolbars dialog box and then click OK.

*Floating
toolbars
arranged so
that you can see
the worksheet in
the background*

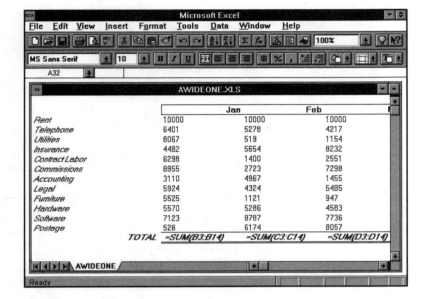

Making Additions to the Toolbar Family

Like Excel, toolbars can be changed to suit your every whim and fancy.
The 13 members of Excel's toolbar family are Microsoft's "ideal" combination of buttons. But what if you prefer using different combinations for
your own work? Maybe you'd like to knock a few buttons off the Formatting toolbar, and then add on a couple of other buttons? It's easy enough
to do. Just customize it.

Here's how you can add a button to a toolbar:

1. Display the toolbar you want to customize.

2. Open the View menu, choose the Toolbars command, and click
the Customize button. Or, open the shortcut menu for the toolbar
you're going to customize, and then click the Customize button.

Excel displays the Customize dialog box.

3. Click the category name that describes the tool you want to add. The categories are organized pretty much by task. The File category offers buttons that do stuff with your files, the Edit category shows you the editing buttons, and so on.

4. In the Buttons list, locate the button you want to add. If you're not sure what a particular button does, click it to display a brief description at the bottom of the dialog box.

5. Drag the button out of the Customize dialog box, move it on top of the toolbar you're customizing, and drop it there. You might have to reposition your Customize dialog box to do this.

6. Click the Close button to return to your workbook.

That's it! You've just added a button to a toolbar. Could it be any easier? I think not.

Other ways to customize toolbars

✔ If those tiny little graphics on each toolbar button are too small to decipher, you can blow them up a bit so they're easier to see. Check the **Large Buttons** check box inside the Toolbars dialog box. **WARNING:** The longer toolbars tend to run off screen when this feature is enabled. Just clear this option if this display quirk annoys you.

✔ To delete a button from any toolbar that's displaying on your screen, display the Customize dialog box; then drag the button off the toolbar and drop it into your workbook. It will disappear into thin air, and Excel will quickly reorganize your toolbar to fill in the missing space. Simple.

continues

✔ To return any built-in toolbar to its original state, click the check box next to its name in the Toolbars dialog box and click the **R**eset button. Any customization you have done to that toolbar is eliminated.

✔ To create a completely original toolbar, open the Toolbars dialog box, type a new name inside the Toolbar Name box, and click the New button. Excel immediately displays the Customize dialog box and adds an empty toolbar to your screen. The name you chose appears at the top of the empty toolbar. Add any buttons you want, and then click the Close button to return to your workbook.

✔ To shuffle the order of buttons on any toolbar that's displaying on your screen, open the Customize dialog box, drag the dialog box out of the way of the toolbar you wish to shuffle, and then drag and drop the buttons to their new pecking order.

✔ To copy a button from one toolbar to another, display the Customize dialog box, press and hold down the Ctrl key, click the button you want to copy, drag it to the destination toolbar, and then drop it. You can use this trick only while the Customize dialog box is open.

✔ To delete a custom toolbar, click its name in the Toolbars dialog box and click the **D**elete button. When Excel asks whether you're sure that you want to delete the toolbar, click OK if you are.

✔ Excel won't let you delete any of its built-in toolbars. After all, they are family.

EXPERTS ONLY

Attaching a macro to a button on the toolbar

The last category of buttons in the Customize dialog box is called Custom. The buttons in this category are fairly generic: they have icons, but no specific purpose attached to them. Excel allows you to attach a macro to any of these generic buttons and then add the button to any toolbar. That way, when you click the button, your macro will run. Here's how to do it.

As soon as you drag a custom button onto a toolbar, Excel displays the Assign Macro dialog box. This dialog box contains the names of all the macros that exist in Excel's personal macro workbook. If you also happen to have a workbook with module sheets that's currently open in Excel, that sheet's macros also appear on this list. Click the macro name you want to attach to the button, and then click OK. When Excel returns you to the Customize dialog box, click the Close button to return to your workbook. Now click the custom button and watch as Excel runs the macro you attached to it.

Suppose, though, that you didn't actually have a macro ready to attach to a custom button. No problem. In the Assign Macro dialog box, just click the **R**ecord button. When the Record New Macro dialog box appears, type the name of the macro, then click **O**ptions and add the shortcut key. Choose OK. Excel begins recording the macro. When you're finished recording, click the Stop Recording button that Excel conveniently displays in the workbook window. As soon as you do, Excel attaches the macro to your custom button. (Wow! Is this awesome or what?!) Now try running the macro by clicking the button.

PART VI

Quick & Dirty Dozens

I HATE EXCEL

Quick & Dirty Dozens

IN A NUTSHELL

- ▼ 12 cool things nobody knows you can do with Excel
- ▼ 12 things you should never do in Excel
- ▼ 12 heart-stopping messages and what to do about them
- ▼ 12 most common mistakes
- ▼ 12 best Excel shortcuts
- ▼ 12 features you can monkey with if you have time to kill

12 Cool Things Nobody Knows You Can Do with Excel

1. **Stashing your favorite workbooks, charts, and macros**

So you have a favorite workbook that you like to work on first thing every morning? What? You have a favorite macro module, too? Then go ahead and tell Excel to fire up those documents each time you start the program on your computer. That way you don't have to select the **File Open** command over and over and over again.

Here's how: Save the workbook files you want to use at start-up time in the XLSTART subdirectory. This subdirectory is just under the directory that contains Excel's important files—usually called EXCEL or EXCEL5 or something close to that. Each time you start Excel on your computer, the program looks in XLSTART for your favorite workbooks. If none are there, Excel displays the blank workbook called Book1. When Excel does find documents in XLSTART, those documents are displayed as soon as Excel starts on your computer.

2. **Finding things when you don't know what you're looking for**

The Find and Replace commands on the **Edit** menu are cool for helping you quickly locate and change things in large workbooks. The basic premise of this feature is that you know what you're looking for and what you want to replace it with. Fortunately, you're in luck when you're not exactly sure what you're looking for but you do have some clue.

Suppose you have been asked to search for every occurrence of a word. You've searched through the workbook several times, but Excel can't find any matches. You know the word's there and you suspect that you've misspelled it. Here's what to do.

Choose the **E**dit **R**eplace command. In the Fin**d** What box, type as much of the word as you know to be correct, and then use a wild-card symbol for the rest. The entry **TOT***, for example, will find *Total*, *Totals*, and *Totally*. The entry ***MBER** finds the words *December*, *November*, and *September*. The entry **????Q** finds all entries that have five characters (including spaces) and end in the letter *Q*. So it finds stuff like *1st Q*, *2nd Q*, *3rd Q*, and *4th Q*.

3. **I need more decimals, please**

When you format your numbers using the Number, Currency, and Percentage formats, Excel displays your numbers with either two or no decimal places. There are no other choices. So what happens when you need to display more decimal places?

Open the Format menu, choose the Cells command, and then click the Number tab. In the **C**ategory list, choose the general format category you want to use. In the **F**ormat Codes list, choose the specific format you want to use. Before you click OK to apply the format, click inside the Code text box, where Excel displays the code you're about to apply. At the end of the current code entry, type the numbers of extra decimal places you want to show.

To change the code **#,##0.00** so that it shows three decimal places, for example, type an extra zero to make it look like this: **#,##0.000**. Now click OK to apply the format. Or, to change the code **0.00%** so that it displays only one decimal place, delete one of the zeros: **0.0%**.

4. **Stopping prying hands from changing things**

Protect your Excel workbooks by safeguarding them against prying hands and fumbling fingers. Every office has at least one pair of these. You know, the snooping coworker who loves to tinker around on your computer while you're away at lunch. It's important that these busybodies be prevented from changing things in workbooks you leave open on-screen.

First, open a workbook and select the cell range in the sheet you want to protect. Now open the Format menu, choose the Cells command, and then click the Protection tab. Inside the Format Cells dialog box, verify that the Locked check box is checked. If it isn't, be sure to click it before you continue. Click OK to return to your workbook.

Then, open the **T**ools menu, choose the **P**rotection command, and then select the **P**rotect Sheet option. In the dialog box, that appears, make sure that these check boxes are checked: **C**ontents, **O**bjects, and Scenarios. In the **P**assword text box, type the password you want to assign to the current sheet in your workbook. Pick something easy so that you will remember it. Now click OK. When you're prompted to verify the password, retype it exactly as before. Click OK to return to your workbook.

Next, open the **T**ools menu, choose the **P**rotection command, then select the Protect **W**orkbook option. In the dialog box that appears, make sure that these check boxes are checked: **S**tructure and **W**indows. In the **P**assword text box, type the password you want to assign to your workbook. Pick something easy so that you'll remember it. Now click OK. When you're prompted to verify the password, retype it exactly as before. Click OK to return to your workbook.

Now, anytime someone tries to change anything in your workbook, that person will be stopped by a message that says, "Locked cells cannot be changed."

To unprotect your document later so you can use it, open the **T**ools menu, choose the **P**rotection command, and then choose (in turn) the Unprotect Sheet and Unprotect **W**orkbook commands. (They're in exactly the same spot in the menu as the **P**rotect Sheet and Protect **W**orkbook commands were.) In the Unprotect Sheet and Unprotect Workbook dialog boxes, type the passwords and click OK to regain control of your workbook.

BEWARE: Don't forget your password because without it, you cannot unprotect your sheet or workbook. Ever. Without exception.

5. Preventing prying eyes from stealing a peek

Guarding workbooks from prying hands and fumbling fingers offers no protection against prying eyes—and we know that every office has lots of these. You see, some Excel information is so private that you'll be forced to swallow your computer whole, lest your Excel files fall into the hands of industrial spies. When your stomach just isn't up to that particular challenge, you can instead assign a password that controls who may open and work with the workbooks stored on your computer's hard drive.

Open the workbook you want to protect with a password. Open the **File** menu and choose the Save **As** command. Click the **Options** button in the Save As dialog box. In the Save Options dialog box, type a password into the **Protection** Password box, and then click OK. You'll be asked to confirm the password by typing it again. After you retype it, click OK to save your workbook with its new password. The next time you (or someone else) attempt to open the workbook on your computer, you have to type the correct password before Excel will open it.

BEWARE: Don't forget your password because without it, you cannot open up your workbook. Ever. Without exception.

6. Juggling several workbooks at once

Whenever you have two or more workbooks open at the same time, it's easy to move information between them by using the Edit Copy and Edit Paste commands. Suppose that you have two workbooks open on-screen—let's call them Book1 and Book2. You start by copying any cell range in Book1. When you're finished, click your mouse inside Book2 to activate its window. Once inside

Book2, click the cell where you want to place the copy, and then choose the **E**dit **P**aste command. Voilà! Your information appears in Book2 exactly as is did in Book1.

Stay alert when the range you're copying contains formulas. When you copy formulas from Book1 to Book2, be sure to bring along all the original numbers that the formulas use in the Book1 calculations. When you do this, Excel will be able to adjust your relative reference formulas correctly, regardless of where you choose to paste the information in Book2.

When you copy absolute reference formulas, those formulas will calculate whatever is inside the same range on the other workbook. Suppose that you copy the formula **SUM($A$1:$A$5)** from Book1 to Book2. When the formula is pasted into Book2, the formula will not change one bit. The answer that the copied formula displays in Book2 depends entirely on whatever numbers happen to be in cell range A1:A5 in Book2.

7. **Range names you can sink your teeth into**

Name a range and suddenly you have a powerful thing at your fingertips. I'm not talking about cell names, either, which sound like stars from distant galaxies. You know the type, names like H1450 or IV397. I'm talking about plain-English names that not only make sense to you and me, but make sense to every stranger who might meander into your workbook one day. Fact is, names like BOB and GOOBER5 are easier (and much more fun) to remember than cell F5 or cell range G6:P23.

To name a cell, or a range of cells, open the **I**nsert menu, choose the **N**ame command, then select the **D**efine option. In the dialog box that opens, notice that your cell address or cell range appears in the **R**efers To box. All that's left to do is name the range. Hmmm. How about Ashley? No, too yuppie-ish. How about Boris?

No, too dark. How about Madonna? Blechhh! I've got it, let's use SALES94 since it's the range that contains the 1994 sales data. Type **SALES94** into the Names in Workbook box and click OK. You have just named your first range.

Now that you've named it, what do you do with it? Good question. Suppose that you need to add all the numbers in that range. Try this function on for size: **=SUM(SALES94)**. Or maybe you need to reformat the values in the range that contains the 1994 sales data. You're down around row 9,000 and your fingers are getting tired from pressing PgDn and PgUp to move around. Here's a faster method. Press F5, click the name SALES94 in the list, and click OK. Excel moves you there pronto. Format away!

8. **Filtering out unique records in a database**

For those of you who are dying for even more ways to manipulate your lists and databases, boy do I have the thing for you. It's called the AutoFilter feature, and it works just like any old filter to remove unwanted stuff from stuff that you want to keep.

First, click inside any cell in or next to a list or database. Then, open the **Data** menu, choose the **Filter** command, and select the AutoFilter option. Excel adds drop-down list boxes next to each name in your field names row. You can quickly create custom displays for the database by choosing an option from one or more of the drop-down lists.

For instance, in a business contacts database you could choose the **92024** ZIP code value from the drop-down list that appears next to *ZipCode* in the field names row. Excel quickly redisplays your database so that only the records containing 92024 in the ZIP code column. Now print that list, and then refilter your database another way. To turn off the AutoFilter feature, open the **Data**

menu, choose the Filter command, and select the AutoFilter option once more. The drop-down list boxes disappear from your workbook.

9. **Checking your spelling in a workbook**

What? A spreadsheet program that can check the spelling of the words in my workbook? No way. Amazing, but true!

To "spell check" your workbook, click the Select All button (it's the blank button at the area where the row heading and column heading meet). Then open the Tools menu and choose the Spelling command. Excel displays the Spelling dialog box. A likely replacement candidate for the first entry it encounters that it doesn't recognize appears in the Change To box. Type in your correction here, or click the correctly spelled version of the word in the Suggestions list, and then click the Change button. Excel corrects the misspelled word and continues checking for other misspelled words.

In workbooks, it's common to use abbreviated words like JAN for January or AVE for average. Excel always stops at these kinds of words because it thinks that you misspelled them. Click the Ignore All button to move past every occurrence of such a word. Excel will continue checking your workbook. When it's finished checking the entire workbook, Excel displays the message *Finished spell checking selected cells*. Click OK to move back to your workbook.

Be sure to save all the spelling corrections in your workbook. Use the **File Save** command.

10. **Toolbars to the right, toolbars to the left**

Toolbars normally appear at the top of your workbook, between the formula bar and the menu bar. You can position a toolbar in other parts of a workbook window, such as just above the status bar or at the left or right side of the workbook. Any area in your Excel screen that accepts a toolbar is called a *toolbar dock*.

To dock a toolbar, drag it to the location where you want to show it, and release your mouse. If you drag the Standard toolbar down the screen and release it near the status bar, Excel will dock it there. If you drag the Chart toolbar to the right edge of your screen and release it, Excel will dock it there.

The only limitation to docking is that Excel won't let you dock any toolbar that contains a list box (like the Standard and Formatting toolbars) at either the right or left side of the window.

11. **Editing two sheets for the price of one**

So you have 12 sheets in the same workbook that you need to edit? And each sheet was created from the same template, right? You're asking yourself why there isn't an easier way to edit a group of sheets that all look exactly the same. Hey, there is!

Open the workbook that contains the sheets you want to edit. Create a sheet group by clicking the tab for the first sheet in the group, hold down the Shift key, and then click the tab for the last sheet in the group. Excel displays all the grouped sheet tabs in the same color. Notice that the phrase [Group] appears in each sheet's title bar. This lets you know which sheets are part of the group you're editing in group mode.

Now, before you do anything else, listen to this. From this point on, anything you do to the *active* sheet is also done to every other sheet in the group. If you type the number 500 into cell F5, that same number is entered into cell F5 of all the other sheets. Change the width of column D in the active sheet, and that same column width changes in every other sheet. While in group mode, anything you do to the active sheet by using the **File**, **Edit**, and **Format** menu commands gets done to every sheet in the group. Absolutely cool, huh?

When you're finished making all your changes, you can end group mode by clicking the tab for any other sheet that's not part of the group. You also can select the Ungroup Sheets command from the shortcut menu available with all sheet tabs in a workbook.

12. Unfilling filled ranges

Do you know how easy it is to fill in a cell range with sequential numbers or with words? Type a number (like 100) or a word (like JAN) into a cell. Then click that cell to make it active. Now drag that cell's fill handle to the last cell in the range, and then release.

Well, suppose you decide that you don't need all 6,000 of the numbers you just filled into the cell range. Suppose that you only need 4,000 of them. You can unfill any cell range that you just filled simply by dragging the cells fill handle backward through the range you just filled. When you drag backward through a fill range, Excel temporarily shades the cells you're unfilling so you know exactly where you are at all times. As soon as you release the mouse, all the shaded cells disappear, as if you never filled them in the first place.

12 Things You Should Never Do in Excel

1. **Never delete files you don't recognize**

Feel free to use the **F**ind File commands **D**elete option to delete workbooks you don't need any more. These kinds of documents end in XLS. But don't ever delete a file you don't recognize, even if it has one of these familiar file endings.

At all costs, avoid deleting any files from the EXCEL directory. That's where Excel keeps the files it needs in order to run. These files have endings like DLL, EXE, HLP, XLM, and REG. If you delete one of them, you better run...and hide.

2. **Never close a workbook without saving it**

I know, it seems unlikely, but the fact is that lots of Excel users have closed workbooks without saving them, only to regret the decision later on.

Excel never forgets. It's the elephant of the software kingdom. When Excel asks whether you want to save changes to a workbook, you better do just that, even if you don't need the changes. That way, the worst thing that could possibly happen is that you'll have a useless workbook saved on your hard drive. Feel free to get rid of it later on, when you've got your wits about you again.

3. **Never start typing without knowing where you are**

Some people get so quick with the keyboard that they can type for long periods of time without needing to glance at the screen. But Excel doesn't warn you when you are typing over something else.

Stay aware of where you are in your Excel workbook, because all it takes is one slip of the hand. You accidentally hit the PgUp key without knowing it. Excel sends you flying back up the page with nary a chirp or click to let you know what's about to happen. So you keep pounding away on your keyboard, unaware that you're typing over all the stuff at the top of your workbook. It's a bummer—believe me, I know.

4. **Never run a Version 4.0 macro while the worksheet that contains the macro is active**

Suppose a colleague or friend hands you a really cool Version 4.0 macro that they just created, and asks you to try it out on your own computer. As far as you're concerned, a macro is a macro is a macro. You load 'er up and let 'er rip. STOP! Don't run an Excel Version 4.0 macro while the worksheet containing the macro is showing on-screen. Always be sure that another worksheet is active before you run a Version 4.0 macro.

Many a recorded Version 4.0 macro has gone down the tubes simply because the worksheet containing the macro—instead of the target worksheet—was active when the macro was started. You're excited because you're eager to test the new macro immediately. You hit that macro shortcut key, look up at your screen, and freeze in shock as you watch the macro munch itself. Rows are deleting everywhere, whole cell ranges are being cut and pasted. Suddenly everything screeches to a halt. Most of what's left on your screen is unrecognizable. You press Ctrl+Z in hopes of undoing all this mayhem, but Excel only brings back the very last row it deleted. You swear you will never record a macro again.

5. **Never start two copies of Excel on your computer**

Program Manager is one of the coolest things about Windows. It has all those little icons that make it so simple to start programs.

In fact, with Excel running on your computer, you can switch back to Program Manager to start a different program. Maybe Word, for example.

Some Excel users switch to Program Manager before they leave for lunch. Suppose that you are one of those users. You come back to your desk an hour later and double-click the Excel icon in Program Manager. Windows starts a second copy of the program on your computer. This gets even more complicated when you try to open the workbook you were using before, the one that currently is active in the other copy of Excel that's running on your computer. This is confusing, isn't it? That's why you should always avoid starting two copies of Excel on your computer.

But when you do it, the best way to proceed is to exit the most recent copy of the program and then switch back to the other one. How the heck do you do that, you ask? Well, first press Ctrl+Esc to display the Task List dialog box. Locate the description of Excel that's nearer the end of the list, click it once, and then click the End Task button.

6. **Never group edit sheets that look different**

The group editing feature saves you tons of time when you have several sheets that use the exact same design layout, such as a multi-divisional company might use to report its monthly financial data, using four separate—but identically constructed—sheets.

Don't use this feature, though, to edit a group of sheets that have nothing to do with one another. Just because one sheet looks great with column C widened to 15 doesn't mean that every other sheet in that workbook you create will. Here's an even scarier prospect. Suppose that you delete column C from the active sheet. Excel immediately deletes the same column from every other sheet you have selected for group editing. But what's the likelihood that four unrelated sheets all need to have column C deleted? "Oops!" is right.

7. Never use spaces to align stuff in cells

Don't use the space bar to align stuff in your cells. It's tempting to do this, especially if you developed the bad habit from years of using word processing programs. When you use the space bar to align words and numbers in cells, things might look lined up on-screen, but they rarely appear lined up when you print the workbook onto paper. Use the alignment tools in the Formatting toolbar instead. For even more alignment options, use the Alignment tab options in the Format Cells dialog box.

8. Never forget your passwords

A forgotten password is a sure ticket to the unemployment line— or at least to the corner of your office with a dunce hat. Without the correct password, you have absolutely no way to get that workbook open. Call every computer nerd you know, and they'll all say the same thing: "Didn't you write down the password somewhere?"

If you use passwords to protect your workbooks, write them down somewhere. Scribble them on a piece of paper and mail them to your aunt in New Delhi for safekeeping. Better yet, get a safe-deposit box at a bank in Switzerland. Whatever you do, don't rely on your memory. You just never know when you might get a bump on your head going to work one day.

9. Never open files you don't recognize into Excel

Here's the counterpart to the warning about deleting files you don't recognize. Don't open a file into Excel if you don't recognize it. The only files you should be working with end in XLS. Everything else is off-limits.

You see, Excel is good about trying to recognize any file you instruct it to open. That's because the program is designed to use certain files that were created with other programs. But we don't care about those other programs right now. Where you will get into trouble is when you do open a non-Excel file, enter or change a bit of data, and then do something innocent like saving the file. (Heck, you have already been warned to save your files as much as possible.) You will permanently ruin files or make other software programs on your computer unusable if you do this. So don't!

10. **Never sort the field names into your data list**

Always be sure to leave the field names row out of the data range you're sorting in a workbook. (Remember? Click the Header **R**ow option button in the My List Has block of the Sort dialog box.) If you don't, Excel will sort the field names row into your data list as if it were just another record. When this happens, the **D**ata Form command won't work properly. And that, after all, is the #1 coolest way of doing that data list thing in Excel.

11. **Never transpose a cell range onto itself**

So you've got a topsy-turvy worksheet and you want to make it look right. Well go do it somewhere else, will ya? Hey, no kidding. When you paste a cell range with the Paste **S**pecial commands Transpose check box checked, don't paste the range onto itself. You might screw things up. Instead, paste the transposed range into a blank area of the worksheet. That way you can compare the transposed data to the original data and see whether it's exactly what you wanted. Only then should you consider moving the transposed cell range back on top of the original cell range.

12. **Never forget to save, save again, and then save once more just to be sure**

Every Excel user who's lazy about saving workbooks eventually resorts to the "fish story" excuse. That's where you claim to have finished a piece of work, but your claim can't be independently verified by an unimpeachable source. In other words, you were working on the fiscal year-end financial report, when all of a sudden the electricity went off, or some bozo put a knee into your computer's Reset button, or the mail clerk walked by and tripped over your power cord.

Bottom line: your work is gone forever, and there's no way in hell your boss is going to believe that you really did the work. Moral to the story? Save often and as if your life depends on it.

12 Heart-Stopping Messages and What To Do about Them

1. General Protection Fault

The "General Protection Fault" message is the one message you hope you never see. It means that something has gone seriously wrong in Windows or in Excel, and Windows can't really do anything about it. Most of the time, this message displays an OK button, an **I**gnore button, and some other meaningless gibberish.

Start by clicking on the **I**gnore button. You might have to do this several times before anything happens. If Excel miraculously comes back to life, immediately save all your work, exit Excel, and exit Windows.

When clicking on **I**gnore has no effect, you must click **C**lose. Windows probably will exit Excel, and you will lose any unsaved workbooks. At this point, it's best to exit Windows and start all over again. If clicking **C**lose has no effect, press the Reset button on the front of your computer, or press Ctrl+Alt+Del to reboot your computer.

2. **Insufficient memory to run this application.**
Quit one or more Windows applications and then try again.

When you see this message, Windows is telling you that you have so many other programs running on your computer that there's no room left to run Excel. Click OK to get rid of this message box. Exit as many of the other programs as you can, and then try again.

If closing other programs still doesn't seem to work, try exiting and restarting Windows. This time, be sure that Excel is the first (and only) program you run when you get to the Program Manager window.

3. **Document is being modified by [*name*]. Open as Read-Only, or choose Notify to be alerted when it is available.**

This error message can give you the creeps; it's not only heart-stopping, but it displays the name of someone you know in the spot marked [*name*]. This message usually appears when you're running Excel from a network and are trying to open a workbook. Here are the two possible problems.

One possibility is that you're trying to open a workbook that some-one else on your network is using at the moment. If you can wait a while, click Notify and Excel will display a message on your screen when that file becomes available. If you need it immediately, click Cancel, go find that person and tell him or her to get out of your workbook, and then try again. If you only need to review the infor-mation in the workbook, click Read Only. This allows you to look at the workbook and even make changes if you wish. You can not save it using the same name, though, so give it a new name when you are finished editing.

The other possibility is that when this message appears, the name in the box is yours. (Talk about really creepy!) In this case, you have probably opened a second copy of Excel on your computer, and you're trying to open the same workbook that's already open in the first copy of Excel. Exit the second copy of Excel, and then switch to the first copy. Your workbook will be there.

4. **[*filename*] was created in a previous version of Microsoft Excel. Do you want to update it to Microsoft Excel 5.0 format?**

This message isn't quite as serious as it sounds. You're trying to save a worksheet that originally was created in an older version of Excel. If you need to keep the file in a format that the older Excel version can use, click **No**. Every time you save the file in the future, Excel knows to use the older file format.

Later, if you decide to save the worksheet as an Excel 5.0 workbook (perhaps to take advantage of its multisheet feature), choose the File Save **A**s command. In the Save As dialog box, choose the Excel 5.0 Workbook option from the Save File as **T**ype list, type your name in the File **N**ame box, and then click OK.

If you don't need to keep the file in the older Excel format, click **Y**es. Excel saves it in the Excel 5.0 format, and you will never get this message again—not from this file, anyway.

5. **Drive does not exist/Path does not exist/Cannot find this file**

These three messages are essentially saying the same thing. Excel doesn't recognize the disk drive, the path name, or the workbook name you typed into the Open dialog box. Check to be sure that you've spelled everything correctly and that the workbook you're trying to open really is located there. Click OK to try again.

6. **Cannot use that command on multiple selections**

Excel is really great about allowing you to do things to disconnected ranges of cells. You can format them, erase their contents, and even copy them. Some things you try to do to disconnected cell ranges cause Excel to go berserk, like trying to cut and paste a disconnected range of cells. You can't. Excel won't let you. So stop trying, and you will never see this message again. Instead, cut and paste things one cell range at a time.

7. **Cannot quit Microsoft Excel**

Just like the little pink bunny in the commercial, Excel sometimes refuses to quit. It keeps going and going and going. This error message usually appears right after you press Alt+F4 to quit the program. (In case you forgot, that's the shortcut key for the File Exit command.)

If Excel is still in the middle of doing something, like calculating a complex formula or running a macro, it won't let you exit. Occasionally, you will get this message when you press Alt+F4 while a dialog box is still on-screen. In any case, be sure to let Excel finish what it's doing before you try to quit again.

8. **Cannot save this file with the same name as an open document**

This message appears whenever you attempt to save a workbook using the name of another workbook that's already open in Excel. Suppose that you choose the Save **As** command from the File menu and, in the Save As dialog box, click the name of a file in the File **N**ame list. Then, when you click OK, the error message appears. What do you do?

Cancel the dialog box by clicking on the Cancel button. Now open the **W**indow menu and click the name of the workbook that's causing the problem. Close it. Now, if you really want to save the other workbook using the closed workbooks name, choose the File Save **A**s command again.

9. **Disk is full**

This message crops up for lots of different reasons. What follows are the most common ones.

Your hard drive has run out of storage room. The workbook you're trying to save will not fit. Delete some files from your hard drive and try saving again. If you don't normally delete files, or if you aren't sure which ones you can delete, try saving your workbook to a floppy disk.

If you got the error message just after you tried saving to a floppy disk, pull the disk out of its drive and see whether it has been write-protected. For 5 1/4-inch disks, there will be a little piece of

plastic tape about an inch from the top right edge of your disk.
Remove it. If you're using 3 1/2-inch disks, flip your disk over to
the side where there's a little black push-tab in the top left corner
of the disk. Slide this tab down. Now try again.

If you still get this error message, or if you're sure that your floppy
disk is not write-protected, you will have to delete some files from
your floppy before you can save the workbook there.

If all else fails, go get a blank, formatted floppy disk.

10. **Incorrect password**

Oops! You typed your password incorrectly. Open the **File** menu,
choose the **O**pen command, and try again. If you still can't get it
open, go call that aunt in New Delhi who has a copy of your passwords. Or was it a safe-deposit box in your Swiss bank?

What, you never wrote down your password anywhere? Better luck
next time. Your workbook is gone. Forever. As in never to be re-
covered unless you can remember your password. Can you say,
"I Hate Excel?"

11. **Selection is too large. Continue without Undo?**

Yes, this message indicates that Excel is getting on in years. It can't
quite tackle those large jobs like it used to. So be careful, because if
you click OK (which means you have decided to go ahead with
whatever it was you were doing before this message appeared),
Excel will not be able to undo it. So if you choose **Edit Undo** or
press Ctrl+Z, nothing will happen. Those 12 rows you accidentally
deleted will remain deleted. If you would rather not take any
chances, click Cancel to get back to your workbook. Then save the
workbook and exit Excel. Start up Excel again, open the workbook,
and try doing that operation over.

12. Replace contents of destination cells?

I know this message is a drag, but that's what got you into trouble
in the first place. You dragged a cell range to a new location in
your workbook, and that new location has stuff in it. If you click
OK, Excel will move the dragged range on top of the other range,
thereby overwriting the other range. Think about this before you
do it. Click Cancel to save yourself from making a terrible mistake.
(Even if you accidentally overwrite the other cell range, you always
can press Ctrl+Z to undo the mistake.)

12 Most Common Mistakes

1. **Excel won't start when I double-click its icon**

The most common complaint about Windows is that it's hard to double-click icons fast enough to get a program started. Double-clicking a mouse button definitely is an acquired skill. You might have to practice this stroke a few billion times before you get it right.

Here's an easier way to start Excel. In Program Manager, click the Excel icon once to highlight it, and then press Enter to start the program.

2. **Sometimes when I type, Excel beeps and flashes stuff**

You're typing along merrily when all of a sudden your computer beeps at you, flashes a menu, or shows some error message that has nothing to do with what you were typing. So you hit Esc a few times and start typing again—everything is fine. What happened? You inadvertently hit the Alt key while you were typing.

The Alt key is located to the left (and sometimes also to the right) of the space bar. Pressing the Alt key activates Excel's menu bar. Normally, if you were accessing the menu bar this way, you would press a single key to open one of Excel's menus. But if you don't realize that you pressed the Alt key, you will just keep typing along. Excel's reaction to all this typing depends on which keys you happen to press next.

If the first key you hit happens to be one of the keys that opens a menu, Excel will pop open that menu. If the second key miraculously happens to be one that starts a command, Excel obediently issues that command and might even open a dialog box. At some point you will hit a key that Excel is not expecting. That's when it beeps at you.

3. **Why isn't my printer printing?**

Here's the situation. You print a sheet in a workbook. Five minutes later your printer is still quietly sitting there. There are no printed pages in sight. You try this a few more times, and it still doesn't work. What gives?

There are two possible explanations. If you're trying to print by clicking the Print button, make sure that you aren't really clicking the Save button. These tools sit side-by-side in the Standard toolbar. If Excel displays a message saying that it *is* printing, but nothing comes out of your printer, your printer is off. Turn it on.

4. **My marquee won't go away**

Whenever you copy and paste in Excel, the marquee remains around the source cell. This is a gentle reminder to you that you can continue pasting copies of that same cell into other parts of the workbook. Unfortunately, it makes most of us think that we did something wrong or left out a step. You know, "Hey Bob, the marquee's still there. What's up?"

Just press Esc to make the marquee go away. Better yet, when you move to the cell where you want to paste the copy, press Enter instead of choosing the **Edit Paste** command. This both pastes the copy and gets rid of the marquee.

5. **Where's the rest of my cell entry?**

When you type a really long entry into a cell, Excel usually lets it overflow into the next cell so that you can see all of it. But if the next cell already has something in it, Excel chops off the long entry at the right edge of its column. Use the **Column Width** command on the **Format** menu to increase that column's width so that you can see everything that's there.

6. **My text stays put when I use the Cut command**

When you choose **Edit Cut** to move the contents of a cell, Excel doesn't remove anything from the cell. To cut the information out, you first have to pick the destination cell and then choose the **Edit Paste** command. Until that time, Excel continues to show the marquee around the cell you're trying to cut.

If what you really want to do is cut the stuff from the cell, as in permanently get rid of it, highlight the cell and press the Delete key.

7. **My Home key doesn't work properly**

Old habits are hard to break. Lots of other software programs let you press Ctrl+Home to move quickly to the top of a document. In Excel, pressing Ctrl+Home only moves you along the current row until it reaches the left edge of the active sheet in your workbook. You have to press Home to get back to the very top of a workbook.

8. **My column suddenly got very wide**
(Or, my row suddenly got very tall)

The dragging technique for highlighting a group of rows or columns is extremely close to the one you use for increasing column widths and row heights. The only difference between these two techniques is where your mouse pointer happens to be when you start dragging.

To select a group of rows or columns, be sure that your mouse pointer looks like a thick, white cross before you start dragging. To increase a column's width or a row's height, be sure that the mouse pointer is shaped like a thin, black cross before you start dragging.

9. **My formula answers look like text instead of numbers**

If you forget to start a formula with the equal symbol, Excel thinks you're entering text. Press F2 to edit the cell, hit the Home key to get to the left edge of the formula bar, type =, and then press Enter to store the entry. The cell should now show a number.

10. **When I select a cell range, Excel erases everything!**

You might experience this horror if you're a new mouse user. The action of selecting a range of cells involves clicking the first cell, dragging to the last cell, and then releasing the mouse. When you click the first cell, don't click the small black handle in the lower right corner of that cell. That's the fill handle, and if you drag it, Excel will fill the entire selected range with whatever happens to be in the first cell. When the first cell is blank, Excel fills your entire selection with blank cells. The proper way to select a range of cells is to place the mouse pointer in the middle of the first cell and drag through the remaining cells.

11. **My workbook just disappeared!**

Fortunately, workbooks don't really disappear unless you tell them to. You probably clicked on the Minimize button ▼ in the upper right corner of your workbook window. Look at the bottom of your Excel screen. You'll see an icon with the name of your workbook just below it. Double-click the icon to get your workbook back. (Or, if you haven't quite licked double-clicking yet, you can click it once and press Enter.)

12. **All the information in my workbook just disappeared!**

You either clicked inside one of the scroll bars or hit the PgDn key. Excel has scrolled out of the workbook area that contains the information you typed. Press Home to get back to the top left corner of your workbook.

12 Best Excel Shortcuts

1. Open Sesame

If you want to open a workbook that you have recently worked on, open the **File** menu. The last four workbooks you opened are listed at the bottom of the menu. Click the one you want.

2. Getting Excel under control

If you have several workbooks open, you can close them all in one fell swoop. Hold down the Shift key, open the **File** menu (notice that the **C**lose command became **C**lose All), and choose the **C**lose All command. Excel closes all workbooks.

3. Draggin' 'til you drop

Dragging and dropping in Excel is the quickest way to copy and move blocks of data around your workbook.

To move a cell range quickly, highlight it, place your mouse pointer anywhere on the perimeter of the highlighted area, drag to where you want to move the data, and drop it there. The moved cell range appears instantly.

To copy a cell range quickly, highlight it, place your mouse pointer anywhere on the perimeter of the highlighted area, hold down the Ctrl key, drag to where you want to copy the data, and drop it there. A copy of the cell range appears instantly.

4. 911 for emergencies, F1 for help

Whenever you're trapped, or lost, or in a bind, or confused, or unsure of how to proceed, or afraid to proceed, or unaware that you need to proceed, or just plain unaware, hit the F1 key. All your answers are there.

5. **Closing Excel or a workbook, lickety-split**

At a recent Indianapolis 500 time trial, it was confirmed that the quickest way to exit Excel and get back to Program Manager is to press the keyboard shortcut Alt+F4. It gets you out in a flash.

During the same time trial, it was confirmed that the quickest way to close an Excel workbook is to use the keyboard shortcut Ctrl+F4.

6. **The shortcut menu shortcut**

You can avoid Excel's Edit and Format menus altogether by using the shortcut menu. Just right-click your mouse in any cell or in a cell that's part of any selected cell range, and Excel will open its shortcut menu. From the shortcut menu, you can quickly cut, copy, paste, clear, delete, and insert data in your workbooks. You also can format numbers, align anything, change fonts, draw borders around cells, and add patterns. Heck, this menu does everything for you but wash windows.

7. **The cell range selection two-step**

Have you ever released your left mouse button too early while you were dragging through a cell range? If you have, then you probably will start all over again in order to highlight all the right cells. Here's an easy way to include additional cells to a range that's already highlighted in your workbook. It involves only two quick key presses.

Position your mouse pointer over the cell you want as the new bottom right corner of the highlighted block. Now hold down the Shift key and click your mouse once in that cell. Excel quickly adds all the in-between cells to the highlighted range.

8. **AutoFit column widths (and row heights, too)**

The best way to adjust column widths in a workbook is to let Excel do it for you. Position your mouse pointer atop the vertical bar at the right side of a column's heading. When the pointer becomes a thin, black cross, double-click the left mouse button. Excel will expand or shrink the width of the column to match the longest entry in that column. To create an autofit row height, double-click the horizontal bar at the lower edge of a row's heading.

9. **Fast font flipping**

The Font list box in the Formatting toolbar offers the fastest way to add new fonts to your workbooks. For some reason, when you have more than just a couple of different fonts installed on your computer, it can take from 5 to 10 seconds for the font formatting options to appear when you choose the Format Cells command, and then click the Font tab. But it only takes about 1/10 of a second for the Font list box to drop down when you click its down arrow.

10. **At the beep, the date and time will be...**

To quickly insert the current date, press Ctrl+; (semicolon).
To insert the current time, press Ctrl+Shift+; (semicolon).

11. **Quick formulas (and text too!)**

If you want to enter the same formula into several cells, select the range that will contain the formula. Type the formula in the first cell. Rather than press Enter to enter the formula, press Ctrl+Enter. The formula is entered into the active cell and all cells in the selected range. Oh, and by the way, this cool data entry trick works for plain numbers and text, too.

12. **Sum speedy formula, huh?**

Oh, and last but certainly not least, the AutoSum button. Where would we be without this one? Just move into the first blank cell after the cells you want to sum, and click the AutoSum button in the Standard toolbar. Excel immediately types a SUM function into the formula bar. It even supplies the range of cells you want to sum. Just press Enter for an instant answer to the function.

12 Features You Can Monkey with If You Have Time To Kill

1. Developing your own style

The longer you work with Excel, the more you'll develop your own style. Not the I-have-a-car-phone or let's-eat-sushi kind of style. I'm talking about the kind where you invent a method of making your workbooks look attractive. You can group together your favorite formats and give them a style name. Maybe you like using an Arial 16-point bold font with a single underline for your workbook titles. You could call this the TITLE style.

To create a style, pick any cell in the workbook and apply your favorite formats there. Now click inside the Style list (it's the box at the left end of the toolbar that always says *Normal*). Type in a new name for your style. To apply this style to other stuff in your workbook, move there and choose the new style from the Style list (click its down arrow to open the list). If you're feeling real adventurous, you can edit your style list entries by using the **Format Style** command.

2. Summarizing workbook data in an outline

Excel can create an outline for your workbook data. With an outline, you can collapse rows and columns together so that only your report titles, headings, and totals appear on-screen. This makes it easy to print summary data instead of the entire workbook.

Select any single cell in your workbook where you've organized data into a table; for example, pick a cell in your budget table or personal expenses table. Open the **D**ata menu, choose the **G**roup and Outline command, and then click the **A**uto Outline option.

Excel shows its outlining tools in the left or top margin of your workbook. To collapse all the rows or columns in your table and show only the titles and the totals row, click the minus button in the left or top margin. To redisplay the detail, click the plus button in the left or top margin. You can then use the row and column level symbols (the buttons with the numbers 1, 2, 3, and so on) in the upper left corner of the workbook to collapse and then expand the row and column details. When you get the exact detail you need, print your report.

To get rid of the outline when you're finished, open the **Data** menu, choose the Group and Outline command, and then click the **Clear** Outline option.

3. **Goal-seeking for fun and profit**

The Goal Seek feature solves formulas backwards. Imagine that the highest price you want to pay (tax included) for a car is $15,000. The sales price is in cell B1—but don't enter anything. You want Excel to figure out that value. In cell B2, enter a formula that calculates the sales tax:

=0.08*B1

In cell B3, enter a formula that calculates the total purchase price:

=SUM(B1:B2)

You want to figure out how much to offer for the car so that when the sales tax is added, the total price in cell B3 is $15,000.

Open the **Tools** menu and choose the **Goal** Seek command to open the Goal Seek dialog box. Type **B3** in the **Set** Cell box; type **15000** in the **To** Value box, and type **B1** in the By Changing Cell box. When you're ready, click OK to solve this formula backwards.

In the Goal Seek Status dialog box, click OK to return to your workbook. In this example, when the sales price is set to $13,888.89, the sales tax is equal to $1,111.11, so the total purchase price is equal to $15,000. You can press Ctrl+Z immediately to get your original numbers back.

4. **Pasting numbers that add up to something**

If you ever have two workbook templates that contain numbers you want to add together, here's one way to do it all at once. (Be sure that the cell ranges you want to combine are the exact same size before you try this.)

Open both workbooks in Excel. Select the range of cells in the first workbook. Choose the Copy command from the Edit menu. Press Ctrl+F6 to show the second workbook. Activate the first cell of the same range in the second workbook. Open the Edit menu and choose the Paste Special command. In the Paste Special dialog box, click the Add button and then click OK. Excel adds the numbers from the first cell range to those in the second cell range. For even more daring calculation escapades, try using the Subtract, Multiply, and Divide options in the Paste Special dialog box.

5. **Insert a painting into a workbook**

You already know that a chart is one type of object you can embed into a Excel workbook, but there are lots of other types of objects you can embed. You can, for example, embed objects that were created in other programs. Let's check out how to do this with the Paintbrush program, because everyone who owns Windows also owns this little beauty.

Open the Insert menu and choose the Object command, then click the Create New tab in the Object dialog box. Click the Paintbrush Picture option in the Object Type list, and then click OK. Excel immediately draws a blank object in your workbook; the object is surrounded by edit handles.

But something else also happens. Excel starts the Paintbrush program and pops it onto your screen right on top of your newly embedded object and your workbook window. At this point you can create a new picture in the Paintbrush window. (If you don't know how to use Paintbrush, check out its built-in Help system. It works just like the one in Excel.) Once you're done creating, open Paintbrush's **File** menu and choose the **Exit & Return To** command. Paintbrush will ask whether you want to update the open embedded object before continuing. Click **Yes** to signal that you do. Paintbrush closes, and you're sent back into Excel. The picture you created now appears inside the embedded object in your workbook. You can drag and resize the Paintbrush object the same way you do with embedded chart objects.

What an artist you are!

6. Using Excel's canned macros

Excel comes with a whole slew of prefab macros called *add-ins* that can do different things for you. For example, there's an autosave macro that automatically saves your workbooks for you, and there's a macro that lets you add notations and summary information to your workbooks. When you start one of these add-ins, Excel adds a description for the macro to one of the menus. The AutoSave macro, for example, gets added to the **Tools** menu. To see what's available on your computer, choose the Add-Ins command on the **Tools** menu. You can use any of the macros that appear in the dialog box that opens.

7. Making workspaces for your workbooks

In Excel, a *workbook* is a collection of worksheets, macro module sheets, and chart sheets. Workbooks are useful because they allow you to group together the documents that belong together. It's like

having a briefcase in which you can stick all of your important folders. When you want to work with a particular group of documents, all you need to do is open the workbook file, and Excel instantly opens every document that's part of that workbook. Workbooks are a time-saver.

You also can create a custom *workspace* file for a group of related workbooks. A workspace is more like an office where you store your various briefcases. To create a workspace, open all the workbooks you want to include. Then open the **F**ile menu and choose the Save **W**orkspace command. Give your workspace a descriptive name like FINANCE.XLW, BUDGETS.XLW, or CASHFLOW.XLW. Later, when you open the workspace, Excel opens all the related workbook documents you saved within it.

8. **Controlling how Excel calculates**

Doesn't it seem like there would be only one way to calculate formulas in your workbooks? Well, Excel gives you not one, not two, but *three* different ways to calculate formulas. Open the **T**ools menu, choose the **O**ptions command, click the Calculation tab, and take a look. You can have Excel calculate for you automatically, you can make Excel wait until you press F9, or you can let Excel calculate some things automatically and others not. As if that's not enough, there are no less than seven other options for fine-tuning your calculations. And you thought adding was as easy as 1-2-3.

9. **Blending colors in the color palette**

When you click the Color tab in the Options dialog box, Excel shows you the various palettes it uses to colorize different parts of your Excel workspace. For special color needs, you can edit a color in the palette by using Excel's Color Picker tool (hey, I don't make up these names, I just report them). To edit a color in the palette,

click the color and then click the **M**odify button. Excel displays the Color Picker dialog box. Feel free to picker any color you think will do the job. To picker a color, clicker it once with your color picker clicker (your mouse). Then clicker OK once to return to the Color Palette dialog box. Your new color appears in place of the one you edited. You can use the new color in cell patterns, text color, or anywhere in a chart that uses color.

10. **Toolbar face-lifts**

Not only can you display other toolbars in Excel and then arrange them all around your workspace for the ultimate in convenience, but you can even add a custom picture to the face of any one of the tools. Before you try this out, you need a picture; create something in the Paintbrush program. When you finish making the picture, save it. Now copy the picture to the Clipboard. (Most Windows-based graphics programs let you press Ctrl+Ins to do this.) Now switch to Excel. Open the **V**iew menu and choose **T**oolbars. Then click the **C**ustomize button in the Toolbars dialog box. Click the tool you want to customize, open the **E**dit menu, and choose the Copy Button Image command. Voilà! A toolbar face-lift in under 10 seconds flat.

11. **The macro, just another object**

Macros are simple enough to start when you give them shortcut names like Ctrl+Z or Ctrl+G. After you create 10 or 20 macros, it can get a little bit confusing trying to remember which shortcut key runs what macro. If it will help you keep track of your macros, you can attach them to objects in your workbooks. Anytime you click the object, a macro runs. Maybe you would like to run a for-matting macro as soon as you click an embedded chart. To attach the macro to the chart, be sure that the appropriate macro sheet is open in Excel, and then right-click the embedded object to display

its shortcut menu. Choose the Assign Macro command. In the Assign Macro dialog box, click the name of your macro and click OK. Whenever you move your mouse pointer over an object that's attached to a macro, you can click that object to run the macro.

12. Taking copious notes

It would seem that creating a report and typing it into a workbook would be all you need to do to document important data. But in this age of telecommunications and high-speed data transfer, we all seem to want to know more about everything. So maybe the Excel workbook's no exception. If you want, after you type a number into a cell, you can attach a lengthy diatribe to the cell so that the 24th-century explorers who one day unearth the workbook will know exactly what it's all about. To add notes to cells, open the Insert menu and choose the Note command. In the Cell Note dialog box, type your earth-shattering news into the Text Note box. Be sure that the address in the Cell box belongs to the cell you want to annotate. Click Add to add the note, and then OK to get back to the workbook. If you really want to make this a multimedia miracle, click the Import button in the Sound Note group and choose a .WAV sound file to add to the note. That way, whenever someone reads the cells note, your workbook will break into the 20th-century rendition of Beethoven's Fifth Symphony.

To view notes you've added to a workbook, open the Insert menu and choose the Note command again. In the Notes in Sheet list box, click the note you wish to read, then read the full text display in the Text Note box. When you're finished viewing your notes, click Close to return to the workbook.

You will always be able to tell which cells in your workbooks contain notes when you do the following: Choose the Tools Options command and click the View tab. In the Show block, click the Note Indicator check box. With this option checked, Excel will display a tiny red box in the upper right corner of every workbook cell that contains a note.

I HATE

Index

Symbols

% (percent) symbol in formulas, 83
* (asterisk) in formulas, 83
+ (plus) symbol
   in formulas, 83
   mouse pointer, 128
- (hyphen) character, 22
– (minus) symbol in formulas, 83
/ (slash) character, 22
   in formulas, 83
< (less than) comparison operator, 210
< > (not equal) comparison operator, 210
<= (less than/equal to) comparison operator, 210
= (equal sign), 24, 83, 199, 210
> (greater than) comparison operator, 210
>= (greater than or equal to) comparison operator, 210
^ (caret) symbol in formulas, 83
100% zoom, 192
200% zoom, 192
360-day calendar, 215-217

A

absolute cell references, 132
Accounting category (number formats), 63
active cell, 13-14
   moving, 16-17
   name box, 16

active workbook, 48
add-ins, 352
addresses (cells), 14
   formulas, 84-85
      editing, 90-91
      row/column deletion, 113
      row/column insertion, 107-108
   name box, 16
   pointing to, 86
addresses (ranges), 31
Align Left/Right buttons (Formatting toolbar), 65
alignment, 65, 142
   centering, 143-145
   numbers, 21
   spaces, 332
   text, 20
   text orientation, 146
   Wrap Text option, 145
All category (number formats), 63
Alt key, 341
arguments (functions), 97, 199
   financial functions, 221-223
   Function Wizard, 200
Arrange Windows dialog box, 183
arranging windows, 183-185
arrow keys, 17, 27
ascending sort, 274
asterisk (*) in formulas, 83
Auditing toolbar, 309
AutoFit (columns), 67-68, 347
AutoFormat, 156-157
AutoSum button (Standard toolbar), 99
AVERAGE function, 202-203

B

Backspace key, 28
Bold button (Formatting toolbar), 57
bold type, 57
borders, 151-154
buttons (toolbars)
   copying between toolbars, 314
   deleting, 313
   inserting, 312-313
   order, 314

C

C prompt, 10
calculations, 353
   AutoSum button (Standard toolbar), 99
   SUM function, 201-202
canceling, 28
   printing, 78
capitalization
   date and time entries, 23
   UPPER function, 214-215
caret (^) symbol in formulas, 83
cascading windows, 184
categories (charts), 246
cell addresses, 14-16
cell references, 24
   absolute references, 132
   relative referencing, 132
cells, 13
   active cell, 13-14
      moving, 16-17
      name box, 16

clearing, 109-110
contents, deleting, 28
deleting, 109
filling, 133-134
    unfilling, 328
inserting, 106
long entries, 342
printing, 77, 161
ranges, *see* ranges
selecting
    by type, 115-116
    entire sheet, 31
    nonadjacent, 32
shifting, 106, 111-112
types, 115-116
Center button (Formatting toolbar), 65
centering, 143-145
chart objects
    formatting, 260-261
    selecting, 252
chart sheets, 251, 262
Chart toolbar, 257-259, 308
charts, 242-243
    categories, 246
    creating with ChartWizard, 243-251
    editing, 253-254
    embedded charts
        deleting, 248
        printing, 262
    formats, 246
    formatting, 255-261
    legends, 249, 258-259
    moving, 253
    opening, 255
    printing, 261-262
    resizing, 253
    saving, 255
    selecting worksheet area, 244
    sizing, 253
    titles, 247, 257-258
    types, 256-257

ChartWizard, 242-251
    editing charts, 254
    navigating, 249-250
ChartWizard button (Standard toolbar), 244
clearing cells, 109-110
clicking mouse, 10-12
closing
    Excel, 346
    windows, 179, 184
    workbooks, 42-43, 50, 329, 345
code, *see* macros
color, 151, 301, 353
columns, 13
    AutoFit, 67-68, 347
    deleting, 110-112
    headers, 301
    inserting, 104-107
    selecting, 31
    switching to rows, 137
    titles, freezing, 190
    width, 66-69, 343
combining ranges, 351
Comma Style button (Formatting toolbar), 64
commands
    Data menu
        Filter, 325
        Form, 276
        Sort, 272
    Edit menu
        Clear, 109
        Copy, 129
        Cut, 125
        Delete, 110, 270
        Delete Sheet, 112
        Fill, 133
        Find, 116
        Go To, 114
        Paste, 125, 129
        Paste Special, 135-137
        Repeat, 102
        Replace, 119
        Undo, 29

File menu
    Close, 50
    Exit, 42
    Exit Windows, 43
    File Find, 51
    New, 50
    Open, 46
    Page Setup, 166
    Print, 76, 160
    Print Preview, 74
    Save, 37
    Save As, 40
Format menu
    AutoFormat, 157
    Cells, 61, 142
    Chart Type, 256
    Column, 68
Insert menu
    Cells, 106
    Chart, 251
    Columns, 104
    Legend, 259
    Name, 324
    Note, 355
    Page Break, 168
    Rows, 104, 270
    Titles, 257
    Worksheet, 106
    repeating, 102
    selecting, 29
Tools menu
    Goal Seek, 350
    Protection, 322
    Record Macro, 288
    Spelling, 326
    Stop Recording, 291
View menu
    Toolbars, 257, 307
    Zoom, 192
Window menu
    Arrange, 183
    Freeze Panes, 189
    Hide, 185
    New Window, 182
    Split, 187
    Unhide, 185

I HATE EXCEL FOR WINDOWS!

comparison operators, 210
context-sensitive help, 34
Control Panel (Printers utility), 174
converting
    dates to serial numbers, 23
    time to fractions, 23
copy operations
    copying and pasting, 129-131
    copying between workbooks, 323
    copying buttons between toolbars, 314
    dragging and dropping, 127-129, 345
    duplicating workbooks, 181
    formats, 136, 142
    formulas, 131-132
    pasting, 129-131
correcting errors, 26-28
    formulas, 93-94
COUNT function, 204-205
criteria (lists), 279-280
Currency category (number format), 64
Currency Style button (Formatting toolbar), 64
customizing
    toolbars, 354
    Excel
        Edit options, 305-307
        Show options, 299-300
        workspace, 304-307
cut and paste operations, 124-126
Cut button (Standard toolbar), 126
cut operations, 343

D

data entry, 18, 329
    date and time, 23
    error correction, 18
    formulas, 24
    functions, 97-98, 198
    lists, 267-268
    long cell entries, 342
    long entries, 20
    military time, 23
    numbers, 19-21
    replacing entries, 27
    text, 19-20
    words, 19-20
Data Form (lists), 276-279
Data menu commands
    Filter, 325
    Form, 276
    Sort, 272
data series, 259
databases, 264-265
    see also lists
date and time, 21-22, 347
    360-day calendar, 215-217
    capitalization, 23
    formats, 21-22
    NOW function, 208-209
    same cell, 23
    serial numbers, 23
Date category (number formats), 63
DATE function, 206-207
DAYS function, 215-217
decimals, 321
    increasing/decreasing decimal places, 64
Decrease Decimal button (Formatting toolbar), 64

defaults
    find operations, 117-118
    printers, 175
Del key, 28
Delete dialog box, 111
deleting, 108-113
    buttons (toolbars), 313
    cell contents, 28
    cells, 109
    charts (embedded), 248
    columns, 110-112
    files, 329
    gridlines, 152
    ranges, 111
    records (lists), 270
    rows, 110-112
    sheets, 110-112
    toolbars, 314
    workbooks, 51-54
    see also clearing
descending sort, 274
dialog boxes
    Arrange Windows, 183
    Delete, 111
    Find, 116
    Format Cells, 61, 142
    Format Data Series, 259
    Go To, 114
    Insert, 105
    New, 50
    Open, 46
    Options, 299-304
    Page Setup, 169
    Print, 76
    Printers, 174
    Record New Macro, 289
    Replace, 119
    Save As, 37, 42
    Search, 52
    Sort, 272
    Summary Info, 38

Titles, 257
Toolbars, 307
directories, 40
displaying
Formula Bar, 299
Formulas, 301
Gridlines, 301
toolbars, 310-311
document window, 16, 178
DOS prompt, 10
double-clicking mouse, 10
draft printing, 170
dragging and dropping, 345
chart title, 258
copy operations, 127-129
move operations, 122-124
dragging mouse, 12
column width, 68-69
Drawing toolbar, 309
drawings, inserting in workbooks, 351
duplicating workbooks, 181

E

Edit menu commands
Clear, 109
Copy, 129
Cut, 125
Delete, 110, 270
Delete Sheet, 112
Fill, 133
Find, 116
Go To, 114
Paste, 125, 129
Paste Special, 135-137
Repeat, 102
Replace, 119

Undo, 29
Edit options (Options dialog box), 305-307
editing
charts, 253-254
formulas with addresses, 90-91
lists, 269-270
macros, 293-294
records (lists), 278
sheets
groups, 331
multiple, 327
effects (fonts), 150
embedded charts
deleting, 248
printing, 262
End key (moving insertion point), 28
entering information, see data entry
equal sign (=), 24, 83
comparison operator, 210
functions, 199
error correction, 26-28
formulas, 93-94
error messages, 335-340
formulas, 94-95
Esc key, 18
Excel
closing, 346
exiting, 42-43
multiple copies, 330
starting, 9-12
troubleshooting, 341
EXCEL directory, 329
exiting
Excel, 42-43
help, 33
Windows, 43
extensions (file names), 38

F

F1 (Help) key, 32, 345
field names (lists), 266
fields (lists), 265
File menu commands
Close, 50
Exit, 42
Exit Windows, 43
File Find, 51
New, 50
Open, 46
Page Setup, 166
Print, 76, 160
Print Preview, 74
Save, 37
Save As, 40
files, 39
deleting, 329
multiple, 186-187
names, 38
opening, 332
fill handle, 134
filling cells, 133-134
unfilling, 328
filters (lists), 325
financial functions, 219-221
arguments, 221-223
FV, 234-235
IPMT, 229-231
NPER, 227-228
NPV, 236-237
PMT, 223-225
PPMT, 231-233
PV function, 225-227
RATE, 228-229
Find dialog box, 116
find operations, 116-118, 320
replacing information, 118-120
floating toolbars, 310
fonts, 58-60, 146-151, 347
effects, 150
point size, 148

I HATE EXCEL FOR WINDOWS!

size, 148
styles, 149-150
TrueType, 149
footers, 172-173
Format Cells dialog box, 61, 142
Format Data Series dialog box, 259
Format menu commands
AutoFormat, 157
Cells, 61, 142
Chart Type, 256
Column, 68
Format Painter button (Standard toolbar), 136, 142
formatting, 139-140
alignment, 142-146
AutoFormat, 156-157
borders, 151-154
chart objects, 260-261
charts, 246, 255-261
copying, 136
copying formats, 142
date and time, 21-22
fonts, 146-151
lists, 270
numbers, 61-64
decimals, 321
ranges, 141-142
shading, 154-156
text
type size, 59-61
type styles, 56-61
Formatting toolbar
Align Left button, 65
Align Right button, 65
Bold button, 57
Center button, 65
Comma Style button, 64
Currency Style button, 64
Decrease Decimal button, 64

Increase Decimal button, 64
Italic button, 58
Percent Style button, 64
formula bar, 16
displaying, 299
Formula Bar check box (Options dialog box), 299
formulas, 23
% (percent) symbol, 83
* (asterisk), 83
+ (plus) symbol, 83
– (minus) symbol in formulas, 83
/ (slash), 83
= (equal sign), 83
^ (caret) symbol, 83
addresses, 84-85
editing, 90-91
pointing to, 86
row/column deletion, 113
row/column insertion, 107-108
blank spaces, 83
cell references, 24
copying, 131-132
displaying, 301
errors, 93-95
exponentiation, 84
operation order, 92
parentheses, 92
ranges, 89
recalculating, 91
shortcut, 347
text, 344
Fraction category (number formats), 64
fractions (time), 23
freezing
column titles, 190
windows, 189-191

Full Screen toolbar, 309
Function Wizard button (Standard toolbar), 200
functions, 96, 198-200
= (equal sign), 199
arguments, 97, 199
AVERAGE, 202-203
COUNT, 204-205
DATE, 206-207
DAYS, 215-217
IF, 209-211
NA, 212
names, 96, 199
NOW, 208-209
parentheses, 97, 199
ROUND, 212-214
SUM, 201-202
UPPER, 214-215
see also financial functions
future value (investments), 221, 234-235
FV financial function, 234-235

G-H

Go To dialog box, 114
Goal Seek, 350
graphs, see charts
greater than (>) comparison operator, 210
greater than or equal to (>=) comparison operator, 210
gridlines, 152
displaying, 301

handles
fill handles, 134
selection handles, 248, 252
headers, 172-173
Help, 32-34
hiding windows, 185-186

Home key, 14, 343
    activating cells, 17
    moving insertion
        point, 27

I-J

icons, 10
IF function, 209-211
Increase Decimal button
    (Formatting toolbar), 64
Insert dialog box, 105
Insert menu commands
    Cells, 106
    Chart, 251
    Columns, 104
    Legend, 259
    Name, 324
    Note, 355
    Page Break, 168
    Rows, 104, 270
    Titles, 257
    Worksheet, 106
inserting
    buttons on toolbars,
        312-313
    cells, 106
    columns, 104-107
    drawings in work-
        books, 351
    records (lists), 270
    rows, 104-107
    sheets, 104-107
insertion point, 27-28
interest rate, 222, 229-231
    loans, 228-229
    monthly, 224
investments, 222
    future value, 221,
        234-235
    net present value,
        236-237
IPMT financial function,
    229-231

K

keyboard
    Alt key, 341
    arrow keys, 17
    Backspace key, 28
    closing windows, 181
    copy operations,
        129-131
    Del key, 28
    End key, 28
    Esc key, 18
    Home key, 14, 343
    maximizing/minimiz-
        ing windows, 181
    move operations,
        124-126
    moving
        active cell, 17
        windows, 181
    PgDn/PgUp keys, 17
    resizing window, 181
    restoring windows, 181
    selecting
        ranges, 31
        window, 181
    shortcut keys
        (macros), 289
    sizing window, 181

L

landscape orientation,
    169
Legend button (Chart
    toolbar), 259
legends (charts), 249,
    258-259

Italic button (Formatting
    toolbar), 58
italic type, 58-59

less than (<) comparison
    operator, 210
less than or equal to (<=)
    comparison operator,
    210
list ranges, 265
lists, 265, 268-269
    Data Form, 276-279
    editing, 269-270
    field names, 266
    fields, 265
    filters, 325
    formatting, 270
    planning, 266
    records, 265
        deleting, 270
        editing, 278
        inserting, 270
    searches, 279-280
    sort keys, 271-272
    sorting, 270-274, 333
loan payments, 223-227
    interest rate, 229-231
    principal, 231-233
long entries, 20

M

macro code, 286
macros, 284-285, 352-354
    editing, 293-294
    module sheets, 286
    personal macro work-
        book, 287, 290, 295
    playing, 292-293
    recording, 288-292,
        294-295
    shortcut keys, 289
    storing on sheets, 291
    Version 4, 330
margins, 75, 170-171
marquee, 88, 342
maximizing windows, 179

I HATE EXCEL FOR WINDOWS!

menu bar, 15
menus
    opening, 29
    shortcut menus, 346
messages (error messages),
    335-340
Microsoft toolbars, 309
military time, 23
minimizing windows, 179
module sheets (macros),
    286
mouse, 12
    clicking, 10-12
    copy operations,
        127-129
    dragging, 12
        column width,
            68-69
    move operations,
        122-124
    moving
        active cell, 17
        windows, 179
    pointer, 128
    selecting ranges, 31,
        344
move operations
    copying between
        workbooks, 323
    cutting and pasting,
        124-126
    dragging and dropping,
        122-124, 345
    ranges, 345
moving
    active cell, 16-17
    between panes, 189
    between windows, 182
    charts, 253
    insertion point, 27-28
    toolbars, 311
    windows with mouse,
        179

N

NA function, 212
name box (active cell), 16
names
    file extensions, 38
    functions, 96, 199
    ranges, 324
    workbooks, 38
        renaming, 40-42
navigating
    ChartWizard, 249-250
    sheets, 114
negative numbers, 21
net present value (invest-
    ments), 236-237
New dialog box, 50
New Workbook button
    (Standard toolbar), 51
not equal (< >) compari-
    son operator, 210
notes, 355
NOW function, 208-209
NPV financial function,
    236-237
Number category
    (Number formats), 63
Number Format catego-
    ries, 63-64
numbers
    alignment, 21, 65
    decimal places, 64
    entering, 19-21
    formatting, 61-64, 321
    negative numbers, 21
    scientific notation, 21
    serial numbers, 23

O

objects, 248
    formatting, 260-261
    selecting, 252
Open dialog box, 46

Open File button
    (Standard toolbar), 50
opening
    charts, 255
    files, 332
    menus, 29
    windows, 182-183
    workbooks, 46-50
        at startup, 320
        shortcut, 345
optional arguments (fi-
    nancial functions), 221
Options dialog box,
    299-304
    Edit options, 305-307
    Formula Bar check
        box, 299
    Sheet Tabs check box,
        302
    Show options,
        299-300
    Window Options,
        300-303
orientation, 169
outlines, 349

P

page breaks, 168
page numbers (printing),
    170
page ranges (printing),
    163
page setup, 168-171
Page Setup dialog box,
    169
panes (windows), 187
    freezing, 189-191
    moving between, 189
    removing, 189
paper (printer), 73
paper size (printing), 170
parentheses
    in functions, 97, 199
    in formulas, 92

partial columns/rows, 106
passwords, 323, 332
Paste button (Standard toolbar), 126
paste operations, 135-137
    copying data, 129-131
    moving data, 124-126
patterns (cells), 154
payments, 222
    interest rate, 228-231
    loan payments, 223-227
    payment periods, 221-222
    term, 224
percent (%) symbol in formulas, 83
Percent Style button (Formatting toolbar), 64
Percentage category (number formats), 64
personal macro workbook, 287, 290, 295
PgDn key, 17
PgUp key, 17
playing macros, 292-293
plus (+) symbol
    in formulas, 83
    mouse pointer, 128
PMT financial function, 223-225
point size (fonts), 60, 148
pointing to addresses, 86
power cord (printer), 72
PPMT financial function, 231-233
principal (loans), 231-233
Print button (Standard toolbar), 76, 161
Print dialog box, 76
Print Manager, 174-175
Print Preview, 73-75, 162
Print Preview button (Standard toolbar), 75
print titles, 164-166

printers, 72-73
    selecting, 162, 175
    setup, 162
Printers dialog box, 174
Printers utility (Control Panel), 174
printing, 76, 160-161
    canceling, 78
    cells, 77, 161
    charts, 261-262
    draft quality, 170
    multiple copies, 161-162
    orientation, 169
    page breaks, 168
    page numbers, 170
    page ranges, 77, 163
    paper size, 170
    scaling, 169
    sheets, 77, 161
        portions, 163-164
    special effects, 168-171
    troubleshooting, 78, 342
    workbook sections, 77
protecting workbooks, 321
protrait orientation, 169
PV function, 225-227

R

range names, 324
ranges, 31-32
    addresses, 31
    borders, 152
    combining, 351
    copying, 345
    deleting, 111
    formulas, 89
    list ranges, 265
    moving, 345
    selecting, 31-32, 89, 346

deselecting, 32
    formatting, 141-142
    troubleshooting, 344
    transposing, 333
    type style, 59
RATE financial function, 228-229
recalculating formulas, 91
Record New Macro dialog box, 289
record number indicator (Data Form), 277
recording macros, 288-295
records (lists), 265
    deleting, 270
    editing, 278
    fields, 265-266
    inserting, 270
    sorting, 271
relative references, 132
removing split panes, 189
renaming workbooks, 40-42
repeating operations, 102-103
Replace dialog box, 119
replace operations, 118, 120
replacing, 27, 320
resetting toolbars, 314
resizing
    charts, 253
    windows, 179
ROUND function, 212-214
rows
    deleting, 110-112
    headers, 301
    height, 343
    inserting, 104-107
    selecting, 31
    switching to columns, 137

S

Save As dialog box, 37, 42
Save button (Standard toolbar), 39
saving, 36, 334
   charts, 255
   personal macro workbook, 295
   workbooks, 37-42, 329
scaling, 169
Scientific category (number formats), 64
scientific notation, 21
screen
   formula bar, 16
   menu bar, 15
   name box (active cell), 16
   status bar, 16
   title bar, 15
   toolbars, 15
scrolling, 17
   font list, 148
   help window, 33
   in print preview, 75
   split windows, 188
Search dialog box, 52
searches (lists), 320
   criteria, 279-280
   see also find operations
selecting
   area for charting, 244
   cells
      all cells in sheet, 31
      nonadjacent, 32
      types, 115-116
   columns, 31
   commands, 29
   printers, 162, 175
   ranges, 31-32, 89, 346
      deselecting, 32
      formatting, 141-142

troubleshooting, 344
rows, 31
selection handles, 248, 252
selection marquee, 88
serial numbers, 23
setup
   page setup, 168-171
   printers, 162
shading, 154-156
Sheet Tabs check box (Options dialog box), 302
sheets, 12
   cells, 13
      selecting all, 31
   chart sheets, 251, 262
   columns, 13
   deleting, 110-112
   editing
      groups, 331
      multiple, 327
   inserting, 104-107
   module sheets (macros), 286
   navigating, 114
   printing, 77, 161
      portions, 163-164
   selecting charting area, 244
shifting cells, 106, 111-112
shortcut keys (macros), 289
shortcut menus (toolbars), 311, 346
shortcuts
   closing Excel, 346
   closing workbooks, 345
   fonts, 347
   formulas, 347
   opening workbooks, 345
Show options (Options dialog box), 299-300

sizing
   charts, 253
   windows, 179
Sort dialog box, 272
sort keys (lists), 271-272
sorting
   ascending sort, 274
   descending, 274
   lists, 270-274, 333
   undoing, 275-276
spell check, 326
splitting windows, 187-189
spreadsheets, 8-9
Standard toolbar
   AutoSum button, 99
   ChartWizard button, 244
   Cut button, 126
   Format Painter, 136, 142
   Function Wizard, 200
   New Workbook button, 51
   Open File button, 50
   Paste button, 126
   Print button, 76, 161
   Print Preview, 75
   Save button, 39
   Undo button, 30
starting
   Excel, 9-12, 341
   Windows, 10
status bar, 16
Stop Recording toolbar, 309
strikethrough text, 150
styles, 349
   fonts, 149-150
   lines, 153
subdirectories, 40
subscript text, 150
subtopics (Help), 32
SUM function, 201-202
Summary Info dialog box, 38

superscript text, 150
switching
    between windows, 182
    between columns/
        rows, 137

T

text
    alignment, 20, 65
    color, 151
    orientation, 146
    wrapping, 145
tiling windows, 184
time
    fractions, 23
    military time, 23
Time category (number
    formats), 64
TipWizard toolbar, 309
title bar, 15
titles
    centering, 143-145
    charts, 247, 257-258
    columns, freezing, 190
    print titles, 164-166
Titles dialog box, 257
toolbar dock, 327
toolbars, 13-15, 307-310
    Auditing toolbar, 309
    buttons
        adding, 312-313
        copying between
            toolbars, 314
        deleting, 313
        order, 314
    Chart toolbar,
        257-259, 308
    creating, 314
    customizing, 354
    deleting, 314
    displaying, 310-311
    Drawing toolbar, 309

floating, 310
Formatting toolbar
    Align Left button,
        65
    Align Right
        button, 65
    Bold button, 57
    Center button, 65
    Comma Style
        button, 64
    Currency Style
        button, 64
    Decrease Decimal
        button, 64
    Increase Decimal
        button, 64
    Italic button, 58
    Percent Style
        button, 64
Full Screen toolbar,
    309
Microsoft, 309
moving, 311
resetting, 314
shortcut menus, 311
Standard toolbar
    AutoSum button,
        99
    ChartWizard but-
        ton, 244
    Cut button, 126
    Format Painter,
        136, 142
    Function Wizard,
        200
    New Workbook
        button, 51
    Open File button,
        50
    Paste button, 126
    Print button, 76,
        161
    Print Preview, 75
    Save button, 39
    Undo button, 30

Stop Recording
    toolbar, 309
TipWizard toolbar,
    309
Toolbars dialog box, 307
Tools menu commands
    Goal Seek, 350
    Protection, 322
    Record Macro, 288
    Spelling, 326
    Stop Recording, 291
topics (Help), 32
transposing
    ranges, 333
    columns/rows, 137
troubleshooting startup,
    341
TrueType fonts, 149
type size, 59-61
type styles, 56-61
    bold type, 57
    italic, 58-59
    removing, 61
    see also fonts
typeface, 147
    see also fonts
typing errors, 18
typing information, see
    data entry

U-V

Undo button (Standard
    toolbar), 30
undoing, 28-30
    sort operations,
        275-276
unfilling cells, 328
UPPER function, 214-215

View menu commands
    Toolbars, 257, 307
    Zoom, 192
View options, 299
Visual Basic code, 294

I HATE EXCEL FOR WINDOWS!

W-Z

What-You-See-Is-What-
   You-Get (WYSIWYG),
   140-141
wild cards, 49
Window menu commands
   Arrange, 183
   Freeze Panes, 189
   Hide, 185
   New Window, 182
   Split, 187
   Unhide, 185
Window Options (Op-
   tions dialog box),
   300-303
Windows
   exiting, 43
   starting, 10
windows
   arranging, 183-185
   cascading, 184
   closing, 179, 184
   document window, 16,
      178
   duplicate workbooks,
      181
   freezing, 189-191
   help window, 33
   hiding, 185-186
   maximizing, 179
   minimizing, 179
   moving with mouse,
      179
   moving between, 182
   multiple files, 186-187
   opening multiple,
      182-183

panes, 187
   moving between,
      189
   removing, 189
resizing, 179
sizing, 179
splitting, 187-189
tiling, 184
workbooks, 12-14
   active workbook, 48
   closing, 42-43, 50, 329
      shortcut, 345
   Control menu, 180
   copying between, 323
   creating, 50-51
   deleting, 51-54
   names, 38
      renaming, 40-42
   opening, 46-50
      at startup, 320
      shortcut, 345
   passwords, 323
   personal macro work-
      book, 287, 290, 295
   printing sections, 77
   protecting, 321
   saving, 37-42, 329
   sheets, 12
workspaces, 352
wrapping text, 145

XLS file extension, 38

zero values, 302
zooming, 192-193
   in print preview, 75